Recollections of
a Sectarian Realist

Recollections of
a Sectarian Realist

A Mennonite Life in the Twentieth Century

By J. Lawrence Burkholder

Edited by Myrna Burkholder

Foreword by John A. Lapp

Based on interviews conducted by C. Arnold Snyder

INSTITUTE OF MENNONITE STUDIES

Recollections of a Sectarian Realist:
A Mennonite Life in the Twentieth Century
By J. Lawrence Burkholder
Edited by Myrna Burkholder
Based on interviews conducted by C. Arnold Snyder

Copyright © 2016 by Institute of Mennonite Studies, Anabaptist Mennonite Biblical Seminary, 3003 Benham Avenue, Elkhart, IN 46517. All rights
reserved.

To order copies or request information, please call 1-574-296-6239, email
ims@ambs.edu, or visit www.ambs.edu/ims.
3003 Benham Avenue, Elkhart, Indiana 46517-1999
http://www.ambs.edu/IMS/

All rights reserved

Library of Congress Cataloging-in-Publication Data

Names: Burkholder, J. Lawrence, author. | Burkholder, Myrna, editor.
Title: Recollections of a sectarian realist : a Mennonite life in the
    twentieth century / by J. Lawrence Burkholder ; edited by Myrna Burkholder
    ; foreword by John A. Lapp ; based on interviews conducted by C. Arnold
    Snyder.
Description: Elkhart, Indiana : Institute of Mennonite Studies, 2016. |
    Includes index.
Identifiers: LCCN 2016050745 | ISBN 0936273569 (alk. paper)
Subjects: LCSH: Burkholder, J. Lawrence. | Mennonites--United
    States--Biography.
Classification: LCC BX8143.B865 A3 2016 | DDC 289.7092 [B] --dc23
LC record available at https://lccn.loc.gov/2016050745

International Standard Book Number: 0-936273-56-9

Printed in the United States of America by Duley Press, Mishawaka, Indiana

Cover design by Mary E. Klassen; cover caricature by Roland H. Bainton

Photos reprinted courtesy of
Associated Press: pages 130, 131
Goshen College: pages 100, 115, 156, 159, 160, 166, 242 (photo provided by
Goshen College Communications and Marketing Office)
The Goshen News: page 165

Table of Contents

Foreword

J. Lawrence Burkholder was a major personality on the North American Mennonite scene for much of the twentieth century. This volume is a rich remembering with numerous insights from a well-lived Mennonite life.

What makes this memoir so fascinating is the geographical spread and the interaction with significant public events from the 1940s to the end of the century. Burkholder was born in 1917 in Newville, a small town in south-central Pennsylvania. He died in Goshen, Indiana, in 2010. Between Newville and Goshen, he lived for a year or more in Gettysburg, Pennsylvania; Croghan, New York; Calcutta, India; Shanghai, China; Princeton, New Jersey; Oxford, England; and Cambridge, Massachusetts.

As a youth, Burkholder was infatuated with the latest technology, the airplane. Before graduating from high school he had earned a pilot's license, which he used for seventy years.

After graduating from Goshen College and Lutheran Theological Seminary at Gettysburg, he pastored in New Bremen, New York. Although ministers were exempt from the draft, he decided that as a conscientious objector he should share in the deprivation soldiers experienced. He left his family in Goshen to become a volunteer overseas relief worker. He ended up in Shanghai in the midst of a civil war. After more than a year of separation, his wife Harriet and their two young children joined him.

After graduate study at Princeton Theological Seminary, Burkholder taught at Goshen College before accepting a call to Harvard Divinity School. While at Harvard he helped establish Mennonite Congregation of Boston and actively participated in the civil rights movement in Boston; St. Augustine, Florida; and Selma, Alabama. In 1970 he accepted the call to become president of Goshen College, a position he held until his retirement in

1984. He is widely remembered as a friend to many students, for numerous thoughtful chapel talks, for initiating overseas study service terms in Poland and China, and for leading a major campaign—the Uncommon Cause—to build the college endowment.

These recollections are of a Mennonite life. Burkholder's parents' families had been Mennonite for several centuries. He was baptized at Diller Mennonite Church in 1929 by a well-known Lancaster Mennonite Conference bishop, Noah Mack. But his early religious nurture also included significant mentoring by William T. Swaim, pastor of Big Spring Presbyterian Church in Newville.

Burkholder was always more than a sectarian. As a student at Lutheran and Presbyterian seminaries, he learned how interdependent the Christian movement is in all its parts. In India and China, he discovered the depth of the Anglican tradition and the shallowness of some sectarians. His decade at Harvard Divinity School as the first chair of its Department of the Church gave him an appreciation for the contribution of traditional New England parishes.

Burkholder made a notable contribution to Mennonite tradition. He filled several pastorates, served widely as a speaker in congregations and conferences, and served on major church committees. He enriched and extended Mennonite theological and ethical thinking in his considerable writings. He challenged the rigidity and self-satisfaction of some traditional thought and practices as well as the newer formulations of John H. Yoder. The church continues to wrestle with the insights Lawrence Burkholder set before us.

Readers will be impressed with the breadth, modesty, and clarity of these recollections. Indeed, Lawrence is worthy of a major biographical study.

We owe much gratitude to Professor C. Arnold Snyder of Waterloo, Ontario, for his extended interviews, now so well edited by Myrna Burkholder, who has also collected photographs helpfully illustrating her father's life.

John A. Lapp
Dean, provost, and professor of history at Goshen College
when J. Lawrence Burkholder was president

Introduction

Work on J. Lawrence Burkholder's memoir began at the urging of historian C. Arnold Snyder, who on several occasions in 2005 interviewed our father in his retirement. I am grateful to Arnold for recording and transcribing those conversations. When the transcriptions were returned, my father and I began to edit them—but as his health began to decline, we set the project aside.

After our father died in 2010, my brother Howard, my sister Janet, and I—with the help of many others—did our best to edit the manuscript in a way that honors his voice. In footnotes scattered throughout the book we provide additional information about people, places, and events dealt with in his text. And because he lived several years beyond the time covered by the Snyder interviews, we include an epilogue that covers events occurring during those years.

This memoir includes a penultimate chapter devoted to J. Lawrence's musings on the important theological and ethical issues a generation of Mennonite leaders wrestled with as they increasingly assumed positions of power and responsibility in church and society. His reflections reveal his quest to hold together a sectarian commitment to Jesus's way, instilled in him by his Mennonite upbringing, and a realism informed by his reading of Reinhold Niebuhr as it resonated with his experience of moral dilemmas encountered in relief work and in leadership roles later in life.

The informal style of J. Lawrence's presentation in this memoir illustrates his gifts for public speaking and conversation. We hope that the readers of this memoir will be enriched, as we have been, by remembering how his experiences shaped his thinking in so many ways.

My thanks to my sister, Janet Burkholder Friesen, for serving as copy editor for the book. Providing additional editorial assistance were Lauren Friesen, Luke Gascho, Linda Gerber, John A. Lapp (who also generously wrote the foreword), Jim Lehman, Gerhard Reimer, Phil Roth, Ben Sprunger, Donald Xie, Don Minter, Mary Oyer, and Melanie Zybala. Also deserving thanks are archivists and staff of these institutions: Goshen College; Harvard Divinity School; Mennonite Church USA Archives; Mennonite Historical Library; Newville Historical Society; Lutheran Theological Seminary at Gettysburg; Princeton Theological Seminary; Shippensburg University Archives. Documents from J. Lawrence Burkholder's siblings—Mildred McDannel Hackman, Evelyn Kreider, and Verna Troyer—also provided useful information.

Thanks also to the executive committee and staff of Institute of Mennonite Studies at Anabaptist Mennonite Biblical Seminary for taking on this project and for additional work in preparing the manuscript for publication. We also owe a debt of gratitude to several AMBS volunteers: to Sophia Austin for her care and diligence in preparing the index; to James Nelson Gingerich for scanning many of the photographs and slides and for formatting the book; and to a fine crew of keen-eyed proofreaders—Ron Kennel, Dot Smucker, Thomas Kreider, and Evelyn Kreider.

Janet, Howard, and I are grateful to our parents, J. Lawrence and Harriet Lapp Burkholder, for the rich heritage into which they brought us and for the legacy they have left with us and many others. We remember both of them with respect and affection. They were dedicated to the cause of Christ's kingdom and gave generously of themselves in so many ways. We take comfort in the fact that our parents are now in communion with God, their Creator, and Jesus Christ, their Redeemer.

Myrna Burkholder

1

Childhood Years in Newville, 1917–36

I was born October 31, 1917, in Cumberland County, Pennsylvania. My parents were Henry Longenecker Burkholder and Mary Seitz Burkholder. We lived in an unincorporated town called West Hill, which consisted of a few houses along the road.[1] When I was

Sign welcoming visitors to Newville, Pennsylvania

1 In her informally published memoir, *West of West Hill: Memories and Reflections*, J. Lawrence's sister Evelyn Burkholder Kreider describes West Hill as a one-street hamlet.

about four, we moved to 89 North High Street in nearby Newville, a beautiful—if nondescript—little town.[2] We were always aware of its place within the Cumberland Valley because we could see Blue Mountain to the north.[3] The mountain became part of the landscape of our home.

For more than twenty years, my father was a professor at Shippensburg State Teachers College,[4] which was about ten miles southwest of Newville. He commuted to school, sometimes by automobile and sometimes by train. The train was pulled by a steam engine, which I found fascinating.[5]

We would like to have known more about my father than was disclosed within the family. We knew that he grew up in Upper Frankford Township on a farm located along Conodoguinet Creek, about four miles north of Newville. We referred to it simply as "the creek." Conodoguinet is a Native American word meaning "a long way with many bends." Spanning the creek were two attractive covered bridges which have since been removed.[6]

My father's father, John W. Burkholder, suffered from melancholia, which we would probably call depression now. His mother, Fannie Longenecker Burkholder, was a small woman who

2 J. Lawrence was amused by the sign welcoming visitors to his hometown, which explains that Newville means "new village."

3 Blue Mountain is a ridge that forms the northern boundary of the Cumberland Valley and the eastern edge of the Appalachian Mountain range. It extends 150 miles through Pennsylvania. The Cumberland Valley is bounded on the south by the South Mountain highlands, a series of small rocky hills. Scottish settlers purchased the valley in 1736 from the Shawnee Indians.

4 Now Shippensburg University.

5 Cumberland Valley Railroad, first used in 1837, came through Newville. The Newville station is no longer there, though the adjacent stationmaster's house is still standing. The railroad's nine-and-a-half-mile corridor between Newville and Shippensburg is now a recreational trail.

6 Conodoguinet Creek was at one time lined with some 140 mills of various kinds from one end of Cumberland County to the other. In 1909 only thirteen of those mills remained, and by now even those are largely forgotten.

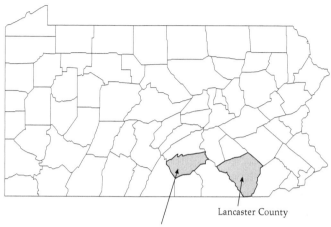

Lancaster County

Cumberland County, Pennsylvania

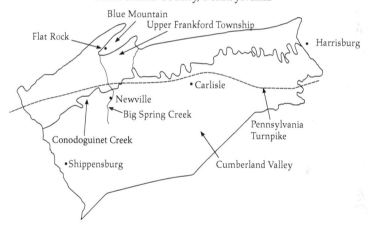

Blue Mountain
Upper Frankford Township
Flat Rock
Harrisburg
Carlisle
Newville
Big Spring Creek
Pennsylvania
Turnpike
Conodoguinet Creek
Shippensburg
Cumberland Valley

J. Lawrence Burkholder grew up in Cumberland County, Pennsylvania, in the town of Newville, from which he could see Blue Mountain to the north. His father, Henry Longenecker Burkholder, commuted southwest about ten miles to Shippensburg, where he taught for some twenty years at Shippensburg State Teachers College.

was simple in her manner and language. There were four children in the family, including Ida and Lizzie, who remained single, and their brother, Ephraim. We do not know whether my father went to high school because he never spoke about it. He did attend Dickinson College in Carlisle, Pennsylvania, and graduated in 1927. It was—and is—a school of some reputation. He also attended New York University for graduate studies.

At age thirty, he married Mary Seitz, an attractive young woman from a farm near Newville. She was from a family of five boys and two girls. Their beautiful family farm is still there. We know that her mother, Elizabeth Baer, was an absolutely wonderful person. Elizabeth came out of the Reformed Mennonite Church tradition, which was very conservative. She married my grandfather, Jacob Seitz, who was an alcoholic. He would leave for extended periods of time, often being returned by a horse that knew the way home. Later in life he had a conversion experience and lived very responsibly thereafter.[7]

Henry Longenecker Burkholder (1878–1938), father of J. Lawrence Burkholder

I was the fourth of five children. Mildred was the first to come along. She was a charming person and was the favorite of my father because she did everything just right. She was a straight-A student, went into the field of education, and began to teach when she was eighteen or nineteen years old. She had advanced through school quickly. She eventually married Emmert McDannel, a United States post office railway postal clerk, and lived most of her life in Elizabethtown, Pennsylvania. He died in 1962, and some twenty years later, in 1983, she married Henry H. Hackman, a long-time acquaintance who was a fellow educator.

My brother, Harold, who was four years older than I, was a handsome young man and a good student; he was much inter-

---

7 According to "The Story of Kenneth Leroy Seitz," informally published in 2004.

ested in sports. He studied at Shippensburg State Teachers College and Goshen (Indiana) College. He went on to become a teacher and counselor at a high school in Peoria, Illinois, where he married Gladys Schertz, an elementary school teacher.

My sister Evelyn Kreider was the third born. She was an energetic person and a good student. She went to Goshen College, worked several years as a home economics teacher, and married Carl Kreider, who later became dean of Goshen College. She is well-known for her gracious hospitality and being an excellent cook.

After me came the youngest in the family, my sister Verna. By that time things had loosened up in our family, so she had what one might call a "normal" childhood. We made a lot of fuss over her, partly because she had such a pleasant disposition. She also went to Goshen College and taught English and music before marrying Dana Troyer, an ophthalmologist.

Our mother was an exceptional woman; her character could not be exceeded in virtue, from my point of view. She and my father lived together compatibly, if not so happily. All his life my father struggled to make something of himself. He got no encouragement from his family to educate himself and received only discouragement from Lancaster Mennonite Conference, which gave oversight to our congregation, Diller Mennonite Church.[8]

Mary Seitz Burkholder (1884–1941), mother of J. Lawrence Burkholder

---

8 Several generations of J. Lawrence's father's Burkholder family members and (later) his mother's Seitz family members attended Diller Mennonite

J. Lawrence Burkholder as a child with relatives in Newville, Pennsylvania. Back row: sister Mildred Burkholder (partially hidden), mother Mary Seitz Burkholder, uncle Warren Seitz, uncle Jacob Raymond Seitz, sister Evelyn Burkholder. Front row: cousin Richard "Dick" Seitz, J. Lawrence Burkholder, cousin Betty Seitz, and brother Harold Burkholder

Unlike Lancaster County, Cumberland County had no Mennonite community to speak of. We were only a collection of Burkholders, Burkharts, Charltons, and a few others who met at Diller Mennonite Church every Sunday morning for a service that never varied. At that time, the congregation numbered maybe thirty to forty members. We had no regular preacher.

At one time we were led by J. Paul Burkhart, a member of the congregation who became educated and was later superintendent for the Cumberland Valley School District. He preached "classy" sermons. He depended on a kind of eloquence that is passé in our everyday conversations. Some of his sermons were beautiful, full of poetry. However, he was silenced because he married someone

---

Church. The church is named after Francis Diller, who came to Pennsylvania from Berne, Switzerland, in 1754, and who lived and died in nearby Lancaster County. In 1790, his widow and three sons moved to the vicinity of Newville. One of them, Peter, donated the tract of land on which the church was built. Later, another brother, Francis Diller, was ordained as a minister.

from the Evangelical Mennonite Church; that is, he married outside the church.

My Sunday school teacher, after I reached the age of twelve or maybe fifteen, was his brother, Mark Burkhart, a high school mathematics teacher in Carlisle who later became a principal. He was a mathematician with a philosophical side. No matter what the Sunday school lesson was about, he would start out with a definition of terms. He used the definitions of religious terms as a guide to ideas. Thereby he was insisting that we understand a form of ontology. He was effective as a teacher. But he too had to

The original building used for services by Diller Mennonite Church during J. Lawrence Burkholder's growing-up years

leave the church because he also married someone from another denomination. To this day I appreciate his approach and now understand ontology to mean an attempt to understand existence in a systematic way. The ontological view of God is of a being whose greatness is beyond our comprehension, and yet our ideas of God can be ordered and expressed in a systematic way.

At an earlier age I was the only member of my Sunday school class and was taught by an older woman who assured me that "it's good to be right and right to be good." As I recall, she often showed me big posters supplied by the denominational publishing house, Herald Press of Scottdale, Pennsylvania. They portrayed biblical pictures, of men with massive physiques carrying grapes as big as pears out of the land of Canaan—or so it seemed to me.

My family went to church regularly, even though Diller Mennonite Church appeared to be dying. The services were stiff, stereotypical, and repetitive. Even so, we knew each other well and interacted with each other after church. My mother, especially, was able to talk with everyone. She was friendly and not outspoken.

Our church was under the authority of Lancaster Mennonite Conference, and we did not experience the Lancaster ethos at its best. We hardly knew its members as human beings, because they were represented to us by only one person, the bishop, who would come twice a year for communion. Before each communion service, conference rules and regulations were read to us. Some of those regulations pertained to clothing, especially for women. During the Depression we were not supposed to be on "relief," and we were not supposed to have life insurance. Several members of our congregation were going into business, and they needed life insurance for equity when borrowing from the bank, so this was an issue for them.

Furthermore, there was the problem of finding marriage partners, since the congregation was so small and was not located near other Mennonite congregations. It was only by traveling to Lancaster County or to Slate Hill Mennonite Church, which was close to Harrisburg, that one might find someone who belonged to the same faith.

The future of that congregation was in peril at that time. There were a few little scandals, and occasionally my parents expressed the desire to move somewhere else to be able to attend another Mennonite church. In that connection, Goshen, Indiana, was often discussed. We made a number of trips to Goshen, one of

them during the sum-
mer of 1935, when
our father taught at
Goshen College. We
were also attracted to
the nearby Fairfield
Mennonite Church, a
General Conference
Mennonite congre-
gation. Sometimes a
choir from Bluffton
College, a General
Conference Menno-
nite Church school
in Ohio, would come
through there, and as
a little fellow I was
much interested in
how those grown-ups
could sing!

J. Lawrence Burkholder (center) with school pals

During my childhood, I was a loner, simply because there was only one other boy in our part of Newville. This boy always had a rope in his hand. He wanted to play "horsey," and he wanted to play horse with me. Of course, I was always the horse. Since he could not pronounce my name, he called me "Wauwence!" That was as far as our friendship could go.

As a boy I was small; I was often called "little Lawrency." An aunt referred to me as "the little pig which was pushed back." And I was also timid. Because of my fear that I might say something wrong, I found it difficult to be in social situations. Additionally, I considered myself physically inferior.

My main points of reference those days were the Sears, Roe-buck and Montgomery Ward catalogs. These catalogs were my Bible. I spent many days and many hours with these catalogs, because I had no other books. Since Newville was such a small town, with only about 1500 people, we had no public library. And the schools were not considered very good, even though they had improved greatly by the time I was in high school.

In those early days I was more or less confined to our home. I was attached to my mother. She understood me, and we had long discussions as we worked together, especially as I worked with her in her garden.

As for my father, I felt that I did not know him well, much less understand him. He went to school every day, came back late in the evening, and then went to his office to get ready for the next day of teaching.[9]

While growing up, I related more readily to nature than to people. I appreciated the topography of Cumberland County. On any day, looking from our backyard to the north, I could see Blue Mountain, which seemed to me like an elephant. The mountain was long and tapered down to what would be the trunk of the elephant. Of course, there was an open space where the eyes would be. This was Flat Rock, a place that could be approached from the

---

9   Henry L. Burkholder was born on October 24, 1878. According to archival information at Shippensburg University (formerly Shippensburg State Teachers College), Henry attended Cumberland Valley State Normal School for two years and graduated in 1901 at age twenty-three. Then he did public school teaching until 1917, when he joined the faculty at Cumberland Valley State Normal School, renamed Shippensburg State Teachers College in 1927. He remained on the faculty until his death in 1938 at age sixty. According to several newspaper obituaries (though unconfirmed otherwise), he was a student at the National Conservatory of Music in Philadelphia in 1919 and a graduate of the International School of Music in New York City (no date). At Diller Mennonite Church he served as chorister for many years and as a teacher and Sunday school superintendent. He served on the board of education in Newville, as was reported in a clipping from a local newspaper in 1935, and he was president of the Burkholder Family Association from 1933 to 1938. We don't know how much education he had before attending Cumberland Valley State Normal School at age twenty-one, or where and how he spent his time between completing his early education and attending Cumberland Valley State Normal School. A good guess might be that he had at least an eighth-grade education and lived at home with his parents, helping them with farming before continuing his formal education.

J. Lawrence Burkholder with his grandson Eliot Friesen (on the left) and his son Howard Burkholder (on the right), during their 2008 visit to Colonel Denning State Park

other side of the mountain.[10] Sometimes we went to that spot, where we could look over the valley for miles and miles. It was beautiful.

---

10   Colonel Denning State Park, constructed during the Depression and formally opened in 1936, is a 273-acre park that includes a manmade lake and a steep, two-and-a-half-mile trail to Flat Rock, which offers a panoramic view of Cumberland Valley. The entrance to the park is located on the inside of the curve of Blue Mountain, just north of Newville. The park is surrounded by the Tuscarora State Forest. In 2008, J. Lawrence visited this park with his son Howard, grandson Eliot Friesen, and daughter Myrna. During this visit he shared a bit of Burkholder family history related to the founding of this park: His father had built a small cabin for the family very near to what is now the park and had a vision for the development of the park. He took the idea to a local state representative. J. Lawrence remembered helping to build the family cabin, and it is mentioned in the 1938 yearbook of Shippensburg State Teachers College as the destination for a spring outing of the Philosophical Society, of which his father was faculty sponsor. It is not known exactly when the family sold this cabin.

I appreciated the rolling hills of Cumberland County, though they were not good for farming. We were envious of Lancaster County, with its wealth and its limestone land. Most of the farmers in our county were relatively poor, although there were some

Laughlin Mill, Newville, Pennsylvania, built sometime between 1760 and 1763

dairy farmers who did quite well. I liked the countryside and especially a nearby creek, which we called Big Spring.[11]

Big Spring Creek emanates from a hillside a few miles south of Newville. It meanders its way into the city limits of Newville.

---

11 Big Spring Creek, thought to be the fifth largest spring in Pennsylvania, is owned and used by the Pennsylvania Fish Commission for Big Spring Trout Hatchery. It is supposedly one of the most famous limestone spring creeks in the world. This stream is known to be part of the historical beginnings of fly fishing in America. Because of the condition of the stream, trout are able to grow in it year round. It flows northward through Newville into Conodoguinet Creek. Of the many mills known to have lined the creek's banks, none but Laughlin Mill remain. Probably the oldest of the mills, built sometime between 1760 and 1763, Laughlin Mill is located within the city limits of Newville and is maintained as a historic site.

Not only is it a beautiful stream, but it is also well-known as a trout stream with a number of dams and deep pools. I enjoyed fishing there, even as a very little youngster. I fished because I liked to eat fish, and fishing gave me time to exercise my dreamy, reflective inclinations. I could sit for a half hour without getting a bite and still thought of the time as well spent.

I was not adept at handling fancy fishing rods, but now and then I would catch a sucker or a sunfish or occasionally a trout. I prized catching trout and took them home. On one occasion I caught a big trout, and the leading lady of Newville, Mrs. Katherine Graham (widow of John Graham, who had served in the Pennsylvania state legislature), stopped her Cadillac and examined that fish. I remember this incident with some pride.

The stream was mysterious to me. I wondered what was at the bottom of it. What was living there? What did it look like? I had never seen a stream that had been drained, so I did not know that the bottom of a stream looks much like the bottom of any field. I imagined what was down there, and I had some thoughts that I later discovered to be somewhat platonic. I thought that maybe what was real was under the surface of the water and wished I could just get in there and look at it. Plato thought that our senses only provide surface knowledge and that reality exists beyond the surface. I wondered how one gets in there to look at reality without disturbing it. Plato does not tell us.

Something else I did was climb a tree behind our house. From that tree I could look over the town to the south and see Blue Mountain to the north. I remember that our house was at the apex of a triangle, as it were, very close to the road. Behind our house, the county had put a stone pile. I had no baseball bat, but I had a sawed-off broomstick. So I would throw those pebbles up and hit them with the broomstick. I became good at it. I peppered the neighboring farmer's field more than he would have appreciated, had he seen me!

Even though our father was an educator, we had few books at home to read. Most likely this lack reflected his own stark background. However, he was a good man. I don't want to say anything that would detract from the quality of his teaching or the character of his person. He taught education classes and penmanship—the Palmer method. My mother, who had only an eighth-grade education and had never taken a course on the Palmer method, had excellent penmanship.

J. Lawrence and his sisters Evelyn and Verna at their home in Newville, Pennsylvania

We did not have much in the way of toys, although I was given a big toy now and then— a scooter, for example. I'm sure that neither my father nor my mother had toys as children, because of the age in which they were brought up as well as the fact that they had had to work so hard even as children.

We lived with the presupposition that as Mennonites we were different. My father was not different by external appearances—when he died he had eight dress suits of fine quality—but my mother dressed plainly, like a Mennonite. In spite of this, she had a liberal spirit and was helpful to many people. It seemed that every hobo in the county knew her and would knock on our door. A hobo with a British accent—Old Johnson, we called him—would always ask whether he could have something to eat and whether my mother had an extra pair of pants for him. I recall a conversation she had with him one time about religion. She never pressed her religion on anybody and was not evangelistic in that sense. I remember he told her that he was a universalist and that everybody would go to heaven. My mother only said, "I hope so!"

Of course, she was well aware of the fact that the citizens of Newville were not by any means perfect. When I introduced Harriet, my wife, to Newville and told her what went on there, she thought it sounded like a kind of Peyton Place! She was correct in that it was a place of many suicides and much sexual freedom.

It was also a church town, with two large Presbyterian churches, two large Lutheran churches, and a Church of the Brethren congregation. Our little Mennonite church was located about five miles outside Newville and had no connection at all with other local churches.

My mother worked hard. She spent most of her time in her garden taking care of the plants and vegetables she sold every spring—cabbage plants, cauliflower plants, and sweet potato plants. Many people would stop by to get a dozen or more plants. I noticed that when a customer bought a dozen plants, my mother would make it thirteen or fourteen plants. If someone requested 100 sweet potato plants, he got 105. Most of the plants were grown under glass, heavy glass that she had to remove, even though she was thin and wiry and somewhat frail. She would often have conversations with customers. The fact that she was dressed plainly was no problem, it seemed.

Once I was given a little express wagon, as they were called then. With it I peddled my mother's vegetables in Newville. Most people had gardens, but I would try to sell a bunch of beets for five

The childhood home of J. Lawrence Burkholder at 89 North High Street, Newville, Pennsylvania

cents, a bunch of carrots for five cents, or stalks of celery for ten cents. It was a good experience for me as a little fellow, because it took some nerve to go to a house and knock on the door. People were kind to me, and I recognized that in them.

I learned so much from my mother about the town and the people in the town. She talked to me so freely! We were great friends, and I don't remember ever being scolded by her, not even once. Since I was always barefoot in the summertime, I had calluses on my feet. I could run over stones and not feel them. And every night before I went to bed, she would wash my feet, usually outside the house. She used a bucket. I appreciated that so much. And I really appreciated her.

People in town, especially the people who came from what was called Smithtown, knew my mother and loved her. We knew a lot about Smithtown. Mr. Smith, an architect and builder from Newville, built some rather inadequate houses just before the Depression, but they were very useful during the Depression, which began in 1929. People who could barely pay rent lived there—poor people, often young families. The houses were built near our home, which probably reduced the value of our property.

The women in the Smithtown community came frequently to my mother's kitchen. They came there with their woes and their problems. She would always invite them to sit on one of our dining room or kitchen chairs. When I came home from school, I frequently found five or six women visiting with my mother. She was not preaching to them; she was simply talking with them. She often gave them a little money, though she had very little herself. Or she would go to the basement and get some canned meat or vegetables. She was always a little concerned about what was referred to as the "social disease." After they left, we would put the chairs outside for a while. I learned about this disease when I was seven or eight years old.

We were brought up to feel that it was virtuous to work hard. While there was satisfaction that came from our hard work, it also produced a family who did quite well in many respects. This gave my mother so much pleasure in life. She enjoyed reading and would study her Sunday school lesson avidly Saturday evenings. She taught Sunday school, and her theology was rather simple—to be sure. Nevertheless, it was authentic and contained an element of social concern, even though she did not know about systems, orders, or public policy, as we might speak of them today.

She obviously had neighbors whom she cared about very much. She did not press herself on those neighbors; they came to her. When she passed away, they came to her funeral. We did not have church funerals in those days, so we had the funeral at our home. Afterward the room where it was held smelled terrible! The many poor people who came to the funeral were obviously not very clean. I think their presence was a wonderful tribute to my mother, even if it could have been viewed otherwise! My mother passed away in 1941 at age fifty-seven, which was rather young.

I believe my mother was almost perfect. I cannot think that she ever did anything wrong except that one time when—she confessed—as a child she had told a lie. She had wanted to become a missionary, but she could not, since she did not have an education. Not many people were becoming missionaries anyway, when she was young. Missionaries represented an ideal.

However, she became a missionary by the way she brought up her children and served her local community. She did not speak negatively. I remember only two times when she got mad. A neighbor farmer sometimes drove his cows past our house on the way to his barn to be milked. He would herd them with his car and bump into them, which skinned their back legs. Oh, that made my mother so furious that she scolded him about it when she bought milk from him.

We also had a neighbor who could not keep his hands to himself when he was in the creek with other people—that is, with young ladies! She really told him off. Otherwise, I cannot think of anyone whom she declared to be wrong or evil in any way.

I should also say that my mother had a brother, Warren Seitz (Uncle Warren, to us), who was in the army during World War I. He was gassed and ended up in a veterans hospital in Coatesville, Pennsylvania, where he died. When we heard that he had died, we retrieved his body from an undertaker in Coatesville. My mother was enough of a pietist to wonder about his soul. She verbalized the fact that she wrestled with the idea that he was being punished. Though never violent, he had psychological problems. He talked loudly and just could not handle life. He never married, and he got syphilis.

My mother held on to the idea that there may be eternal damnation, even though she said when we came back from retrieving my uncle, "I hope he is in heaven." She hoped everyone would go to heaven. I remember Karl Barth expressing the same hope in more sophisticated terms!

We were a religious family, which mostly was a matter of morality—of being good, being no embarrassment to anybody, and helping other people. I just assumed as a youngster that I would become a preacher or a missionary. I was a good little boy, even though I had my little bad thoughts now and then.

When my mother was selling plants, she put the money in a certain place—coins, not many dollar bills—just change. Once when I was eight or nine years old, I snitched a dime and went to the feed store nearby, where they had a case of candies. I got two big Hershey bars for a dime. (Maybe my punishment is that I am now diabetic.) Of course, I felt guilty, but I did not say anything to anyone about what I had done. About two days later, my mother told me a little story about herself. At one time, when she was on the farm, the Seitz family got a bag of rock candy. It was considered very good candy at that time—better than chocolate candy—and she ate some of it. Her brothers accosted her for eating from the bag, and she told a lie. She said, "I did not eat any of it."

That story was about helping me understand that I was not a thief. It was a form of grace. At that time I did not know anything about grace as a theological doctrine, even though I felt it from my parents. It was about her forgiving me without destroying my self-respect as a child. I learned much about life from her.

All of us children noticed that there was a large book in my father's library called *The Origin of Life*. It was a medical book about reproduction, and it had all kinds of images in it—of the naked human body, male and female, and of the birth of a child. It was funny that this book was supposedly never "read" by any of us, but it looked kind of worn out! Of course, it was "referenced." Even an uncle found out about it and wanted to see it. Sex was not talked about at home, although my mother did tell me a couple of things, which was wonderful of her. I felt as if I was a friend of hers, even when I was young.

My relationship with my father was good but somewhat strained. Although I rarely spent much time with him, he paid maybe too much attention to my report cards, which were not always so good. My family said I was a dreamer. With my mother I worked hard, which included picking up stones in the garden, among other tasks. In spite of that effort, my father probably wanted more tangible evidence of my possibilities as a human being.

One time he told me that I should learn to use a shovel. I took it to mean that he thought that I would never amount to anything. He did not intend to be cruel, I am sure, but he did reflect his background. It made me wonder, even then, to what extent we can transcend those influences into which we are born. I am nevertheless grateful for my father and respect him highly. He had his struggles.

We always had financial limitations, not in the sense that we were in debt, but rather in the sense that there was little for extras. Sometimes someone would come to our house to sell us something, but my mother just did not have the money for it. However, I am sure I am reflecting the times in which we lived. They were hard.

During my childhood, I did develop a certain fascination with several dimensions of life that were new at that time. One was aviation. If I saw the picture of an airplane in a magazine or newspaper, I would cut it out. I was just enthralled with the idea of flying. I imagined myself flying an airplane over mountains, one after another. I talked to my mother one time about how many mountains there are in the world, and from that we got into a discussion about infinity. She said, "After one mountain, there is another mountain. After one valley, there is another valley." Of course, I asked her whether they ever stopped. She said, "Well, I do not know."

I guess one answer could have been that they go around the world and come back, but that was a little beyond our thinking at that time. However, as a child I did ponder infinity. I once asked her whether there is something so small that it cannot be divided. She did not know the answer to that one. When I was alone, I would think about lots of things. I thought of nature as being not just beautiful but enchanted.

I also dreamed of the possibility of my landing an airplane right behind our house. One time in about 1926 or 1927, when I was nine or ten years old, a man did actually land in a nearby field. He landed in a Waco biplane with an old, old 0X-5 motor. The pilot was a barnstormer from Butler, Pennsylvania. When he landed he broke the propeller, which meant that he had to stay there until he could get somebody to take him to Harrisburg to buy another one. I had a chance to talk with him, and he let me sit in the airplane, and he even let me move the control stick while sitting there. He told me that to make the plane to go down, I should push the stick forward, and to make the airplane go up, I should pull the stick back. What an amazing experience for me! I wondered whether I could ever become a pilot. That was my dream: to become a pilot.

Eventually the pilot got the propeller, which I helped him replace by holding a wrench for him. When he was finished, he got in the airplane and took off. I was rather wishing he would have taken me for a ride, but he did not offer to do so. In those days, an airplane ride was expensive! I knew that my Sunday school teacher, Mark Burkhart, had paid fifteen dollars to take a five-minute airplane ride at the county fair.

I loved airplanes primarily because of what they could do. They could go up or down, left or right—every direction but backward. Such freedom—to go left or right when one wanted to do so. I felt that if I could look down from above, in a way I would be transcending my situation as a little boy, with all its limitations. I saw it as a kind of salvation. Salvation has been thought of as a kind of freedom from the limitations of this world. To me, taking off in an airplane was an almost metaphysical situation.

I tied together that understanding of flying with seeing the beauty and topography of the county. I knew of many, many hills and rock formations and streams in the area, particularly Big Spring Creek, and it was my ambition to fly over them.

In 1927 Charles Lindbergh made his famous flight. I was completely captivated not only by his feat but also by Lindbergh as a person and by his airplane. I read about him, and of course when his book, "WE," was published that year, I read it. I thought that he was almost like a son of God. He was slender, as I was then. I was hoping that when I grew up, I might look like him. Of course, I would learn to fly an airplane too. He was famous, and I thought that I would enjoy being famous also! I remember that when his son was kidnapped, I even looked down the Conodoguinet Creek to find the baby! This was pure imagination, of course. I was also much impressed by his wife, Anne Morrow Lindbergh.

Lindbergh was simple, in a way. He was a person of integrity, of great courage, and of bravery. He could fly an airplane, even though he could only see out in front of it by looking through a periscope. And he could fly fifteen or twenty feet above the water, or maybe thirty or forty feet during his flight to Europe.

I thought Lindbergh was a great person, and he had a great influence on me as a youngster. That said, I was somewhat disabused of some of that admiration during World War II, when his political views and details about his moral life were made known.

Something else that came along at that time as a wonder to me was the radio. Imagine just pulling music and voices out of the air! Radios operated so simply! Preaching against radios came from Lancaster Mennonite Conference, so we as Mennonites were not supposed to have them. Nevertheless, my father knew that one of his former students at Shippensburg State Teachers College was selling radios in Harrisburg. So we went there, selected one, and brought it home. It was a Majestic. I think this was in about 1926, when I was maybe nine years old.

I remember that we spent our evenings with the radio, an activity that included trying to find as many stations as possible. We would then tell our neighbors about what we found. We listened to KDKA from Pittsburgh and WHP from Harrisburg. We even listened to WJZ from New York City, which we could get quite frequently in the morning.

Every morning I turned on the radio and listened to Dick Leibert play the pipe organ at Radio City Music Hall in New York City. He played popular music—even jazz music, which I liked up to a point. The pipe organ was a mystery machine. I wondered about those pipes and how they worked. Now and then he played something I thought was especially beautiful, Handel's *Largo* or Schubert's *Ave Maria*—both somewhat sentimental and simple, not to be compared to Bach. Being able to listen to the music meant so much to me, and I enjoyed it.

On the radio I also heard on Sunday mornings many of Harry Emerson Fosdick's sermons. I did not understand all of them, but I could understand some of what I heard. I remember his saying over and over, "Behold, I stand at the door and knock," because that was the way he began his sermons. And I knew that he was broadcasting from First Presbyterian Church in New York City, and later Riverside Church, also in New York City.

Another program I enjoyed on Sunday mornings was The Children's Hour, hosted by Milton J. Cross, in which little children would perform. The world was opened up to me through radio. I began to think of things outside the little place, the little county, where I lived. I loved the radio, and I thought that a radio station was something enchanted.

We began to get a daily newspaper, except for the Sunday edition, which we were not allowed to get, even though it was published on Saturday. Ours was a Sabbatarian community with rules dictated more by local Presbyterians than by Mennonites. Mennonites were serious about Sundays as well. I remember that one Sunday morning at my church, as a very little boy I ran and skidded my feet along a carpet that was getting shiny. I was scolded—not by my family, but by somebody from the church—for running on Sunday!

We also never thought of playing ball or swimming on Sunday. One Sunday we went to visit my uncle John Seitz, who had been sent by Lancaster Mennonite Conference to be our minister for a while. He and his family lived on a beautiful farm along Yellow Birches Creek near Messiah College in Grantham, Pennsylvania. That Sunday afternoon we went swimming. I felt uncomfortable about doing so and was hoping that Jesus would not come and catch me swimming! I did not understand how it was possible that Uncle John would allow swimming on Sunday.

Maybe the teaching about not swimming on Sundays came more from the Presbyterians than the Mennonites. There was a strict Presbyterian minister in Newville named Reverend Love, who had a son, Charles Love, a schoolmate of mine. Reverend Love was a disciplinarian of the strictest sort.

Sunday afternoon was a drab time. There was nothing to do except read, and we did not have much to read. The idea of watching televised Sunday professional sports was completely unthinkable at that time. We were taught that Saturday was a day of preparation for Sunday. That was the day to read the Bible, although we did not always do so, except for my mother, who would study her Sunday school lesson. And how she studied! She studied a commentary or two and would often introduce some rather novel questions the next day.

Of course, we were imbued with the idea of the "two kingdoms." That did not come through as a doctrine—something theologians would talk about—but it was something we felt and lived. We just assumed that we were different, as Mennonites, from other people in town. At the same time, we did attend non-Mennonite churches occasionally.

We sometimes went to the Sunday afternoon vesper services on the lawn at Big Spring Presbyterian Church, which overlooked Big Spring Creek and was next to a large cemetery.[12] We also went

---

12 Big Spring Presbyterian Church was built as a log cabin in Newville in 1737 on eighty-nine acres of land donated to the Presbyterian church by

sometimes to their Sunday evening services and to those of a local Lutheran church. We—especially my mother—knew the ministers in these churches; she often talked with them. We respected non-Mennonites and were ecumenically minded. Nevertheless, we—especially our mother, who nearly always wore a covering—were recognized as Mennonites.

My father's two sisters, Aunt Ida and Aunt Lizzy, lived two blocks from us. When we went into town, we always went past their house. They were usually sitting on their porch, from where we were scrutinized. My father helped them in many ways, because they were unmarried and without professions or jobs. There were no factories in town, except one—a knitting mill. My father helped Aunt Ida become a practical nurse. When a baby was born somewhere, she would "go out on the case," as we called it, and that gave her something to do. Babies kept coming along. Since the work did not provide her an adequate income, she helped her sister, Aunt Lizzy, bake pies and bread to sell in town. They also took in washing. They were never dependent on us financially and got by, just barely. They were concerned about us children—maybe little bit overly concerned, even though from their perspective they had our well-being in mind.

Some of the conditions of our life since then have been transcended by Mennonites entirely. We thought of being Mennonite mostly in negative terms. Frequently we would go to non-Mennonite churches as a kind of relief. Other people seemed more free and friendly. And yet we were not sure that they were "good," as it had been defined for us. Big Spring Presbyterian Church was beautiful. It had high ceiling arches, a red carpet, and a pipe organ. I loved the pipe organ and went there primarily to hear it.

We also sometimes attended Zion Lutheran Church, where my mother often discussed theology with Rev. Paul Kelley, the minister. He introduced her to the idea of grace, which she passed along to me: the belief that we could be forgiven, if we would

---

the Laughlin brothers, who had built Laughlin Mill on Big Spring Creek. On this land the church platted the town land and sold the lots. The church building was rebuilt in 1789 as a stone structure.

repent. Or as Old Johnson would have said, even if we do not repent. That was an issue that challenged my thinking.

Something that made an impression on me was the death of Walter Heiser, which happened when I was six or seven years old. I never knew him personally, but I knew he was a little boy about my age who had lived in another part of town. When I got to his home for the funeral, I heard some people speaking favorably of him. And they made comments about his "being with the angels" and "being with God." To me he looked peaceful in the casket, even though he was dressed in long brown pants and black patent leather shoes, neither of which I had ever seen on a youngster before. Well, I had never before seen patent leather shoes on anybody, not even little girls!

When the minister conducted the funeral, he said what a wonderful little boy Walter had been and how he was now in the arms of Jesus. Everyone was saying such complimentary things about that little boy that I kind of wished I could die so that they would say the same of me! Seriously though, this experience did expose me to death as a fact of life. I did not brood about it, but I was more aware of it now. As I later found in being exposed to the existential thought of Søren Kierkegaard, I became more aware of the finiteness and insecurity of everything and the limits of our existence. Also the minister said, "He's now in heaven, where nothing changes." I had to reflect on that too.

I'm not sure how I got to that funeral; I don't remember my parents being with me. It was the first one I ever attended, and it made a huge impression on me. When one is so young, experiences accumulate: one learns of this and of that. Then one thinks of this and of that. This was where I was introduced to death as a possibility and an inevitability.

As a boy I was also interested in rocks. There were a lot of different kinds of rocks in Cumberland County. People nearly cursed the rocks because it was difficult to farm around them. We made a distinction between a slate-rock farm and a granite farm—or rather, limestone farm land. Frequently I would help my father's brother, Uncle Ephraim, who was a farmer. He had two horses,

Daisy and Nell. Daisy had a good temper, and Nell had a bad temper. I got behind her one time and was nearly kicked.

The farm was on a big hillside, and I did what I could to help Uncle Ephraim with his gardening and harvesting. Here again, my father came to his brother's rescue. As the Depression was starting, the farm economy was so bad that my uncle found it necessary to try to borrow money from my father, who did not have it to give him. Instead my father got him started with truck farming, raising celery and taking the produce to sell in Carlisle. My father was gifted at helping people find some way of making a living!

Another member of our church was also having a difficult time farming and was having marital troubles. My father got him started making brooms. My father had a most imaginative mind in that respect.

My father could have been a carpenter—but he became a professor, though none of us ever knew exactly how. He made money during World War I by raising a fine strain of leghorn chickens. He also sold hatchery eggs, a dollar a dozen. Apparently that is how he made enough money to buy the house in Newville into which we moved when I was three years old. My father had a difficult life in many ways, but he was respected professionally.

Unfortunately, he was not able to finish his doctoral degree from New York University before his passing at age sixty in 1938. In 1927, when I was ten years old, he went to New York University in New York City to work on his doctorate. He invited me to come and stay with him for several weeks during the summer of that year. He stayed near the university in a hotel located on Dominick Street near the entrance to the Holland Tunnel. He had a little kitchen in his room.

During that visit, I saw a side of my father that I had never appreciated before. He was warm and understanding. He allowed me to run around the city, even though I was so young. I carried the address of the hotel in a little notebook in case something happened to me or I could not find my way home.

When wandering around the city, I found something that gave me great satisfaction. I found in the Pennsylvania Station an airplane: a Ford Tri-Motor. It was possible to walk on the scaffolding around the airplane and look in its windows, where I could see the pilot's seat in the cockpit. Oh, I spent so much time there. I wanted to touch that airplane. To me it was almost like an ark; it was beyond this life. I wondered whether the time would come when I could sit in a fine airplane like that one.

That summer I got acquainted with a few boys who lived near the hotel in the area around Varick Street and who were as tough as could be. They liked to play stick-ball, a game played in the city. The rules and the general design followed baseball, but for bases they used lamp posts or street corners. I could really hit that ball! I had learned to hit stones with sticks, but now I was hitting balls! I was quite good at their game, so they wanted to know where I came from and where I had learned to play so well.

I also saw a little girl there who I thought was very nice. She was maybe eight or nine years old, a little younger than me. She came up to me and said something like, "You're good!" That was the beginning of a little infatuation between us. Her name was Evelyn Vesh, and that is all I knew about her. She was called Evie. I think she kind of liked me, or she at least liked the way I hit that ball. Maybe this was just a little early experience of fame!

I enjoyed being in New York City so much. I felt free. I could just come and go when I pleased. My father had put great confidence in me that I could find my way back to our hotel room.

At that time, though, I found out something about my father's prejudices, philosophically speaking. Philosophically, he was a follower of Herman Harrel Horne, under whom he worked at New York University. Horne was an idealist and stood in opposition to the pragmatism of John Dewey. Of course, I could only appreciate my father's point of view. I did not understand pragmatism philosophically. Instead I had the general idea that if one is an idealist, one is committed to certain abstract ideals, which—since they were put there by God—were to be obeyed, always and consistently! According to John Dewey, on the other hand, one never knew for sure what was right. And I thought that was an excuse for doing whatever one wanted to do. I thought that maybe John Dewey was not as sincere as my father.

My father was a strong Republican. When Herbert Hoover became president, his picture was placed in a window in our home. In the 1920s the Democrats were not strong in Newville; it was a Republican town.

My father did well in school; he got mostly A's. He was always hindered by economic necessity—by having a family of five children. Nevertheless, he was highly regarded as a teacher and was always reading.

In general, I would say life was good, and I am glad to have been brought up where at least there was structure and law. My family violated few church laws—except perhaps a prohibition on having a radio! For that, my father did not have to make a confession at church. In fact, confessions were seldom made in church. Instead people just quit coming to church. We did not cast out many people. It was just understood that when you did not do what Lancaster Mennonite Conference said to do, you stopped attending and went to church somewhere else.

Change took place gradually among those Mennonites. For example, when Harriet and I got married, my mother wore a head covering but no longer a plain Mennonite cape dress. And how did most Mennonites eventually get rid of the women's head covering? We just did it. That is how change has taken place in the Mennonite church for centuries! We cannot look to a Mennonite conference for official decisions.

Our congregation's leaders did not push the radio prohibition. Radios just came slowly into our homes. When Bishop Noah Mack and his wife, Biddie, came to our place twice a year, they did not say anything to us about our radio. I was baptized by Bishop Mack when I was twelve years old, and he never asked me to line up with anything. I knew anyway what I was supposed to do.

Even though there were no church rules against flying, once when Bishop Mack and his wife were sitting at our table and I was just learning to fly at about age fourteen, Biddie pointed her fin-

ger at me and said, "Young man, sometime you will come down."
I was smart enough to say, "Yes, every time I go up."

As a youngster I was overly sensitive and scared much of the
time, especially when I went to church. I could feel the tension.
There was tension with Lancaster Mennonite Conference all the
time. Within our congregation, between certain major families
there was also a little tension, which I could feel. I don't think
others were as sensitive to these tensions as I was.

The year I turned twelve, 1929, was quite a year for me.
Several interesting things happened. One was that I got a bicycle. I had wanted a bicycle for years but was unable to have one,
because they cost so much! There was a bicycle on sale for twelve
dollars from somebody named Jesse H. in Shippensburg. I bought
his Columbia bicycle, which was a good one, and did I ever ride it!

I then got a summer job delivering groceries for a young
entrepreneur, Walter Dunbar, who was starting a grocery store. I
worked for him six days a week and every day delivered groceries
on my bicycle all over town. That job enabled me to get into many,
many houses—at least into the kitchens—where I observed the
class structure of the town.

This was near the beginning of the Depression, and I saw
how hard it hit many people in our little town—though not all, to
be sure. I was in the homes of many people with real need. I knew
what they ate. I knew who ate butter and who ate margarine, and
who ate mush and who ate mush and sausage. I also knew there
were people in the town on Parsonage Street who had thick breakfast steaks, while elsewhere some older women had them cut thin.
On Parsonage Street, where the wealthy tended to live, residents
were apparently rather unscathed by the Depression.

I also discovered the African American community. There
was a small Black community in Newville. Only two students in
my entire public school experience were Black. One of them was
a very good baseball player and played on the team I played on.

A lot of people at that time were out of work and had nothing. Many of them were charging their groceries, at some risk to
Walter Dunbar, the owner of the grocery business. I got to know

every street in Newville—every brick, it would seem—because I was constantly going all day long, delivering groceries. Then on Saturday I would work in the store, waiting on customers. It was a great deal of responsibility for a twelve-year-old. I ingested a good bit of the ambiance of the time, and as a result I assumed that the world would always be poor. I thought the Depression had come to stay. I knew, because my father said so, that the only person who could help us would be President Herbert Hoover.

At the age of twelve I was also converted—if conversion is the right term. The ministerial society in Newville invited an evangelist, Rev. Luther Knox Peacock, to come from Pittsburgh to preach at Big Spring Presbyterian Church. He came from one of the seminaries there, most likely Western Theological Seminary.[13] I thought he preached good sermons and went there every evening to listen. I usually sat in the back, because the back seats had cushions! I would listen to his sermons and the invitation given afterward. "Hitting the sawdust trail" is not the proper phrase for what happened at that church, but a good many did go forward when given the invitation to do so. Among them were some of the leading citizens of the town, including several bankers and a painter who had often painted our house.

One evening the sermon was entitled "Little Man up a Tree," and Reverend Peacock said that we ought to be willing to help the Lord. This sounded right. Sitting in front of me was the leading banker of the town, Mr. Hewlett, with his son. His son was a minister who had come home and was now pleading with his father to go forward. When the father did go forward, I went along. It was nothing that resembled a great confession of sin: I knew I was not perfect, but I also knew I was not carrying a huge load of sin. It seemed like the right thing to do—like the normal thing to do. I was alone in this, in that no other member of my family was there with me.

I was met at the altar by the minister of the church, Rev. Franklin Wheeler. He shook my hand and asked me to sign a doc-

---

13 Now Pittsburgh Theological Seminary.

ument related to church preference. I did not know what to write, so I simply said, "I have not decided."

Frankly, it was a combination of things that led me to go forward. I liked Big Spring Presbyterian Church—its architecture, its high ceiling, and its pipe organ. (I was back in Newville not too long ago and saw that its sanctuary table is still there, with the large pulpit behind it, and the same artwork behind the pulpit!) I also liked the sermons. I just liked everything. I thought it represented me. Then the question was: Would I join a Presbyterian church? I talked to my mother about this, and she said, "It is up to you."

I decided that I would remain a Mennonite—that is, Mennonite in the formal sense. I think I did so primarily because my father had warned me that every twenty-five years there is a war and that I would not want to fight. So it would be more reasonable for me to be a conscientious objector as a Mennonite than as a Presbyterian.

Several years after I was baptized, Big Spring Presbyterian Church got a new minister, Rev. William T. Swaim, who happened to be a pacifist. He grew up in the South in a prominent Presbyterian family and went to a Presbyterian college, where he had roomed with an African American student. He was a wonderful man, and my parents knew him quite well. My mother in particular had many conversations with him, so he had a huge influence on my family.

Because of Reverend Swaim, I thought again about becoming a Presbyterian. The problem for me with doing so was that on Sunday mornings, when the other members of my family went off into the country to Diller Mennonite Church, I would need to go to church alone. It was a little too much for me as such a young person to anticipate being separated from my family in that way. I decided to remain a Mennonite.

When I joined Diller Mennonite Church, I was not given any catechetical instruction. After the sermon, Bishop Noah Mack baptized me. I did declare that I had wanted to be baptized, but I do not remember how word got to the bishop. I do not remember with whom I talked about this, and I do not remember who was pastor at our church at that time, because we had so many!

Ministers were visiting our congregation all the time, which must have been a burden for Lancaster Mennonite Conference. And we could be critical of them, though they were critical of our congregation as well. We were a group of individuals, many of whom were aspiring businessmen and educators who were a little out of sync with the Lancaster ethos! The conference did not understand us, and we just did not understand Lancaster conference thinking. Nor did we know what it meant to live in a Mennonite community where we would have ordinary daily relationships with others like ourselves. At Diller, we were individual families who came together only on Sundays.

After the sermon on the Sunday of my baptism, it was announced that I should come forward. And I did. Actually, I was sitting up front already. That is all I remember. It was no big deal; it was just done.

I was prepared a little theologically, though, because as a child I had attended Bible school sponsored by the churches in town. There I had learned a great deal about the Westminster Catechism, which I had memorized—even though it did not mean much to me. At this Bible school we were not told many Bible stories, although I already knew the stories quite well.

One time I had the opportunity to go to church with my mother's sister, Aunt Sue Seitz. It was a fundamentalist church in West Hill, where she lived. While there, I went to a Sunday school class in which they were studying the Old Testament. I was able to tell Old Testament stories and impressed them with how much I knew. I knew, for example, the stories of Joseph and Abraham. I did have quite a good ear. I lived in an adult context, except for being with my brothers and sisters. As a result, at an early age I began to think like an adult in some ways. I was not totally mature by any means, but I began to think rather serious thoughts at a young age—maybe too young.

All at once when I was twelve years old, I began to grow taller and could handle a baseball glove well enough to play second base on the town team. We played quite well with other town teams. Soon I became the catcher. I was able to catch fast pitches. Our team was called the Chevrolet team because the manager of the team sold Chevrolets.

I would say that the team was representative of our town but not of my Mennonite faith in all respects. I remember that once when we played Belleville, an Amish and Mennonite community north of Cumberland County, a good many of the members of my team got drunk. Maybe I was thirteen or fourteen when that happened. I played baseball from the age of twelve and then all through high school and college.

I could handle a baseball glove well, but I had one problem. By the time I was in high school, I was so tall and thin that I had difficulty getting down on my knees to catch the ball, as catchers need to do, and then throw it to second base. I could pitch quite well in the springtime, but by the time July came around, my arm had begun to give out on me.

When it came to striking the ball in those days, no one could explain exactly how best to do it. It was done by natural impulse and ability. My problem was that I always struck late. I had a fairly good batting average anyway. As a right-handed batter, I hit balls out to right field, often between first and second base.

I was a good enough baseball player that I was looked at by professionals at one point. I loved baseball, and I would have liked to become a professional baseball player. One problem for me was that I would have had to play on Sundays, which conflicted with the beliefs I had grown up with.

If chosen, I would have played on a professional farm team for the Philadelphia Phillies. The farm was located in Harrisburg, Pennsylvania, on an island in the Susquehanna River. I never made it, so I never had to make a decision about playing for the team.

I took my first airplane ride at age twelve, when someone at the county fair offered people rides for a penny a pound. I weighed a little over a hundred pounds, so I think the ride cost about a dollar and ten cents. The flight consisted of the take-off, a three-sixty turn, the landing, and that is all. The plane was an old Curtiss Robin, three-place, closed cockpit monoplane, but what a thrill it was! The pilot sat in the front with the control stick, and two people sat behind him.

I remember seeing an advertisement for a plane of that kind in the *Saturday Evening Post*. It described two businessmen who had bought an airplane in support of their business. Well, the idea of using an airplane for business purposes was a new phenomenon! I thought flying airplanes was only for fun. Though I did not realize it, commercial airlines—including United Airlines and Pan American Airlines—were already in existence in the 1920s.

I enjoyed high school. I was not very good in math or chemistry, but I was very good in history. I had a wonderful history teacher named Russell B. Henneberger. He was the first teacher whom I especially admired and who taught me something about history. He was also a good singer and had leads in several dramatic presentations in town. He was a handsome man and a good Christian, though I do not know his denomination.

It was during this time that—partly by accident—I learned to fly. There was a little airport east of us, between Carlisle and Harrisburg, where a pilot and his wife lived in a mobile home. I visited the pilot once and looked at his airplane, which was an old Jenny OX-5. (OX-5 refers to the engine.) It was an engine that was unreliable and had a bad reputation. Unfortunately, it was about the only engine at the time that was available for biplanes—a Curtiss Jenny in this case. One time the pilot took me up and let me take the controls. He let me fly the plane until near touch down. I have never forgotten that great experience!

He invited me to take a trip with him to Washington, DC, in that little biplane. Since an OX-5 engine flew inconsistently, we never flew over towns. We would always fly around them, just in case the motor stopped! The speed for cruising with that plane was about 1200 revolutions per minute (rpm), whereas full throttle was about 1400. In comparison, modern planes cruise at about 2200 to 2600 rpm. When we were moving along, we could hear every cylinder as it fired—like in a little tractor. We only hoped that the cylinders would continue to fire while we were flying!

When we arrived at Washington, DC, we landed at an airport located across the Potomac River near Washington National Airport. The pilot let me fly the plane from Frederick, Maryland, back to Carlisle.

This pilot could not pass the physical examination in Cumberland County for some reason, so he went to Washington, DC, to take it. There came a time when I noticed he always landed the plane rather awkwardly. He would come in fast and hit the ground with the front wheels, which (thankfully!) were solidly attached to the airplane. They were not intended to do anything but give support to the airplane when it was on the ground. He attempted to land one time at an air meet in Harrisburg and had to go around three times before he could land. He would always bounce rather severely. After I had learned a few things from other sources about flying, I came to the conclusion that he really did not know how to fly well.

Eventually this little airport was bought by a man named Wilson from Boiling Springs, Pennsylvania, who had several other planes. He took me up on flights with him a few times, but he soon let me fly alone.

In Newville, we had the Memorial Day tradition of having someone fly an airplane over our town to drop flowers on the Big Spring Presbyterian Church cemetery. In 1933, when I was in high school and was about fifteen years old, I applied for the job and got it. I then rented a plane and filled the cockpit with flowers. Since I was paid by the American Legion for the flight, it was hardly what a pacifist should be doing. But before World War II, every Memorial Day was devoted to the hope for peace. Since pacifism dominated the mainline churches then, I did not think that what I was doing was in any way supportive of war. I saw it as a celebration of the fact that we would have no more wars. This was a liberal pacifist perspective at that time.

I flew from the airport, which was twenty miles from Newville, to the cemetery where the Memorial Day parade was forming. When I flew over the cemetery, some of the flowers I dropped got into the cemetery and others did not.

Harold, my older brother, was working for the summer as chauffeur for Mrs. Katherine Graham, widow of the Honorable John Graham; she was the leading lady in town. She always led the Memorial Day parade in her black LaSalle. When I flew over the cemetery and dropped flowers, her car was parked in the driveway of Big Spring Presbyterian Church, about fifteen feet from the large monument where her husband was buried. A bunch of the flowers I had just dropped happened to fall right on her husband's grave! My brother said to her, "Isn't that marvelous?"

Of course, it was purely by accident that the flowers landed where they did, but it appeared as if I had honored her husband in this way. She said in a southern accent, "Oh, yes, that's marvelous. Have him come to see me."

That evening, when I returned from the airport, I went to see her. She invited me in, and we had a conversation. She told me that Admiral Richard Byrd, Jr., had once sat in the seat where I was sitting. Admiral Byrd is the famous pilot who made Arctic flights. He had come to get support from her—she was a wealthy woman—for his flights. I felt greatly honored. And when I left, she gave me five dollars, which was a lot of money at that time. For the moment, in a remote way, I felt as if I were in a class with Admiral Byrd! I have some photos of that flight that appeared in our local newspaper.

I enjoyed flying so much in those days, even though I was doing so illegally. At that time nobody paid much attention to licensing. If a person had a license, fine; if not, one just did a little flying now and then. I did not go far when flying.

My interest in flying was interrupted during the summer following my junior year in high school. Reverend Swaim from Big Spring Presbyterian Church came into Walter Dunbar's grocery store where I was working on a Saturday night and said that he had received an emergency call to go to a church in Pittsburgh. He was supposed to preach a sermon there the next evening. In those days, Presbyterian churches always had Sunday evening services.

He asked me if I would be willing to preach for him the following night. I was just astounded. Why would he ask me to do anything like that? We had had fine conversations before, but I had never spoken in public. I had read the Sunday school attendance roll at my church but had never given a speech there, never. I reluctantly said, "Yes, I will do it."

The audience at the church that Sunday evening consisted mostly of older ladies, as I remember. Somehow I got a sermon together. I do not remember what I preached about. It so happened that there was a man in the audience by the name of Harry Cox, a brother to our family doctor, Paul Cox. Harry was a missionary from Africa, with an African inland mission, a somewhat fundamentalist mission. He was impressed by what I said. He came to me and said that he would like to send me to Moody Bible Institute in Chicago for the summer.

I did not know anything about Moody Bible Institute. Furthermore, I was planning to take on a little job at the local airport, where I would be servicing planes. There I could at least have gotten in a few hours of flying. I would maybe become a real pilot, I thought. In spite of having that opportunity, my sense of religiosity or commitment came through, and I said, "Sure, I'll go."

I got on the train, along with my brother Harold's girlfriend, Gladys Schertz, who was from Illinois, and went to Chicago. I believe I attended Moody Bible Institute for about seven weeks. This was in 1935, when the Depression was felt so deeply. I roomed with an ex–prize fighter, Joe Catalino, from West Virginia. He often came into our room, said "Hi, Burk," and then hit me on the shoulder. His aim was to return to and evangelize West Virginia. He was a recent convert; we had many conversations.

I did not enjoy the classwork at Moody Bible Institute much, but I did enjoy the city. I wandered around to look for museums. I especially enjoyed concerts by the Grant Park Symphony Orchestra given at Grant Park. I thoroughly enjoyed the music of Beethoven, Brahms, Bach. I attended those concerts regularly.

I enjoyed the good food at Moody Bible Institute. At that time I was hungry all the time, as I was still a growing boy. I volunteered to work in the kitchen, which meant that I could eat extra food. Happily, I had plenty to eat that summer.

I also went swimming in Lake Michigan frequently. Occasionally I attended the Mennonite Home Mission on Sundays. My future wife, Harriet Lapp, would work there several years later.

Next to Michigan Avenue was a place called Bughouse Square. It was where all the revolutionaries set up their soap boxes and gave speeches. Because of the Depression, the speeches had Depression themes, and a few of the speakers were probably communistic. I spent some time listening to them, but not too intently.

One time I was listening to a speech on a Sunday afternoon, and standing beside me was a handsome, well-dressed man. We got into a conversation—I do not know how, because I was young and naive. Soon he said, "Well, it is lunchtime. Would you like to have lunch with me?"

Of course, I could not turn down that offer, so we went over to a nearby hotel, where they had a wonderful cafeteria with everything good, including steaks, chops, and seafood. He said to me, "Eat whatever you want." So I did. And then, when we were finished eating, he said, "We'll just walk over to my hotel."

After we walked into his hotel room, he said, "We can go swimming."

Since I did not have swimming trunks, he said, "Ah! Here are some trunks."

He handed me a pair of trunks, and I started undressing. Then he said, "You're so handsome."

I said, "Whoa, I've never been told that before."

Then he said, "You have nice legs."

I had never heard of homosexuality. I did not know there was such a thing. But soon I figured out that something was happening there. I said, "Well, if you'll forgive me, I'd like to leave." And I left. That was my first and last experience of that kind. He was very kind, when one considers my innocence. The experience introduced me to a certain dimension of life and social existence that I had not known about before.

That summer I learned something else—about myself. I was supposed to go out and do some street preaching with other students. I did not know how to do it and did not know what to say. I could not speak with integrity. Nevertheless, I had a Bible with me and read little Scripture verses out loud. That was as far as I could go with it. I felt that I did not fit in with the school. I wrote a rather pathetic letter to Reverend Swaim to ask him whether I should come home. And he said that I could, but he said, "Since you understand the situation, maybe you could just stick it out."

I stuck it out for the summer. I went to nearby Fourth Presbyterian Church, which had a good organist. I sang in the choir for a short while and had the opportunity to practice directing a little. Overall, being at Moody Bible Institute in Chicago was a fairly good experience. I have to wonder, though, whether I should have stayed at home to go flying instead!

Not long after that summer, a relative of my mother was killed in an airplane crash. He had joined the air force and was flying a little stubby-winged Boeing, a fighter plane, over a girlfriend's house in Idaho when it stalled out and he was killed. I went to his funeral at a Presbyterian church in nearby Carlisle and heard the minister say that the deceased was now sailing in the skies above heaven. He gave a graphic view of heaven: not golden streets, but wonderful skies.

Another relative, a cousin, Henry Stoner Baer, was also a flyer. He learned to fly a Curtiss Condor, which was an old passenger biplane. In September of 1934, he was flying in Cleveland, Ohio, when he took off and either stalled or had engine problems. He was killed. That was difficult for me to take. I had been with him sometimes at a little airport near Carlisle, where he had flown a nice little airplane which I had also flown. He was a big, tall, handsome man, as were many of my Baer-Seitz relatives.

I went to his funeral, which was held in an ultraconservative Reformed Mennonite Church in Plainfield, a little village near West Hill. The church is now gone. The minister said that my

J. Lawrence Burkholder as a high school senior in 1936

cousin was "unsaved" because he had never joined the Reformed Mennonite Church, not because he was a bad person or because he had joined the air force.

This congregation was part of an ultra-conservative group that came out of Lancaster Mennonite Conference. According to my mother, they believed that the only people who were saved were the members of their denomination. My grandmother, Elizabeth Baer Seitz, had belonged to that church before she was married.

I graduated from high school with fairly good grades. Reverend Swaim gave our graduation speech at a local Lutheran church, and his topic was "The University of Hard Knocks." It was an interesting sermon, but I could not fully understand it. He prophesied that there was going to be a war in the near future. It was 1936, when there were signs that it could happen because of strains in Europe. Though he correctly anticipated World War II and thought it was coming, he could not completely explain it. Even so, what he said was sobering.

The issue of war was one reason I went to a Mennonite school, Goshen College. It would have been much less expensive and easier to go to Shippensburg State Teachers College, where my father taught. Academically it would also have been less challenging. I never did like to study foreign languages and could have gotten through Shippensburg without having to do so.

One of the big decisions of my life was therefore made primarily through the influence of Reverend Swaim. He always kept in touch with me while I was in college. Every summer when I came home, we played tennis or golf together. He turned out to be not very successful in his ministry, because he was ahead of his congregation on social issues. He had been an excellent seminary student and had married the daughter of a professor from Western Theological Seminary in Pittsburgh. He eventually left the ministry to become a promoter for Presbyterian retirement homes, one of which is located on one of Newville's beautiful hills.

I am glad that I decided to go to Goshen College, though I could have gone in many other directions, such as becoming a pilot with a commercial license. With only fifty hours of flying, I could have been ready for a commercial job. We were told not to trust our instruments and rather to fly by contact. We were supposed to land without looking at the air speed indicator, because it might be wrong. So one flew by instinct, or with whatever athletic ability one had.

In those days, we really dressed like pilots. We wore high leather shoes, britches with a flight jacket, goggles, helmets, and scarves. The clothes represented a romantic ideal that we were always trying to fulfill. I remember when I got my first goggles. They were expensive, and did I ever prize them! At that time aviators were considered to be a little bit above the normal cut! We were famous just for being able to fly an airplane. Often at table discussions, someone would ask, "Have you ever been up?" Then all would tell about their first experience of having ridden in an airplane. Now discussions about flying are so humdrum, so boring.

In those days, pilots had only a few instruments, including a tachometer for measuring revolutions per minute, an altimeter, and a temperature gauge. When flying, we looked over the nose of the airplane and hoped that the engine would not quit. It was so exciting to fly somewhere, and to find one's way back was considered an achievement!

An engine did quit on me once, but it happened so recently, about seven or eight years ago, that I hesitate to mention it. I was flying an ultralight plane when the throttle wire broke near the carburetor. I was coming in for a landing, and it was getting dark. I pushed forward with the throttle but got no response. The engine would not come out of idling mode. I had to decide whether I would go over the approaching power wires or go under them. I thought I could go over them and did so. I landed safely and just pushed the plane back into the hangar. I am thankful that with all my flying, I never had engine failure apart from that one time.

2

College Years and a Ministry in Croghan, 1936–44

I went to Goshen College in 1936 and got my bachelor's degree in three years. I was in a hurry in those days and went to summer school at Shippensburg State Teachers College. I rushed through college for financial reasons and because I wanted to get married. I met Harriet Lapp at Goshen College, when I was a freshman and she was a senior. We had a fine time together. We enjoyed going to concerts, and we both liked music. Although I could play the piano a little, she could sing and play the piano well.

We were both interested in the church. We decided to serve the Mennonite Church in some capacity but did not know where. At that time, the Mennonite Church had no seminary, and there was no way of going into ministry except by being chosen "by lot" or doing mission work.

Harriet had grown up in India, where her parents were missionaries.[1] It was assumed by

J. Lawrence Burkholder and Harriet Lapp, on a 1939 visit to J. Lawrence's home in Newville, Pennsylvania

---

1 Harriet's parents, George J. and Esther Ebersole Lapp, went to Dhamtari, India, as missionaries in 1905. Their three daughters were Lois Lapp Camp

Harriet Lapp Burkholder with members of her family: stepmother Fannie Hershey Lapp (1882–1963), Harriet, father George J. Lapp (1879–1951), and sister Lois Lapp Camp (1907–99)

people who knew her—including her father, George J. Lapp, and stepmother, Fannie Hershey Lapp—that she would return to India as a missionary. At one time she thought of being a medical doctor or a nurse. She did not beg me to become interested in India, but it was more or less assumed at one point that she was going to India, and I would go along as her husband. For some reason, I was not attracted to the idea of going to India. She showed me the book *Building on the Rock*, "written by missionaries" (Scottdale, PA: Mennonite Publishing House, 1926), about Mennonite mission work in India. It did not move me. Nevertheless, we continued to

---

(1907–99) who was born in Igatpuri, India; Pauline (1910–13) who was born in Dhamtari, India, and who died of diphtheria; and Harriet Lapp Burkholder (1915–2007) who was born in Calcutta, India. In 1917, two years after giving birth to Harriet, Esther died of black water fever. George then returned to America with Lois and Harriet, who lived with friends and relatives for two years. During one of those years, 1918–19, George was interim president of Goshen College.

go together, and she agreed that if we were married, I could follow my inclinations.

I wanted to be a minister like Reverend Swaim. He was my model, even though I did not want to become a Presbyterian minister. What did it mean to become a Mennonite minister? At that time ministers were not supported financially by their congregations and were usually chosen from within the congregation before being ordained.

Harriet majored in Bible and biology and graduated in 1937. She then took another semester of college to complete a bachelor of theology degree, graduating in 1938. She studied Greek and was better with it than I was. I majored in history under Guy F. Hershberger. I took everything he taught and enjoyed his classes very much. I made good grades, but I did not like studying German.

After Harriet graduated, she went to Mennonite Home Mission in Chicago for about a year and a half, where she worked with, among others, Anna Yordy, a long-time mission worker. I frequently visited her in Chicago. She was not entirely happy with her work, but she had good friends there who worked with her, and I had a lot of respect for the work that they did.[2]

After I graduated from college in 1939, we were married on August 20 in Manheim, Pennsylvania, in the home of her step-

---

2 The work of the Mennonite Home Mission in Chicago was begun informally in 1893 by a group of Mennonite young people, many of whom were students in Chicago. At the time of its closing in 1957, the mission was located at 1907 South Union Avenue, which was later in the path of an expressway. The mission effort then became Englewood Mennonite Church, now located at 832 West 68th Street in Chicago. Harriet's parents, George J. and Esther Ebersole Lapp, and her stepmother, Fannie Hershey Lapp, were among the many young Mennonites who worked at the mission before embarking on foreign ministries. George was there from 1902 to 1904 and it was there that he met his future wife, Esther Ebersole, who was in nurse's training at Passavant Memorial Hospital in Chicago but was briefly involved with the work of the mission. George's second wife, Fannie Hershey Lapp, worked at the mission in 1909.

J. Lawrence and Harriet Lapp Burkholder's wedding on August 29, 1939, in Manheim, Pennsylvania, with J. Lawrence's family: Carl and sister Evelyn (Burkholder) Kreider, brother Harold Burkholder with fiancée Gladys Schertz, J. Lawrence and Harriet, sister Mildred Burkholder, sister Verna Burkholder, and mother Mary Seitz Burkholder

grandparents, Amos and Lavina Hershey, the parents of her step-mother, Fannie Hershey Lapp.[3]

Even though I thought I was smart to have gotten my college degree in three years, I had no idea what to do after graduation. I finally decided to go to Princeton Theological Seminary in Princeton, New Jersey. Dean Harold S. Bender of Goshen College had gone there, and I hoped he could help me get in. He did.

---

3 Fannie Hershey had lived and worked at various locations in India. She married George in 1920 in Manheim, Pennsylvania, at the home of her parents. They then returned to India with daughters Lois and Harriet. George and Fannie retired to Goshen, Indiana, in 1945 after forty years of service in India. George then became director of Bible correspondence for Goshen College until his passing in 1951. Fannie died in 1963.

On our honeymoon we went to Princeton, where we found a place to live for the next year. Harriet worked in the Princeton University Library. Unfortunately, we had few financial resources, as we were still feeling the effects of the Depression, which our country was just starting to come out of at that time. I worked part-time at an A&P grocery store. Somehow we made it. We spent no more than three or four dollars a week for groceries.

We lived near the Westminster Choir school on Pine Street. Because of our love for music, we went to the school often to hear their choir or an organ recital. I went to some football games and sold programs to get in free. Princeton was an interesting little town. And as I remember, 1939–40 was the year of the World's Fair in New York City.

That year I learned that I am more interested in some theological issues than in others. I took a course in apologetics, in which we discussed naturalism and its many forms. I studied enough in that course to doubt whether much of what was reported in the Old Testament happened. I doubted that the Old Testament narratives were history. I wrote a paper to that effect for Henry S. Gehman, professor of Old Testament.

At the same time, I appreciated the New Testament and made a distinction between the New Testament and the Old Testament on matters of faith. Of course, I did not understand the Old Testament in its historical context, because I was not allowed to look at it in that way. At that time, Professor Gehman would not take a position on such matters himself, but he did introduce us to Julius Wellhausen's theory of documentary strata in the books ascribed to Moses (the Torah). The documentary hypothesis proposes that the five books of Moses were constituted by later redactors from four main distinct sources, the Jahwist, the Elohist, the Deuteronomist, and the Priestly (JEDP). Princeton Theological Seminary was just making the transition from its earlier conservatism to what might be called crisis theology or neo-orthodoxy, which accepted the principles of the Wellhausen hypothesis.

Because of my theological questions, I began to wonder whether I wanted to be a minister after all, even though I wanted to continue my studies. At the end of the year, we were out of money and had no family resources to help us. My father had died in 1938, and my mother was at home without much money. My father died one year before his retirement fund would have accrued to her. Social security as we know it did not exist then. My mother's sister, Sue Seitz, moved in with her from West Hill.

To be closer to my mother, Harriet and I moved in the fall of 1940 to Gettysburg, Pennsylvania, where I went to Lutheran Theological Seminary at Gettysburg. I just showed up, because I did not know I needed to apply! The dean said, "So you're a Mennonite?"

I said, "Yes, the Mennonite Church."

"Is that a church or a sect?" he asked.

"Well, we call it a church," I answered, because I did not know what "sect" meant!

A few circumstances made it financially possible for us to go to Gettysburg. Walter Dunbar, the grocer for whom I had worked in Newville as a youngster, had gone out of business because of the Depression. He was selling insurance and living in Gettysburg. He was unmarried and had to have a place to live. We worked out an arrangement with him in which he rented from us a particular room in the house where we were living. Harriet worked in a G. C. Murphy five-and-dime store, and I worked at an A&P grocery store. With those three forms of income, we were able to make it for two years.

I preached frequently at Fairfield Mennonite Church, which I considered a quite liberal (General Conference) Mennonite church congregation. It was the church of good friends of ours, Howard and Ruth Musselman.

I was challenged by much of the theology of Gettysburg seminary at that time. I wondered if their Lutheranism was dealing with the facts of life, particularly when it came to their talk of Jesus being "in, with, and under the sacraments." Coming from Mennonite tradition, I argued that the communion host was simply a symbol.

I found the professors admirable, including Professor John Aberly, who belonged to the Boston school of "personalist" theology. He believed in a personal God and explained that the purpose of Christianity is to build up personhood. He had spent most of his life in India as a missionary, and I saw in him a genuine concern and love for others.

I also learned about the term *grace*, which I had not heard much about before. At least, I had not heard the term explained in a way that I understood. It was illuminating to learn about the concept of grace. The term *agape love* was also getting attention theologically, and it was an amazing discovery for me as well. Other theological issues that I was exposed to while at school were related to the problem of evil.

At that time I was thinking favorably about pacifism as a political alternative. Professor Raymond T. Stamm, a product of the University of Chicago school of thought, was the New Testament professor at Gettysburg. He was interested not only in the New Testament but also in its implication for political reality. This was 1941–42, when the United States had become involved in World War II. He was a pacifist at that time.

At the beginning of the war, we had not heard much about the European treatment of Jews and about the death camps. I was an enthusiastic, strongly convicted political pacifist. I was still listening to sermons on the radio by Harry Emerson Fosdick, who was a pacifist, and Frederick Stamm, a United Church of Christ minister from New York City, also a pacifist. Reverend Swaim from Newville, with whom I kept in contact, was still a pacifist during the early part of World War II.

About that time I had to register for the draft, which I did as a conscientious objector. As a seminary student, I was not called up for military duty, and I was able to finish my theological education at Gettysburg. I completed a bachelor of divinity degree in 1942, and I think I may have graduated second in my class. First in the class was Robert H. Fischer, who became a professor of church history at Lutheran School of Theology, Chicago.

Then what to do? I did not know. There was a rather isolated conservative Mennonite community in Upstate New York, in the vicinity of a little town called Croghan. These folks sometimes called themselves Amish, even though they belonged to the Conservative Amish Mennonite Conference. The first settlers had emigrated in 1833 from the Palatinate, a region in southwestern Germany, and spoke French when they came to New York. The strictness of the conference to which they belonged—about clothing, among other things—was a problem for some of its members. These members broke away from the conference and formed a new congregation called First Mennonite Church of New Bremen, established November 11, 1941, with seventy-six charter members. Their bishops from the (Old) Mennonite Church were S. C. Yoder, president of Goshen College; David A. Yoder, Elkhart, Indiana; and Simon Gingerich from Wayland, Iowa.

This congregation was located near Watertown, New York, and was about twenty miles from the Thousand Islands in the St. Lawrence River. It was dairy farming country, and the land was good only for farming and logging. Since the

J. Lawrence and Harriet Burkholder with daughter Myrna, born 1941 in Gettysburg, Pennsylvania

congregation needed a minister, S. C. Yoder contacted me about going there.

Would I go there? I did not know anything about these people. Since I did not have any other work, I decided to do so. Immediately after I graduated in June of 1942, Harriet and I and our first child, Myrna, who had been born in Gettysburg on July 25, 1941, went from Gettysburg to Harrisburg, Pennsylvania, where we took a train to New York City. We changed trains at Grand Central Station and went from there to Utica, New York. We were met in Utica

J. Lawrence and Harriet Burkholder with daughter Myrna at First Mennonite Church of New Bremen, New York, 1942, during J. Lawrence's pastorate there

by one of the leaders of the congregation, Ben Zehr, with his wife, Suzanna, and their two daughters. He was in the lumber and construction business and was the leader of the congregation. He was the one who drew together the dissenting group. We grew to view him as a peacemaker.

What would I do to make a living? The congregation had no provision whatsoever for my support. So Ben Zehr gave me a job in his sawmill, where I worked five days a week in addition to preaching on Sunday mornings. The people in the congregation were delightful, but culturally I had to make a rather complete 180-degree turn. There was no music there, or books, or a library—nothing in the community of a cultural nature. What did we do? We talked cows, lumbering, and maple sugaring. We also talked about babies and big families.

These folks were genuine. A sense of humor accompanied their conservatism. There were quite a few plain coats in the congregation, and they wanted me to start wearing a plain coat, but I pleaded with them to let me wear a plain vest with an ordinary black business suit. During our first year there, we visited every household. We had to go after milking, which was finished at about eight o'clock each night. We put Myrna in a collapsible baby coach, and she was often sleeping by the time we arrived. Our purpose was not to make a pastoral visit but rather to get acquainted and just talk. Sometimes we had prayer, though not always. It was our way of entering into and becoming part of the community.

We did go to several musical concerts in Watertown. One thing we had of a cultural nature in our home was a record player that played 78 rpm records. We had one album, a recording of Beethoven's piano concerto no. 5, known as the *Emperor Concerto*. We played it so often that to this day I cannot listen to it.

We simply tried to identify with the community. I advanced to working in the sawmill's accounting office. While I did not really enjoy the job, it helped me get to know members of the congregation who worked for Ben Zehr's construction company as carpenters and masons. They lived ordinary lives. We ate their food, enjoyed being with them, and experienced them as wonderful people. Only two people in the congregation had college degrees: Kathleen Zehr and Charlotte Zehr, the two daughters of Ben and Suzanna Zehr.

I began to run out of sermon material because I did not have time to read. I did not get *Christian Century* or any other theological magazine; I could not afford such periodicals. We were given one offering a month. Once a month the visiting brother, Simon Lehman, stood up to say, "Now this is the Sunday when we give a freewill offering to go to our minister." That offering would amount to $15–$18, which paid our rent.

Since we had no automobile when we arrived, a fine person in the congregation by the name of Sam Yantzi, who had a car dealership, gave us an old Chrysler.

One member had inherited a big farm with a herd of about 125 cows—a lot of cows for that time. He said to me, "Lawrence, do you have life insurance?"

"Yes, I have something with Presbyterian Life and Casualty. It isn't much, but it is something," I answered.

Then he said, "What will it pay out?"

After I told him that I did not know, he said, "We can't have that here."

So I gave up my life insurance. I did not even contest it. Maybe he figured that he had some insurance in the form of cows and land.

We had a rather delicate relationship with the older, more conservative churches in the area. Many families were split down the middle, with some staying with the older churches and others joining ours. These congregations are still there, although they have really changed since then. I had to enter into as favorable a relationship as possible with the ministers of those churches.

When I had on my vest with a lay-down collar, I looked like a Catholic priest. Croghan was considered a Catholic community and had a Catholic seminary. Seeing the monks walking by, one would have thought it was medieval times. Sometimes when I encountered them in the streets, we had little conversations. I always walked through town to get our mail. It helped me get to know others, with whom I developed friendly relationships.

We started a congregational Sunday school program, for which we got Sunday school quarterlies, and we had a summer Bible school. I organized a little boys choir, which sang quite well. One little fellow who sang beautifully later became a leading banker in Watertown. Much of what is commonplace now in church was new to them. And some of the young people began to attend Goshen College or Bethel College, a General Conference

Mennonite Church college in Newton, Kansas. Even today, the people from that congregation who later moved to Goshen, Indiana, get together every year, with up to a hundred people attending!

At that time, because of World War II, young men were being drafted into the military. All Mennonite young men had to do to pass the board examination for conscientious objection to military service was quote Bible verses. I taught some of the men in the area a few verses they could say.

The older (Old) Mennonite Church leaders in the area were just not able to speak with the draft board. They could not articulate their ideas about pacifism. The draft board was tough. These church leaders looked to me to enter into dialogue with the draft board about war. The chairman of the draft board was a gunsmith of German background named Jack Wolschlager. He strongly held the just war theory and challenged me to provide a convincing answer. We had quite a few conversations about our views on war.

Wolschlager brought up with me the horrors of the emerging situation in Europe with respect to Nazi death camps. Germany in 1943 was advancing, so our whole nation was mobilized for war. We were all living on food stamps. I had to face the fact that the actions of Hitler and Stalin were leading to great human suffering and death. I wondered what the future of the world would be if they were not stopped. My own pacifism was being tested.

Surprisingly, I had been told at Lutheran Theological Seminary at Gettysburg, under the instruction of J. Roy Strock, that the way to approach evil was simply to be good and goodness would be rewarded by the decline of hostilities. And I believed that there are circumstances in which that could be true. I wondered, though, if that could be true in this case.

One of my coworkers at the A&P grocery store in Gettysburg was killed in the war. He had become a pilot and was shot down. Wolschlager told me that my proper place was to become a bomber pilot, if I could. The military was training pilots in Utica, New York, about seventy miles south of Croghan. (I had stopped in at the Utica airport several times to fly a Waco F2.) Wolschlager was encouraging me to go back there and tell them I wanted to fly or learn to be an instructor. I knew I was not good enough to be an instructor, but I could learn to be one. Like many things in those days, it would have been done in a rush.

I imagined that I would be flying over the continent of Europe to drop fire bombs on cities. I could not do that. It just was not in me. I did not have to remember the Sermon on the Mount or the teachings of Jesus to find a principle that would make me morally bound not to do this. It was a feeling I had; I just could not do it.

At the same time, I had a hard time contemplating what it must be like to be living in Hamburg or Berlin, or another European city, when the bombs dropped. It was a major conflict for me. How was it possible to get out of a conflict of an ultimate nature such as that? I felt that I could find a way around it, if I could not find my way out of it.

In the spring of 1944, I read an article by American journalist Theodore White (then a correspondent for the weekly news magazine *Time*) about starvation and cannibalization in Honan Province[4] in China. I knew that the General Conference Mennonites had a mission in that province, though the (Old) Mennonites did not have a mission anywhere in China at that time. I read about the bombing of Chungking,[5] the Chinese provisional capital, which had no defenses against the Japanese who were proceeding west to Hanku.[6] That was more than halfway through the mainland of China, just where the mountains start.

Something told me that I should go there. This was now later in 1944. For some reason, though it may have been providential, Mennonite Central Committee (MCC), the relief and service organization for Mennonite-related denominations, decided that somebody should go to China to do relief work. They sent S. Floyd Pannabecker, a former China (General Conference) Mennonite missionary and educator to China, and Robert Kreider.

---

4 Now Henan Province.

5 Now Chongqing.

6 Now Wuhan.

Robert Kreider got only as far as Durban, South Africa. He had to return, because a law had just been passed by the US Congress that prevented Civilian Public Service (CPS) volunteers from serving outside the US. (Later, from 1946 to 1949, Kreider served as director of MCC's postwar relief work in Europe.)

Since I, as a licensed minister, was exempt from being drafted, I volunteered to go to China to work with Mennonite Central Committee—after processing this decision with the congregation and with Harriet. We left Upstate New York in October of 1944. By this time, we had a second child, Howard, who was born in Lowville, New York, in July 1943.

3

Relief Work in India and China, 1944–48

In October of 1944, I started my journey to China. I left my family with the understanding that Mennonite Central Committee would support Harriet and our two children, and I would get $10 a month in spending money. Harriet and our children moved to Goshen, Indiana, and lived for a year with Florence Amstutz and her four children. Her husband, H. Clair Amstutz, was in Puerto

During 1944–45, Harriet, Myrna, and Howard Burkholder lived with the Amstutz family at 312 South Fifth Street, Goshen, Indiana, while J. Lawrence was in Calcutta.

My Dear Little Myrna,

Here is a another letter all for you. How I would like to see you and Howard again. Mother tells me in her letters that both of you are growing to be so big and strong. Someday I will come back to live with you and mother and then we will do many things just like we used to do. Do you remember how we used to go to church together and Daddy would preach; we would take rides in the boat and Daddy would fish?

Did you have a good time at Christmas? Mother tells me in her letters that you got a lovely doll and a crib. How I would like to see it, and your train and all the other nice things which were under the Christmas tree Christmas morning. You should be a very happy little girl since you have such a good mother, so many little friends like John and Alan with whom you can play.

Do you remember how you went on the train to St. Paul to see Uncle Ezra, Aunt Lois, Dickie and Johny and Evelyn and the baby. I'll bet you had a good time playing in the snow, and riding on the sled. When Daddy was a boy he was especially fond of sliding down big long hills.

I am especially glad to hear that you can sing so beautifully. I would like to hear you sing "O Come All Ye Faithful" and "Silent Night" They are among my favorite songs. I wish that you would learn to sing many nice songs about Jesus. And don't forget to say your prayers at night.

I travel on the train almost every day. In India the trains are much smaller than the kind which you rode to ST. Paul. Here the trains do not go very fast. Every day I see many air planes. Do you remember the time that Daddy wanted to take you up in the air plane but you were afraid? I know that you would not be afraid any more.

Not long ago I was walking through a village when I saw a little girl who could not walk because she had a sore foot. She was a little girl just about the same size as you. I looked at her foot and it was red and swollen. She wanted me to give her some medicine but I put her foot in hot water and then put salve on it. Now she is much better and is very happy. Now she can run and play like other girls do.

Be sure to give Howard a good big kiss and a hug for me. I love both you and Howard and Mother very much. I would like to have a letter from you. I would suggest that you tell mother what to write and she will put it in an envelope and send it to me. Some day you will go to school where you will learn to write also and then you can write letters for yourself.

Your Daddy

Undated letter written by J. Lawrence Burkholder to daughter Myrna after Christmas 1944

Rico doing alternative service as a physician. The second year I was gone, Harriet and the children lived in an apartment near several helpful relatives on South Eighth Street in Goshen.

I went to Baltimore, Maryland, to wait about a week for a ship that was part of a US naval convoy. It would travel across the Atlantic Ocean, through the Mediterranean Sea, and across the Indian Ocean to Calcutta,[1] India. When I got to Calcutta, I needed to stay in India, because it was impossible to get into China at that time. The Japanese occupied all of Eastern China and part of

---

1 Now Kolkata.

Central China up into Manchuria.[2] The Japanese had started their Manchurian occupation already in the 1930s.[3]

Traveling to India was most interesting. There were about eighty ships in our convoy. We were not very afraid, even though there were German submarines—U-boats—all around us. If a ship ran into mechanical problems and fell behind, it was targeted by the U-boats. Ours was a new ship, the *SS Benjamin Peixatto*,

From left to right: Mennonite Central Committee workers in India in 1945: Clayton Beyler, J. Lawrence Burkholder, Ralph C. Kauffman, and Harold Sherk, director from Canada

---

2 Now Heilongjiang, Jilin, and Liaoning Provinces.

3 The conflict known as the Second Sino-Japanese War started in 1937 and ended in 1945 with the end of World War II. Japan was trying to secure from China access to raw materials for industrial purposes and economic resources related to food production and inexpensive labor. At the same time, China was experiencing a civil war caused by the ideological split between the Communist Party and the Kuomintang or Chinese National People's Party led at that time by Generalissimo Chiang Kai-shek. Full-scale warfare erupted in 1946 and continued until 1949 with the establishment of the People's Republic of China under the leadership of Mao Zedong, Chairman of the Communist Party of China.

but we were afraid it would break down, because ships frequently did. I was often afraid, despite strong faith and self-confidence. As we approached the Mediterranean, we went through the Strait of Gibraltar, which hugs the north coast of Africa and which I found to be intriguing.

I was accompanied on this trip by two other MCC workers, Clayton Beyler and Ralph C. Kauffman. We did a lot of talking, thinking, and playing checkers. The northern coast of Africa looked so good to us; we would have enjoyed going ashore. After we left the Mediterranean and went through the Suez Canal, our ship was on its own. Even though there were a lot of Japanese subs in the area, we were not attacked.

We arrived at Colombo, Ceylon,[4] and went into the harbor, where the ship anchored. Somebody came out in a little tender and said through a megaphone, "Your orders are to continue immediately."

We then lifted anchor and went up the eastern side of India in the moonlight, with Japanese subs everywhere. Although this was a dangerous situation, our experience was not unique. There were many other military situations at that time that were more harrowing than ours.

The most dreadful anticipation of military involvement I witnessed was in Baltimore when we were waiting to sail. I entered into a conversation with a handsome African American university graduate who was in the merchant marines. He was assigned to a ship that was going to northern Russia, where 80 percent of the boats were being shelled and were sunk in the cold waters there. And it was January. He showed me a picture of his wife and kids and said, "I'll never see them again, I'm quite sure."

By comparison, our situation was not that dangerous, and we did reach Calcutta safely, via the Hooghly River. Since we could not get into China right away, I was assigned to the Bengal Christian Council Relief Fund. At that time, Calcutta also served as a travel hub for Mennonite missionaries.

---

4 Now Sri Lanka.

I had a rewarding but sobering experience in Calcutta during the year I spent there. It was the time of the Bengal famine. Every morning there were bodies lying around—of people who did not survive. Many of the men in Bengal Province[5] had left their families in search of food and never returned. This circumstance brought a large number of widows and children into the city. We started to distribute rice and build bamboo huts for them. I had an Indian assistant, Joseph Eliezer, who was a Christian of a kind I could understand but knew I was not. He saw God in everything that happened. As a homeopathic doctor, he had a little medicine (a few kinds of pills) which he gave to anyone who would pray with him. Then he would say, "Now I know you will be better." He was an absolutely honest person, a sincere Christian in a simple, unsophisticated sense. I had to admire him.

I was so lonely, because of being separated from Harriet. I could not command any particular pity for myself, since Calcutta was just full of British and American soldiers who had come back from the front in Burma and China.

I frequently attended Sunday afternoon vesper services at nearby Saint Paul's Cathedral, an Anglican church. Some of the soldiers who attended were shell shocked. We heard many sermons of comfort for those who were victims of the war, particularly the British victims of war.

In Calcutta, I stayed at Lee Memorial Mission near a British hospital where Harriet had been born. I attended a Baptist church, where I preached several sermons. I also frequented the Dum Dum Airport, where I talked to pilots, including a few of the pilots for General Claire Lee Chennault's Flying Tigers. On one occasion I was looking at a navy patrol plane, a large plane with a big 650-horsepower engine. The pilot said, "Would you like to take a ride?"

"Oh," I said, "I would be very glad to do so."

He said, "Well, my base is 'out there' somewhere; I'll take you to it and then bring you back."

---

5 Now Bangladesh and West Bengal.

We got into the air, and he let me fly his plane, which I enjoyed very much. He let me maneuver it; then he did a few aerobatics before we landed at his base. To this day I do not know where we were. He was met by his commanding officer when we landed, and the officer said, "Who is this person with you?"

As it turned out, it was against regulations for me to be with this pilot, because I was a civilian. Therefore, the officer would not let the pilot bring me back. So it was three days until I returned on my own to Calcutta!

Being in India that year gave me a chance to visit Harriet's parents, Bishop George and Fannie Lapp, who were living as missionaries south of Calcutta near Raipur in Dhamtari. I was with them twice, once for Christmas in 1944, shortly after my arrival in India, and once again before their return to the States in May of 1945.

My relief work in Calcutta was of the simplest kind, the toughest aspect of which was that I got dengue fever. We had rice to distribute for anyone who wanted it. We also had lots of building material and fabric for men's dhoties. Those asking for any of these things did not need to have any paper qualifications. We just gave to them until we did not have any more. I compare that with the time later on when I became director of Church World Service in Shanghai, China. That was a highly bureaucratic, politically sensitive situation. We ran into dilemma after dilemma. In India, I did not run into any such dilemmas when giving out rice. If and when I did not have any more, I just did not have any more, and the people melted into the countryside.

While I had a good year, my being gone was difficult for Harriet, because she had the care of our two young children. When I left, Howard was about a year old and Myrna was about three years old. Harriet did not complain, because there were many other families in similar situations. At that time, all of life was experienced as a kind of emergency.

The recent war in Iraq was horrible, of course, but most of us were not affected strongly by it. We still went freely to movies and concerts, and we still ate what we wanted to eat and went to school regularly. Most of us were living as usual; some people were even making more money than ever. That war did not affect us in ways that war affected us then. In 1944 we felt we had to approach our work sacrificially and not complain.

Ralph C. Kauffman, with whom I had traveled to India, later became a professor of psychology at Bethel College[6] and died in 2004. He was an interesting person, a true nonconformist. He stayed where I did at Lee Memorial Mission, which was run by fundamentalist Methodist missionaries who had certain rules of conduct and propriety which they expected us to keep. One of these was to dress properly.

Ralph would always come to lunch in the shortest of shorts. Even on a day when they were celebrating some particular British holiday, he came dressed that way, when everyone else was dressed up. He was defiant of tradition. Of course, he could not stand their fundamentalism at all. It was expected that we would stay for a prayer meeting every night after dinner. I did sometimes, although not very often, and he never did.

Ralph even defied Indian tradition. A person of any prestige or a foreigner was called *sahib*, which he resented. He was an egalitarian of the first sort, a Mennonite egalitarian. One time he was taking his trunk from the Methodist girls high school to Lee Memorial Mission. To do so, he had to go through Wellington Square, where there would be many local people sitting and chewing peanuts or doing something like that. Instead of getting a bearer to carry his trunk, he carried it himself. There he was, with his short shorts and a khaki shirt, bearing a big trunk on his head. The people watching him laughed and laughed. They wondered why any sahib would do that.

He was intentionally mocking tradition, even an Indian tradition, and turning it back on them, though not in a malicious way. Maybe he acted without much forethought. I admired him for doing what he did, even if it did scandalize people at Lee Memorial Mission.

---

6 North Newton, Kansas.

Ralph was put off by some missionaries, as was I. One missionary at the mission was an avid stamp collector, and all he did, or so it seemed, was write letters back to his supporting people and work with his stamp collection on the veranda.

I should say, though, that I appreciated the manner and demeanor of the Mennonite missionaries I met while in India, including Harriet's parents. They had an unassuming, humble, dignified, soft-spoken manner which I thought was recognizable. And they were also interested in feeding the poor, whereas the fundamentalists at Lee Memorial Mission thought this kind of activity was a waste of time. I had a higher regard for Mennonitism in the foreign field than I did back home, where we got waylaid about superficial issues like head coverings and plain coats! These issues were not a problem on the mission field. Thus I found a kind of integrity among the Mennonite missionaries in India.

One of my jobs in Calcutta was to go to meet a nightly plane that came from Kunming, China, one that "flew the Hump." Many missionaries were being evacuated from Western China at that time. What a courageous group of missionaries they were—including outstanding surgeons and educators! Some of them also just put me off terribly with their fundamentalism and braggadocio. It seemed they felt that to go out to do mission work was to occupy countries, as if they were a military force claiming, "This is our country!"

Even though I had an interesting year in India, it turned out to be a long year for me; I used to count the days. However, it was a time of growing up for me. I had never before assumed official responsibility for anything in which I had to give reports, keep accounts, and see something through in an orderly way. I also realized that I was more of a city person than a country person.

One day when I was examining a relief program in the Ganges Delta, some distance from Calcutta, a little Indian girl came up to me and took my hand. She pulled me, because she wanted me to go somewhere with her.

We came to a little hut, and she took me inside. The odor was just terrible. She then led me to a little woman in rags in the corner, whom I presumed was her mother. She had a big ulcer on her head and no hair, and there were maggots in the ulcer. The little girl wanted me to help her, but I did not know what to do. My first thought was to get a nurse, but because of our distance from Calcutta I could not do so.

I did happen to have with me a little bit of sulfa powder. (Remember, this was before penicillin.) Sulfa powder was something that had been developed in veterinary science. Without knowing if it was really the right thing to do, I put some of it on her ulcer, gave the little girl some money, and left. She was such a thin child.

Of course, I began to worry about what was happening to that woman. I tried to get a nurse to visit her, but nobody would go. So I went back myself and found that she was a little better, even though the stench was just as bad. I helped her relocate to another portion of the hut, where she could get more fresh air, and I put some more sulfa powder on the ulcer. Then later I went back again and found that she was still alive. Eventually I got her some rice from one of our rice kitchens and helped her get a new bamboo hut. I tell the story not because I was in any sense virtuous but only because I remember it!

I did a lot of bureaucratic work in Calcutta and later in China, most of which was detached from the actual operations. During my total career as a relief officer, I signed many documents that released large amounts of food, especially when I was working with the United Nations in China. I hope that all of this saved lives. But it was the life of that one woman in the Ganges Delta in India that I remember, because it was not a bureaucratic action that saved her life. It was just my being there for her that made the difference. Who knows but what she may have starved eventually. I still remember that case with some satisfaction. I hope that at least the little girl grew up and was able to make something of herself.

In August of 1945, I was in Calcutta at a Young Men's Christian Association center having lunch when I heard about World War II coming to an end and the dropping of the atomic bombs on

Hiroshima and Nagasaki, Japan. I was with someone (I forget who it was), and I said, "We're going to come into a new age now with the atomic bomb."

I had not known that these weapons existed, but I could just imagine their potential. I was scandalized by the fact that the United States used the bomb in Japan, not once but twice. Immediately I wondered why it would not have been possible to use an atomic bomb in water somewhere or in a mountainous area, where it could have scared the Japanese into surrendering rather than killing them. I felt that if a so-called civilized democracy could use the atomic bomb in the way that the United States had used it, what right did we have to preach to others about its nonuse?

Now with the end of World War II, I could go to China. I went there under the auspices of Mennonite Central Committee and Mennonite Board of Missions and Charities. My commission under MCC was to go to Chengchow[7] or Kaifeng in Honan[8] Province to do whatever needed to be done for MCC there.[9] Mennonite Board of Missions, headquartered in Elkhart, Indiana, wanted to start a mission in China, so they deputized me to help find a place. We eventually established a mission near Chungking[10] in the city of Hochwan[11] in Szechuan[12] Province.

On December 28, 1945, Clayton Beyler and I left for China by China National Aviation Corporation (CNAC) in a C-47 transport plane with passenger accommodations. We "flew the Hump" across the Himalayas between northern Burma and China. The

---

7 Now Zhengzhou.

8 Now Henan.

9 Starting in 1946, MCC sponsored forty workers in China, most of whom did relief work in the chosen area of Honan Province with headquarters in Kaifeng, the provincial capital. However, by January of 1948, they had all evacuated from there, relocated to Shanghai, and regrouped as they found new volunteer work in Shanghai and elsewhere. By December of 1951, all MCC work in China had ended.

10 Now Chongqing.

11 Now Hochuan as part of Hechuan District.

12 Now Sichuan.

only way the United States could take supplies to Western China during most of World War II was to fly over the Hump. Actually, we flew around the Hump, in the sense that we flew around the mountains. Leaving from Calcutta, we flew to certain bases along the Irrawaddy River, which flows from north to south through Burma. Then we flew from there to Kunming, which was in the southwestern province of Yunnan. I was glad when we had completed the flight.

"Flying the Hump" referred to taking the route from Calcutta to Kunming developed by General Claire Chennault and the Flying Tigers, a nickname given to the pilots from the American Volunteer Group (AVG), most of whom had learned to fly in the US Navy, Air Force, or Army. They flew in behalf of the Chinese government to stop the invasion of the Japanese. They shot down or destroyed about 300 bombers, many of which were shot down in the air in China. Some of them were destroyed in what is now called Northern Thailand. At one point, the Flying Tigers wanted to make me a chaplain, but I refused.

Flying Tigers pilots have said that when one was flying over the Hump on a clear day, of which there were few, at every point one could see aluminum from planes that had crashed. Pilots in the US and British air forces had crashed so many times, because they and the airplanes were just not prepared for that kind of flying. For example, the pilots never knew where they were, because there were no electronic aids at that time. When the wind came from the south, it blew the planes into the Himalayas.

I knew one pilot, C. Joseph Rosbert, who crashed into a hillside and survived. In later years, I met up with him whenever I went to a Flying Tigers reunion in Oshkosh, Wisconsin. I have an autographed book that he wrote in his old age, entitled *Flying Tiger Joe's Adventure Story Cookbook.*[13]

The Flying Tigers were an amazing group of pilots who learned much from General Chennault. He was a native of Louisiana who went to China to help Generalissimo Chiang Kai-shek and the Nationalist government, the legitimate government of

13 Franklin, NC: Giant Popular Press, 1985.

China at that time. General Chennault had developed certain aerial combat techniques and a P-40 fighter plane with a nose painted to look like shark teeth with an air scoop underneath. It was in that kind of plane (thus the nickname) that the Flying Tigers flew in China.

The Japanese flew by the book and did what they were commanded to do, regardless of the circumstances. Since the AVG planes were able to fly higher than the Japanese bombers, General Chennault's P-40s would swoop in from above and pick them off, one after another. The Japanese planes at that time were heading for Chungking in Szechuan Province or Nanking[14] in Jiangsu Province or a Burmese target, including Rangoon,[15] which they later actually took. I learned to know AVG pilots who had shot down a certain number of these planes—always planes, they said, not people! Since General Chennault's headquarters were at the Methodist mission in Chungking, I learned to know him quite well.

In any case, Clayton and I made it to Kunming safely by flying the Hump. As passengers, we were impressed with the pilots who flew us there. So many of the air force fliers at that time had only two or three hundred hours in the air and had flown bombers, which were not flown at that altitude and under those conditions.

From Kunming, we flew north to Chungking, the wartime capital, as we called it. In 1937 the Chinese government had moved westward to Chungking from Nanking in Jiangsu Province. The government had little offices scattered all over the city. It was a strange city.

We landed on an island in the Yangtze River. As we came out of the clouds, I looked out of the window and saw that we were swiping past a playground and a school. I did not know it then, but I was told later that we had just flown over a cable stretched across the river. That cable was a dangerous trap for airplanes

---

14 Now Nanjing.

15 Now Yangon.

as they came in. DC-3s were flown in high, and then, with flaps fully down, were able to stop at the end of the runway. We were very successful. The runway consisted of stones: huge rocks put together as if they were a wall.

After we got off the plane and crossed the river, we had to go up three hundred steps to the level of the city. I knew that I could not climb those steps while carrying my luggage. Then a Chinese woman tied my suitcases together, threw them over her shoulder and onto her back, and went right up those steps, all of them! Even though I was young at the time, I was exhausted from just

Photo of street scene in Chungking, China, taken by J. Lawrence Burkholder in late 1945 on arriving in China

getting to the top. That woman's strength was somewhat indicative of the strength, courage, and stamina of the Chinese people in general and particularly in Northern China.

To get oriented, Clayton and I stayed for about two weeks at a facility belonging to China Inland Mission, an interdenominational Protestant missionary society. At that time, the roads were muddy, and there was always the possibility that Japanese airplanes would bomb the area. We visited various institutions, because most of the universities from the east coast had moved to this part of China, locating either at Chungking or Chengtu,[16] a city close to Chungking. We were thrilled to be able to inform our wives by telegraph that we had made it safely from India to China.

We wanted to move on, and we did eventually get to Kaifeng by way of Hankou,[17] the capital of Hubei Province. We flew as passengers to Hankou and then north by rail through Honan Province to Kaifeng, where Mennonites were setting up a Mennonite Central Committee operation.

In itself, getting there by rail was interesting. It was now January of 1946, and very cold. There was a general condition of starvation in Honan Province. We traveled in an open, flat railcar. We would like to have left the flatcar occasionally, because sometimes when we would stop in a little village we could see some vegetables and maybe a little piece of meat hanging at what they called a restaurant. Since we could not leave the train for fear it would leave without us, we traveled on it for three days and got very hungry and felt very uneasy.

While traveling, we saw the Chinese prairie and old cities. At that time, every city of any size was enclosed in a wall with three or four gates located at various places in the wall. Occasionally, as we looked over the horizon, we did notice church steeples with crosses on them. They were evidence that Christian missionaries had been there and had established churches. This area had been a stronghold for the Lutheran church, but Catholics were strong there also. These steeples represented the work of Christian missions that had been in China for more than two hundred years and had been accepted by most Chinese people.

We finally came to Kaifeng. A few MCC workers had arrived earlier. These included S. Floyd Pannabecker, whom I learned to

---

16 Now Chengdu.
17 Now Wuhan.

know and appreciate very much. I think he was an extraordinary Christian, very devoted, ready to run risks with the rest of us. He had a good relationship with the Quakers who were also there. We actually lived with the Quaker unit, though we found that there were certain psychological and theological differences between the Mennonites and the Quakers. Some Canadian missionaries were also living and working in the area.

We Mennonites did not know what form relief work should take in that setting. Additional MCC relief workers came, but it took them quite a while to organize and get going, particularly with the Yellow River project. In order to protect themselves against the Japanese at one point, the Chinese opened the dikes of the Yellow River and flooded vast areas. As a result, a lot of land was no longer productive. Several of our MCC workers, along with young volunteers with Brethren Service Committee, were engaged in restoration of that area in 1946–47 through what was called "The Tractor Project."[18] These volunteers not only helped restore the land for farming but also trained local people to use the tractors brought there from the United States for this purpose. They did good work.

In 1946, the war between Chinese Communists and Nationalists was just beginning. Our unit ran out of money. Since telegraphic communications were broken, the only way to get money at that time was for someone to go to Shanghai. So they sent me.

I first took the train to Nanking. There I stayed with a Disciples of Christ missionary by the name of Miner Searle Bates, a historian of missions. He was a brilliant man, a man of great integrity who had been influential in responding, so far as mis-

---

18 Chinese officials and planners from United Nations Relief and Rehabilitation Administration negotiated with Brethren Service Committee to send fifty tractor trainers to work in several locations to introduce Chinese farmers to the use of tractors for farming. The trainers were there from September of 1946 until the closure of UNRRA in December of 1947. They trained 660 students in the use and repair of farm equipment and helped restore 49,000 acres of land for farming. See Howard Sollenberger and Wendell Flory, compilers, *History of the UNRRA Brethren Service Unit* (Elgin, IL: Brethren Service Commission, 1948).

sions are concerned, to "The Rape of Nanking," the Nanking massacre by the Japanese in 1937. At that time, he was teaching history at the University of Nanking, which was quite an impressive institution.

I was his guest, and he quickly gave me a liberal education in recent Chinese history. He then took me throughout Nanking, showing me this street corner and that street corner, this building and that building, and telling me the story of the Rape of Nanking, when several hundred thousand people were killed within a few days. This mass murder occurred after the Japanese captured the city. He said babies were thrown up in the air and caught with bayonets on the way down, and the Nanking River, which flows through the city, was red with the blood of corpses. It was an awful event.

He and others, some of whom were German Nazi sympathizers, formed a committee known as the International Committee for the Nanking Safety Zone. They proposed to the Japanese that a certain location outside the city be a place of refuge for the Chinese to escape the slaughter. It is thought that maybe as many as a quarter million people were saved by that effort.

As a Disciples of Christ missionary, Bates was also in charge of a home or a hostel for young women. One time a Japanese regiment came to his property and demanded that they be allowed to enter. He was a pacifist, typical of liberal Protestants of that time. After all, the major denominations became pacifist officially before World War II, and he was still of that persuasion. He opened the door and the commander demanded entrance. He said "Over my dead body" and took a swipe at the commander with his fist. For some strange reason, which he could not explain, the officer backed off and left, and with him the soldiers who had come intending to rape, torture, and kill the residents. So he lived to tell the story, and the women there were not molested. He did not suggest that pacifism is wrong and a military or physical response is right. He did say that it is a mystery to him that he was not killed. This made a deep impression on me.

Nanking was a beautiful place. A monument to the famous Chinese leader Sun Yat-Sen was located on Purple Mountain, as it was called, just outside of Nanking.

Bates eventually moved to Shanghai and organized what was called the Joint Committee of Thirty, which consisted of thirty outstanding intellectuals in Shanghai. He chose me to be one of them, which I could not understand, because I did not think of myself as an intellectual! I had never taught; I had just been a country pastor. I felt gratified to meet with university presidents and deans and others from Shanghai University. Bates then went to the United States and became professor of missions at Union Theological Seminary in New York City. I appreciated him. He was a dry lecturer, a man of facts and figures, but one could be sure that he was right in what he claimed. He is one who survived the Rape of Nanking.

I followed Bates to Shanghai in February of 1946 and reported to the American Advisory Committee, the operating agent for Church World Service (CWS) in China, because Mennonite Central Committee had been in communication with this organization. CWS continues to be a large interdenominational Protestant organization that serves churches by doing relief work. Its headquarters are in New York City. It is a counterpart to Catholic Relief Services, which has its headquarters in Baltimore, Maryland.

Robert T. Henry was the director of the American Advisory Committee. He was a Methodist missionary who had been in charge of a Methodist school elsewhere in China. Now he was doing relief work and was short of staff. He had a good Chinese staff, some remarkable people, one of whom I felt especially close to and for whom I had a high regard. Since the American Advisory Committee needed people who would deal with the Chinese customs authorities, American insurance companies, and the Catholic church, I was his only option! Dr. Henry said, "Can't you stay and help me?"

I did so then, with the permission of MCC. I was placed in charge of the Material Aid Section, which was responsible for the importation and distribution of American donated relief supplies to five hundred Christian mission and educational organizations in China.

Dr. Henry had an excellent secretary, Diana Tsu, a graduate of Smith College. She and I got along well. I was given the kind of work for which I had no background. Often Dr. Henry would come out of his office and ask whether the shipment had gone yet to so-and-so in such-and-such. He would name a Chinese person and a Chinese city I had never heard of. This was awkward for me. One of my assistants, a refugee from Germany, had been a clothing manufacturer in Berlin. He was Jewish and had a J tattooed on his wrist. He had been a multimillionaire but now had nothing.

I lived in an apartment with other American Advisory Committee workers—an apartment that later became the apartment where Harriet and I and the children lived. The address was 6 Young Allen Court, and it was not far from the Hwangpoo[19] River and the Garden (Waibaidu)

J. Lawrence Burkholder in Shanghai, China, in 1947, with his Material Aid shipping staff. J. Lawrence was working for the American Advisory Council, operating agent of Church World Service in China. From left to right: Mr. Neustadt, Mr. Chu, Mr. Zung, and Mr. Kob.

Bridge. It was near the post office where the Japanese had tortured prisoners, a place with an awful reputation. This was Shanghai.

Our apartment had no furniture to speak of, just a few chairs. We tried to heat it with a drip-stove, a little stove in which oil

---

19 Now Huangpoo.

would drop on charcoal. We could barely heat one room that way, and the room's walls were cold. It was miserable.

Something that I (and later my family) suffered from was lack of good food. Even though I had money from MCC, I had to exchange it at the official rate. My purchases cost me about ten times more than they would have if I had used the prevailing black market exchange rate—the "real exchange," as some called it. It took courage to buy a lemon or an orange, which I knew I needed but which cost so much. The $10 a month that I got for living expenses was hardly enough for me to go out and get a meal. Thankfully, I got one fairly good meal every day at the office, where a caterer brought in Chinese food.

In spite of these complications, my work gave me a fine learning experience. I negotiated with Chinese customs officers and insurance companies and bought certain items for relief purposes. I helped handle a lot of money. It was a time when missionaries and professional people were coming back to China, since World War II was over, and it was no longer necessary to enter China from India by way of the Hump. It was now possible to enter China through Shanghai, Tsingtao,[20] Peking,[21] and several other places, including Hong Kong.

One time, through the services of our office, I helped an American dentist get his dental chair and all his supplies through customs. By the time he got all of these items through customs, someone offered him an absolutely fantastic sum—$40,000, I think—for all of it. He sold it and went back home a rich man! The exchange rate was so unstable and unpredictable that it was difficult for us and for the Chinese. The rate of exchange could go up so fast that money would depreciate drastically in one day.

For example, I took to China with me a very beautiful military-style coat with a wool lining. I sold it when I was in Chungking, because I knew I would not be working in Northern China. I got the Chinese equivalent of $300 for it, even though it had

---

20 Now Qingdao.

21 Now Beijing.

cost me only about $125 from Wanamaker's department store in Philadelphia. By the time I got to Shanghai several days later, what had been the equivalent of $300 was then worth only about $25. We had to be aware of inflation all the time. Because of the devaluation of money, when I traveled I would often have to put bundles of money on one side of the suitcase and my personal items on the other side.

Because of this unreal situation, the only way that the Chinese could save money was in the form of gold bars. Any cash they had, they would exchange for gold bars. Some people did this for many years. We had quite a large staff of about fifteen people, and they would bring their gold bars to the office for safe keeping. Some of them had the equivalent of several thousand US dollars, which was a lot of money then!

At one point Chiang Kai-shek's son, Chiang Ching-kuo, a government official, decreed that all gold had to be turned in for Chinese cash, which meant that the Chinese people on staff would lose their savings. I called them together and opened the safe to give them their gold bars, because in Nanking some people who had withheld money were shot. I had to do this not only for their own safety but also to protect the reputation of the American Advisory Committee. We could not hold gold. It was a tragic situation for them, but they understood. It represented a kind of tragedy that was happening there all the time. As I wrote to Harriet, "This is the greatest swindle that's ever happened." The *New York Times* made a similar statement.

Many people had invested in valuable artifacts such as tapestries, carved ivory, pottery of various kinds, and silver or gold inlay. They could keep those items, even though the gold bars had to be turned in. To be sure, many who had gold bars did not turn them in; they had ways of hiding them. I did not tell the staff what to do with their gold. We were suspect. I felt rather selfish and protective in doing what I did and have felt bad about that situation ever since.

I was in charge of the Material Aid Section for quite a while, but I also went to the airport occasionally to see some of General Chennault's Flying Tigers. Since the war was over, they had become associated with China Air Transport (CAT), a new airline organized by General Chennault. Its purpose was to transport relief supplies and remove refugees from Western China to Central China or to the eastern coast of China. I was much interested in that process. I thought that what they were doing was good.

Since General Chennault knew that I liked to fly, he made it possible for me to do so. I got to know his pilots well, and they let me fly with them, which I enjoyed. After all, these were two-engine planes. By standards at that time, they were large planes. These were DC-3s and also C-46s. The C-46 was developed by the US Air Force for the specific purpose of transporting supplies across the Hump. It was a larger plane with big engines and was easier to fly than a DC-3. The DC-3 was an awesome airplane and a mainstay, but it just did not have the power needed to carry big loads.

I was a guest of General Chennault at a social gathering on one occasion. He was adept at doing magic tricks. At one point in the evening, someone said, "Show us one of your tricks." He agreed to do so and moved a couch away from the wall and then put a big fruit bowl behind the davenport, out of his sight. Next he stood at a certain distance from the davenport and threw the cards one at a time into the big bowl. Each card would stall above the dish, just as an airplane would have done, and it would then float down into the bowl. After he threw the first card, he said, "Tell me if the card went into the bowl." It did, and all the others went into the bowl steadily thereafter. It was a puzzling trick.

Because of my association with General Chennault, I was able to get a good many deals for the American Advisory Committee. At one time I knew that there were many missionaries in Peking who were trying to vacate to Shanghai, so I contracted with General Chennault to get them and bring them back. I made a little money—a couple hundred dollars, for doing so. This was a lot of money, compared to my $10 a month from MCC. I never told anyone from MCC about making money like this. Now it is no longer a secret I am trying to keep!

People were coming back to China from all directions. Many baptisms were taking place in various churches, including Young John Allen Memorial Church[22] in Shanghai. The minister, Rev. Z. T. Kaung—who baptized Chiang Kai-shek several years after he married Madame Chiang Kai-shek (Soong Mei-ling) in 1927—came from this church. The church was located just next to our apartment, as was Soochow University School of Law.

After two years of my being away in India and China, on October 15, 1946, Harriet arrived in Shanghai with our two children. She had been getting along as best she could with them on her own. Arrangements were made for her to come to China on the Marine Lynx, a troop carrier ship being used to transport a large number of missionaries and business people. Since the boat was not designed as a passenger ship, the accommodations for passengers were meager. Harriet and the children had gone to San Francisco expecting to leave for Shanghai soon after their arrival. Since there was a dock workers strike, they spent an extra three weeks there occupying themselves at a park every day. Myrna was five years old and Howard was three years old.

On board, Harriet became acquainted with some fine missionaries. Men and women stayed in separate dormitories. Both children got seasick. The adults helped one another with the entertainment of children as they crossed the Pacific Ocean.

When the boat arrived, Harriet and the children were in line on the deck and were ready to go down the gangplank to meet me, their father and husband, after two years' absence. Something went wrong on the ship—I do not know what—and the passengers were held all day. Harriet and the children had to stand in the sun while waiting. I could see her, and she was crying. The children did not understand what was happening. Eventually, they were allowed to leave the boat in the evening, and we went back to our apartment together.

It was a great reunion, but we did not have a place of our own, because our apartment had been turned into a hostel for Mennonite relief workers as they came into China, and for Rus-

---

22 Now Jinglintang Church.

sian Mennonite refugees who were going in the other direction. We had only a bedroom to ourselves and needed to share meals with about a dozen others. Even so, Harriet and I were happy to be together again. She had survived the trip, and we spent two years in China together thereafter.

By that time, I had become associate director of the American Advisory Committee in China. Our office had just received a donation of canned goods—thirty thousand cases—from the United Nations, which were made available to us the very day that Harriet and the children arrived. I was hoping that I could take a few weeks off to spend time with them, but I could not. These were army and navy surplus canned goods brought from the South Seas to Shanghai for relief purposes. The shipment included thousands of cases of ice-cream mix, of all things!

An incredible amount of money was coming into our office to support our effort. I remember receiving a check for a million and a half dollars! I had never handled this much money. I went down to the bank and made the telegraphic transfer.

I was over my head administratively. Our secretary, Diana Tsu, knew how to handle administrative work. I had replaced Robert Henry, who had to go home because of illness. Another man in our office, Bill Mitchell, was very experienced, but they chose me to be director instead, which I could not understand. I had all the problems and the joys that went along with the job. These included the responsibility of finding housing for the staff; seeing that that they were paid well and protected from and by the police; working out deals with insurance companies; and sending supplies all over China by boat, ferry, and air.

We had to move the thirty thousand cases of canned goods across the Hwangpoo River from UN warehouses to our warehouses. To do this, I had to hire coolies. They were well organized and knew how to take advantage of the situation for their personal benefit. When moving the cases from the warehouse, they threw them on the ground inside the warehouse; they called that a godown. If a case split open, they took the loose cans. Then they took the cases to the door of the warehouse and dropped them again.

After someone else picked them up and threw them again, maybe a few more cans spilled out. When they took the cases across the river on barges to the other side and transported them to our warehouses, they did the same thing again. Not surprisingly, the day after a moving operation, we found our canned goods—coffee, ice-cream mix, canned fruit, and tomato ketchup—all over Shanghai!

We rationalized that their doing this was helping the local economy. We found poor people setting up little stands on the street corner, selling these items to make a little money. I figured that maybe this was the best use of the canned goods. At least we were not paying a lot of money for transport, and we were reimbursed generously from insurance companies for the loss! I was responsible for collecting insurance and tried to be as sympathetic as I could be to the insurance companies. However, I knew they were making so much money because transportation of all kinds of things to

J. Lawrence Burkholder standing in front of an imperial guardian lion statue at Forbidden City in Peking, China, taken during a family vacation in July 1947

Europe and Asia, especially Europe, had opened up after the war was over.

One issue for us was what to do with so much ketchup. We required all institutions receiving canned goods from us to take ketchup with everything else. So ketchup was shipped all over China!

The director of the coolie operation nicknamed me after my telephone number, because they heard me make so many telephone calls from our warehouse to our office.

Our family finally had time for a nine-day vacation in Peking in July of 1947, after we got the thirty thousand cases of canned goods distributed. Little Howard still did not know me well, so I spent a lot of time with him. He was a cute little fellow. Myrna remembered me.

I had been deputized by Mennonite Board of Missions and Charities to try to find a mission field for (Old) Mennonites, and I traveled extensively for that purpose. These travels included a trip into South China, where I stayed with several missionaries from China Inland Mission. When they heard I was looking for a mission field for Mennonites, they became unfriendly. I noticed that was the general attitude among many missionaries of the conservative sort. They had a tendency to think that they occupied a certain area solely for their evangelism efforts, as if they owned it—not realizing, of course, that there were many millions of people to go around.

On one return trip in May of 1947, I left from Hankou and spent several days traveling into Jiangsu Province. I got into some serious storms and floods while riding on a truck. The truck stopped in a small village consisting of only about ten huts. I slept in one of those huts but had no food that evening. After the rains and flooding receded, the truck went on without me during the night. I was all alone and unable to speak the language. I stayed in the village for another day. I did have a little to eat—a few duck eggs and some rice. I did not know where I was, except that I was in a mountainous area.

I wanted to keep moving, so I tied my two suitcases together with a little rope, put them on my shoulder, and started to walk north. I walked for nearly a day. In the evening, when a truck came along, I stood in the middle of the road and stopped it. The soldiers got out and apprehended me with their guns. I tried to tell them that I wanted to go to Shanghai. I said, "Shanghai! Shanghai! Shanghai!"

They put me on the truck, which was full of money and was manned by soldiers and had a machine gun on the front. On the way, it stopped as the soldiers started to fight among themselves. They positioned their guns as if they were ready to shoot at each other. Oh, they were loud! I did not know what the fight was about, but they eventually reconciled enough to all get back on the truck and go on to Hangchow,[23] a city not too far from Shanghai. It was a beautiful place with a famous lake and quaint, ancient buildings. I stayed there for one day and then took a train to Shanghai.

When I got home, three days later than expected, I found that a search for me had begun, because Harriet had notified the police and the American consulate of my absence. I tried to walk into our apartment, but it was locked. I knocked on the door, and my little son, Howard, opened it. He barely knew me, since we had been separated so long. Harriet then came to the door and found that I had a red beard and looked a mess!

I made another trip to a Mennonite Brethren mission in Shaanxi Province. There I met an older man, Brother Henry Bartel. When I told him what my purpose was—to look for a mission field for the Mennonites—he, too, was a little frosty.

While there, I nearly lost my life. I had been put up in a little cottage outside their main building. I went to bed and was half asleep when I realized that my head was just splitting. I did not know why; I could hardly get awake. I struggled and struggled to regain full consciousness. Finally, I realized that I did not have enough air. When I opened the door to the cottage, I discovered

---

23 Now Hangzhou.

that someone had put a charcoal burner just inside the cottage and closed the door. I had nearly suffocated.

When there, I went with Brother Bartel on a little preaching trip. I remember that his text was evangelistic. Since he spoke in Chinese, I could not understand what he was saying. He did tell me what he was talking about: he was talking about Jesus. His audience had never heard of Jesus. He told them a little about Palestine, which was far away in the West, and that Jesus was the Son of God, was raised from the dead, and was now ruling the world. The idea of the Lordship of Christ came through to me—its universal, even cosmic implications.

This was not an entirely new idea to me, though I had not realized its significance. It led me to look at the theology of the books of Ephesians and Colossians. Brother Bartel told the Chinese people that Jesus was their Lord. I thought that was rather interesting, partly because they had no idea who this Jesus was. I guess that was the manner of evangelism at that time.

I did not get to visit the local Mennonite Brethren mission church, because I was not there on Sunday. I was informed in a gracious but definite way that this area was certainly not where the (Old) Mennonites would want to establish their mission.

I was eventually able to help find a location for (Old) Mennonite mission work, in Hochwan, which was located about sixty miles up the Kialing[24] River from Chungking in Szechuan Province. At the suggestion of the Methodist mission, I made a trip to this place with J. D. Graber, general secretary for Mennonite Board of Missions and Charities. Later, a Methodist missionary leader took Don McCammon, one of the first of five (Old) Mennonite missionaries to China, and me to look at the area. It seemed to be a place where people spent a large amount of time playing mahjong, a game of skill, strategy, and an element of chance. The land was beautifully abundant, with rice and fruits of all kinds, including oranges. I thought it would be a delightful place to be a missionary. After we recommended this location, the missionaries found a place in this town to live and work. They had a short but

24 Or Jialing.

Street scene with Mennonite missionary Don McCammon, with whom J. Lawrence Burkholder explored Hochwan in 1947 as a location for future mission work

worthwhile missionary experience in Hochwan from 1947 until 1951, when the Communists took over the area.

Don and Dorothy McCammon, Luella Gingerich Blosser and Eugene Blosser (after his marriage to Luella), Ruth Bean, and Christine Weaver began the mission work. Dorothy later wrote a little book entitled *We Tried to Stay*,[25] which describes their experience in China. Don was captured and later released and expelled by the Communists; six months later, Dorothy and their infant daughter, Julie, were allowed to leave China as well. If there had been no war, they could have stayed longer, and it could have been a productive ministry. Among other projects, they ran a medical clinic.

I made a good many trips flying on weekends with China Air Transport (CAT). I was not qualified as a multiengine pilot and did not have a multiengine rating. In fact, I did not even have a license at that time. So I took a flight examination in a little Piper Cub, and I got the second private license given by the National-

25 Scottdale, PA: Herald Press, 1953.

ist government. The examiner, who gave himself the first license, took me up, and we flew around a little bit. We did this and that, some aerobatics—everything I could think of that he might want me to do—and I was given that license.

I was not qualified to fly the large CAT airplanes, although I did so occasionally. Since some of the flights were routine, I could relieve copilots who were tired or sleepy. At least I had the occasional opportunity to fly an airplane!

The Lutheran Church of China bought two DC-3s, army surplus airplanes. The missionaries called them Saint Peter and Saint Paul, because they robbed parts from Peter to give to Paul! They hired a copilot from Germany (he is no longer living), and another pilot now living in Milwaukee with his Japanese wife; Harriet and I visited them frequently. The airplane, Saint Paul, flew supplies and passengers—mostly missionaries, as long as I was in China. In fact, it once made a trip to Norway for a meeting of the World Council of Churches. I would have liked to go along, but I could not get away from my work. No one was thinking of me as a minister anyway, since I was an executive handling a great deal of money and goods.

The situation in China was changing because the Communist troops, who had for many years occupied Manchuria, were now sweeping down over North China. One time a pilot and I tried to make a landing in Peking on a long cinder patch extending out from a moat surrounding the Imperial City. We flew toward that patch, which has been enlarged and surfaced since then and is now known as Tiananmen Square. The Imperial City was not as elaborate then as it is now, with the picture of Mao hanging on the Gate of Heavenly Peace at the end of the square.

The question was whether we could land there and get out safely, because the city was surrounded by troops. We touched down our wheels as soon as we could beyond the moat, but it was evident that we would never be able to get out. It was too short a runway. This meant giving it the gun and going on, which we did.

We knew people were starving in that location. Later on, we had some meetings to determine whether it would be possible to get a smaller plane in there. We decided it was an unrealistic idea and asked what good it would do, even with a smaller plane.

Life in general seemed a little crazy then! The pilots were sometimes careless about what they would attempt. They seemed to think, "No one is going to stop us, so let's do it!" This attitude resulted in too many accidents. These pilots had been in combat and were conditioned to fly in less-than-normal flying conditions. Sometimes they took off with overloaded planes. I know one pilot who was killed because he took off without removing the stabilizer in the back—a crude instrument to stabilize the tail surfaces. He crashed on take-off.

At the time we had no Instrument Landing System (ILS); these instruments were nonexistent. The only aid we had to identify a city was a vertical electrical signal that went straight up. We would home in on that signal and fly over it. As we did so, a dial on our instrumental panel would turn around. Then we would follow written procedures from an instruction book for landing in relationship to that signal: so many feet of descent per minute in a certain direction. We followed the instructions and hoped that when we came out of the clouds the runway would be there for us. That was the kind of risky flying we did. When we had to do something like that, I was not flying. I was in the back of the plane somewhere and knew what was happening.

I once got a telegraphic message from a Presbyterian mission located in the northern part of Jiangsu Province. They reported that there was fighting between the Nationalists and the Communists, and that their hospital was full of wounded soldiers, both Nationalist and Communist. They were out of medical supplies, including morphine and surgical gauze. I called an Episcopalian doctor, Augustine W. Tucker, whom I knew well from St. Luke's Hospital in Shanghai. He said he could get things together quickly for us. This was on a Friday evening.

I had to call General Chennault to ask if any pilots were available from Shanghai for this flight. He said, "This is the weekend. We don't have any pilots, unless you can find them." I went from hotel to hotel to try to find the pilots. It was not difficult to imagine what they were doing: some of the hotels were really brothels. I found a pilot in the Palace Hotel. I told him about the situation and that we ought to fly the next day, Saturday. He said, "Can't make it. Can't make it."

I persisted and said, "Well, how about Sunday?"

Finally he agreed to leave on Sunday morning. Then I found a copilot for him, a man who was with a woman in a hotel across the street. Next we found a mechanic to get the airplane ready and loaded—properly so. Last, but not least, we had to make sure we could find the hospital! It was located in a small town far from a large city. There is nothing like the topography of China to confuse a pilot: rice paddy after rice paddy, village after village—particularly in the northern part of Jiangsu Province, three or four hundred miles north of Shanghai.

The copilot brought his prostitute girlfriend with us. She was a white Russian, a young woman, nice and attractive. I sat in the back of the plane with her. I remember that I had not had any breakfast and was dead tired. I was supposed to tell them where the hospital was located. I had made arrangements with a missionary from there to put a white sheet on the flat roof of the hospital, if it was safe to land on a nearby runway that the Japanese had built for themselves years earlier.

The pilots and I searched for a long time. We noticed burning villages and concluded that this was probably Haichow.[26] Then we finally found the hospital with the white sheet on its roof. With villages burning nearby, we wondered whether it was safe to land. We could not find the blacktop flight strip. We just saw grass growing up everywhere. We finally found a flight strip, but we were seeing it from very high up, and we could not fly any lower for fear that we would pick up ground-fire.

At one point we decided to land. I was standing behind the pilot and the copilot to watch what was happening. When we landed, we started throwing off the supplies as fast as we could. The young Russian woman was helping us. Then we started the engines, intending to leave, because we thought we had to get out

---

26 Now Lianyungang.

of there as quickly as possible. As we were doing so, we saw a jeep coming toward us with a white flag on it. We saw that it was someone with a basket hanging on a hook from a fishing pole. It was a basket of southern fried chicken and biscuits, which we were able to pick up and then eat after we had flown off. We also received several bullet holes on the back of the tail during take-off!

I experienced the fall—or the Communist liberation—of Mukden, Manchuria.[27] I was there as the copilot of one of General Chennault's DC-3s to help fly refugees to Peking. I stayed at the Railway Station Hotel, but the town was almost empty, a ghost city. I went to a nearby restaurant to get some breakfast and met a Russian man with broken English, who said to me, "I have nothing, and I am being broken. I must get to Shanghai." I also met there a young Russian prostitute with scabs on her legs. I said I would try to get both of them to Shanghai.

I do not remember how I got to the airport from the restaurant, because there were no taxis or cars in sight. I think I went by pedicab. When I got to the airplane we were to use, it was packed full of refugees who had made their way onto the plane. We could not get them off, so the pilot, who was an ex-marine, told me to "clear the cabin." I went into the plane and used all the Chinese words I knew to get some of them out, but I was not successful. So the pilot gave me his revolver. I said, "I can't use it."

He swore at me using some vintage-type words. Then he and I went into the cabin and pushed out some of the people. One person we had pushed out of the plane was an old woman with bound feet. I could hardly do it, but I had to.

Others were crawling over the wings, so we could not start the engines, for fear of slicing them to pieces. Eventually we got in the air, even though the plane was overloaded. Shortly after we got into the air heading south, we heard a commotion in the back. I went back there and found a man screaming, "Tai, tai, tai"—"Wife, wife, wife." Apparently I had pushed out his wife. The other people in the plane told him to shut up. There was not much

---

27   Now Shenyang in Liaoning Province.

grace in what had happened. We went to Peking and left some of the passengers there and saw to it that those who wanted to go to Shanghai got there.

On another occasion I was again flying with refugees from Mukden to Peking and happened to be flying with a famous pilot who had shot down four Japanese fighter planes and destroyed five on the ground. He was James McGovern, referred to as "Earthquake McGoon" in *Time* and *Life* magazines, where he was later celebrated. His copilot wanted to take a break or sleep, so he let me take the copilot's place.

The plane was carrying government officials who wanted to leave because they knew the city was going to fall. While flying, McGoon and I had time to converse. (I knew something about him, but I did not think he knew anything about me.) He eventually let me take control of the plane and soon fell asleep. I knew the general direction in which we were flying, I knew the compass heading, and I knew the chosen altitude. I was trying to keep the plane going straight and level.

After about an hour or so, McGoon awoke and asked, "Where the hell are we?"

I replied, "I don't know."

He called back to the pilots of another plane following behind us, and they said, "We're right on course."

Then he said to them, "This damn preacher can fly this plane straight and level better than I can!"

Except for the swear words, I loved to hear that. Thankfully, we were heading in the right direction toward Peking.

McGovern stayed with Civil Air Transport (CAT) after the dissolution of the American Volunteer Group (AVG). His plane was shot down one time by the Communists. He landed the plane dead-stick—without motors—on an island in a river in South China. His captors put him in jail for about six months and then let him go. He ended up in Hong Kong.

He was a big, overweight fellow and was called Earthquake because he talked so much and so loudly. He played tricks on everybody and could fly superbly. He had a reputation among pilots as a risk-taker, though he always came through. A pilot friend of mine from Milwaukee, Felix Smith, met him in Hong Kong, and what was he doing but eating! He often ate lima beans, because he liked them so much, as Smith pointed out in his book entitled *China Pilot: Flying for Chiang and Chennault.*[28]

Later McGovern relocated to Haiphong, Vietnam. His plane was hit in May of 1954, in Dien Bien Phu, where planes were being shot to pieces. He had just dropped off supplies for the French, when a shell hit his plane and seriously crippled it. The plane staggered seventy-five miles into Laos, but a wing of the plane snagged the peak of a hill. The plane then cartwheeled and turned into a ball of fire and smoke. Just before that happened, he radioed another pilot and said, "It looks like this is it, son."

In 1948, during our last nine months in China, I worked with the United Nations Relief and Rehabilitation Administration (UNRAA) as a liaison between private (nongovernmental) organizations (NGOs) and the UN. My title was director of the National Clearing Committee.[29] Through that assignment, I met some high officials. One was General George C. Marshall, whom I met in Chungking.[30] With his Bible in hand, he attended a Sunday school class that I also participated in. I didn't meet Chiang Kai-shek, although I met some high officials in the Ministry of Social Affairs for the Chinese Nationalist government.

In early 1947 for a week I was a guest of Yan Xishan, a warlord and governor of Shanxi Province. Whenever I have men-

---

28 Washington, DC: Brassey's, 1995.

29 The UNRRA office in Shanghai was located at the Chin Chiang bank building. The agency was founded in 1943 and became part of the UN in 1945. Within a few years its UN functions were transferred to several UN agencies, including the International Refugee Organization and the World Health Organization. As an American relief agency, it was largely replaced by the Marshall Plan, which began operations in 1948; see http://en.wikipedia.org/wiki/United_Nations_Relief_and_Rehabilitation_Administration.

30 The Marshall Plan, which helped Europe rebuild and modernize after World War II, was named for George C. Marshall, who was Secretary of State in President Harry S. Truman's administration.

tioned to a Chinese person that I had known him, they would say, "Oh, he is a famous old man." People from Oberlin College knew him, because they had set up a university within his province. He threw a banquet in my honor because I had been sent there by the United Nations. He had heard that I did not drink, so he gave me grape juice, for which Shanxi Province was famous. As a Nationalist governor of Shanxi Province, he was kicked out by the

J. Lawrence Burkholder in 1947 with Yan Xishan, governor of Shanxi Province

Communists. The Flying Tigers tried to help him by dropping food for him. Eventually he ended up in Taiwan and is venerated to this day. He was a colorful old warlord.

Yan Xishan and I talked mostly about the Communists who were occupying the countryside at that time. The peasants were for the Communists at night and the Nationalists by day. His armies were enclosed within the constabularies, so it was a constabulary kind of military. The Communists roamed the countryside freely.

He was opposed to Chiang Kai-shek, whose railroad tracks were not able to connect to those in Yan Xishan's province because they had been constructed with a different gauge. Later the Communists had to stop and transfer from the one gauge to the other when they approached his province. He was very much for education but knew nothing except a monarchical kind of rule. He was in many respects enlightened and interested in foreigners and was open to missions.

About two hundred people attended the banquet given in my honor. He thought I would be bringing a lot of money from the United Nations. Our connection could have turned into something, had the Communists not invaded his capital city, Yangqu,[31] at that time. Life within the capital city was kept going for only a few more weeks.

For a little while, I was commuting between Nanking and Shanghai every day, back and forth by plane. My absence was difficult for Harriet who, in addition to taking care of the children, needed to help the MCC relief workers who were evacuating from Kaifeng to Shanghai.

Once when I was in Shanghai, I got a telephone call from the American ambassador, John Leighton Stuart, who said that a group of Mennonites was stranded in another city. Somehow he had heard of me and wondered whether I could do anything to help them. I learned that they were fifteen German-speaking Russian Mennonites who had fled eastward from Turkestan through the Gobi Desert into China.

I got in touch with MCC and was told to help to bring the refugees out. I tried to go to Urumchi,[32] near the border between Russia and China, where they were staying with relatives. I only got as far as Lanchou,[33] located in the northwestern province of Kansu.[34] There I learned that the refugees were mostly little children and their mothers, whose husbands had been killed by the Communists.

---

31 Now Taiyuan.
32 Now Urumqi.
33 Now Lanzhou.
34 Now Gansu.

We were eventually able to take them to the MCC center in Kaifeng, where they stayed for a little while. At that time, J. D. Graber, general secretary for Mennonite Board of Missions and Charities, was visiting the center. He baptized some of the group during his visit. While I was instrumental in at least making the first contact and assuring them that MCC would help them, another man, Nicholai Goossen, who was living in Shanghai and who had originally belonged to their group, was in contact with them as well.

Getting them out of China was quite an undertaking. Talk about problems! For years they had been suffering because of living on the move and losing members of their group who had been imprisoned and killed. Eventually, when they got to Shanghai, an MCCer named John Friesen—a tall German-speaking man from Illinois—made arrangements with the officials from the Canadian consulate to get them passports. The passports were available on a Friday, and the ship was to leave three days later, on a Monday. In the meantime, they had to have medical examinations, get inoculations, and take care of everything else. John was good at helping them with all these requirements.

On one of his trips to the city, John got out of his truck and left his little briefcase inside the cab. When he returned from his errand, the briefcase was gone. When he told these refugees that their passports were lost, some—particularly the children—went into hysterics. Maria Wiebe, who was effectively the leader of the group, believed in prayer and that a miracle would help them, as it had before. Actually, it did seem miraculous that they had made it all the way from Turkestan to Shanghai.

John went back to the Canadian consulate and reported to them about what had happened. They did not offer to reissue the passports. They said, "Well, that's too bad."

John persisted and told them, "You've got to be able to issue duplicates. We need to have them right away."

They said, "We can't possibly do that, because we can't get through to Ottawa in a matter of a few hours, and they're going to have to have medical examinations again and all the rest. So they can't make it in time for this boat!"

John, who had big feet, put his foot down and said, "I will not move until we have the passports."

The Canadian officials got the message and went to work to reissue the passports so that the group was able to leave on the boat as planned.

After sailing first to Hong Kong and then to the Philippines, the group made it to San Francisco. From there they went to British Columbia in Western Canada, where they settled. They had children and now have grandchildren. Their names were Wiebe, Maier, Schellenberg, and Goossen. Maria Wiebe, a widow, married Willy Jantzen and moved to Kitchener, Ontario. When we lived in Massachusetts, she and her husband visited us. Now both have died. They were fine people.

Overall, these immigrants did well in British Columbia. Later I had the pleasure of meeting with them there several times. I felt that there was an unusual distance between the parents from the group and their children who were born in British Columbia. The children were out on their own, doing what they wanted to do—not going to Mennonite colleges. They were completely assimilated. Some of them had become quite wealthy with real estate investments. They should be appreciated for their success, despite the differences between generations.

In April of 1948, our family got permission from Church World Service to move to a Blackstone apartment building in Frenchtown, as it was called. We lived there until we left China. We moved because we really could not stand the pressure of sharing our lives with so many others in such close quarters.

Our Blackstone apartment building had been a French concession. We got to know other missionaries who lived in the building. We had a cook while there, and his wife helped take care of our children. Myrna attended Shanghai American School.

It was becoming very tense for everyone in Shanghai, because the Communists were approaching the city. Harriet and I had many decisions to make. We wondered whether we should stay and try to live under Communist occupation. By the time the Communists were approaching Shanghai, we were exhausted. Myrna had purpura—blood pooling under her skin—which we were told was a result of vitamin C deficiency. Our daughter Janet had been born on August 18, 1948, and was only three months old when we decided to leave. We brought her home to the United States in a little basket in November of that year. We left on a transport ship under the custody of the US Navy.

Burkholder family departing Shanghai, November 1948: infant Janet, Amah (holding Janet), Harriet, J. Lawrence, Howard, and Myrna

During our last days in Shanghai, we were relieved to see some Nationalist soldiers in and around the city. But about six months after we left Shanghai, in May 1949, the Communists took control of the city. In spite of our fatigue, we were a little embarrassed that we had run out on other workers.

I left my secretary, Diana Tsu, in charge of our office. The Communists, when they took Shanghai, came in and inspected all our books to look for some kind of discrepancy in our bookkeeping that would give them occasion for an arrest. They could not find anything. That was not a tribute to my management or handling of finances; it was a tribute to the careful work of the Chinese staff.

When we returned home, even with our weariness, we realized that our experience in China had been very exciting. We had been dealing with emergencies for those two years. I felt that even though I had not accomplished much in light of the enormity of the problem, some people were still living who otherwise would have died. Our relief work had served as the conduit for the delivery of thousands and thousands of tons of canned goods to needy people, especially through donations from the United Nations.

4

Post-China Years in Goshen and Princeton, 1949–55

After leaving China, Harriet and Myrna and Howard and Janet and I came back to Goshen, Indiana, though we were not sure what to do next. My first thought was to pastor a church somewhere. I was considered for a church in Iowa, but they were not quite ready to have a full-time minister. At that time some Mennonite congregations were, in principle, against having a full-time minister.

While I was in Calcutta, I had received a letter from Ernest E. Miller, president of Goshen College, asking whether I might be available to join the faculty someday. I did not take the inquiry too seriously because I never imagined that I would teach. I thought that for that kind of work, one had to know more than I did, had to be brighter, and had to have more education than I did. I had not thought of myself as an intellectual. Rather, I thought of myself as a sensitive person but not one who could make arguments supported by organized data!

When I got back to Goshen, President Miller again asked me to join the faculty. I said, "At least I have to get a master's degree in theology, if you want me to teach that subject."

We did not have any money, but we were given a gift of $2,500 by the C. H. and Emma G. Musselman Foundation in Pennsylvania. Howard Musselman and his father, I. Z. Musselman, were owners of Orrtanna Canning Company and made the gift available to me without my asking. It enabled me to go to

Princeton Theological Seminary for one year to earn a master's degree. While I went there, Harriet and the children stayed in Goshen and lived with her father and stepmother, George and Fannie Lapp, now retired from mission work in India.

1803 South Main Street, a house built by George J. and Fannie Lapp in the 1940s, located across from the Union Building at Goshen College, Goshen, Indiana. Harriet Burkholder, daughter Myrna, and son Howard lived with George and Fannie for one year in 1950, while J. Lawrence attended Princeton Theological Seminary, Princeton, New Jersey. After George J. Lapp died in January 25, 1951, the J. Lawrence and Harriet Burkholder family returned to live in this house until 1961.

I studied ethics while in Princeton and wrote a thesis on social responsibility, a subject which was in the air at that time. The World Council of Churches and the National Council of Churches in New York City were talking about this issue. I knew Mennonites were not concerned about that area of politics or social responsibility, although I was ready to give them a lot of credit for what they were doing with relief work, including the China programs.

Howard, Janet, and Myrna Burkholder, Christmas 1950. Photo taken while Harriet and the children lived in Goshen, Indiana, with George J. and Fannie Lapp while J. Lawrence Burkholder attended Princeton Theological Seminary for a year.

I have not seen a copy of this thesis since then and do not have a copy of it. I do not know what I called it.[1] I do not know whether anyone read it, although I guess someone would have had to do so. While at Princeton, I wrote several term papers for Professor Paul Lehmann, who was quite impressed with what I wrote. On the basis of that work, I was ready to apply for a doctoral program. I came back to Goshen to teach the next year.

When I returned to Goshen to teach, my problems started. I was not willing to sign a doctrinal statement in which the leading article was about the verbal plenary inerrancy of Scripture. President Miller had kept in touch with me during my year in Princeton. Even before I returned, there was evidence of resistance to hiring me. Eventually I got a letter from Harold S. Bender, dean

---

1 A copy of J. Lawrence Burkholder's ThM thesis, obtained from Princeton University archives, bears the title "An Examination of the Mennonite Doctrine of Nonconformity to the World." It is dated 1951.

of Goshen College Biblical Seminary, inviting me to teach for one year only! He indicated that after that year, my case would be taken up *de novo*. I remembered the Latin expression *de novo* as meaning something like "from the beginning" or "beginning again." I think my brother-in-law, Carl Kreider, dean of Goshen College, was instrumental in my return. At least he was not opposed to my teaching there. I decided to come back to teach.

I still did not know whether I should be trying to teach. I did not know what would be expected of a college teacher. And I did not know whether I could express myself theologically.

Photo from the Goshen College yearbook, 1951 (page 9): S. C. Yoder (president emeritus and professor of Bible), J. Lawrence Burkholder and his father-in-law George J. Lapp (director of Bible correspondence department)

What a teaching load I was given: Old Testament, New Testament, Philosophy, and Fundamentals of the Christian Faith. I had to teach them all! I had never had a course in philosophy, and I did not know the difference between metaphysics and groundbreaking! I had a very good textbook, which consisted of citations from modern philosophers. I read from the text the night before a class and then presented the material. William Klassen, a good friend who was in that philosophy class, remembers an incident that I do not remember. He said that one time when a student asked a question that I could not answer, I said, "Oh, I don't know, so let's come back to that tomorrow!"

When teaching Old Testament, I did not know what to do with Genesis. I knew that in a literary sense there is a fundamental change after the first eleven chapters. The twelfth chapter begins with Abraham. I felt that the story of Abraham was history, but the rest of the book was poetry or parables containing religious teachings with many subtleties, as well as material that addresses questions about the beginning of history, the beginning of the world. I did not know much about scientific theories. No one was even talking about the Big Bang theory then. I knew enough Latin to know that *ex nihilo* means "out of nothing." The world was made out of nothing. And I knew that that in itself is absolutely unique, because nothing else was made from nothing.

When it came to the story of the Garden of Eden, I did not know how to explain it. Was it about "real" sin, or was it about sexuality gone wrong? I wondered about the tree in the center of a garden. It looked to me like a divine sting operation. I said so in class, although I should not have. And was there really an ark? I could not entertain all these questions. I could not spend the entire semester on them either.

One of my students was Clarence Bauman, who later became a professor of theology and was as bright as could be. He knew more about the Bible than I did and was ready to correct me at times, and quite properly so. Once we were discussing the story of Balaam's ass, which talked. I found it to be quite amusing and chuckled about it in class. He corrected me for doing so.

Actually, I had a fairly conservative interpretation of the Old Testament and did not really understand the documentary hypothesis. I knew it existed, because Professor Henry S. Gehman had mentioned it when I studied at Princeton in the early 1940s. I also heard that Dean Bender was opposed to it. I knew that there were two accounts of the creation story, to be sure, even though I did not know how that might have happened. Actually, I enjoyed teaching the Old Testament class, because I was learning a lot while doing so.

The issue of the signing of the doctrinal statement, including the leading article about the verbal plenary inerrancy of Scripture, was still there, and I still would not sign it. My appointment had been for only one year. Lo and behold, it went quite well, even though I was almost frazzled from it. Then I was asked to teach another year. I went to President Miller and said, "I don't quite understand the situation. Am I on probation?" He said, "I guess you are."

I should have asked about how to get off probation. Instead I just went on teaching. I taught until I left for graduate school in 1953. I left without the security of knowing whether I could return.

We had no money saved for graduate school. For teaching at that time at Goshen College I was offered $2,200 a year. Dean Kreider went to President Miller and said, "It's got to be more than that." It was then decided to give me $2,400 a year! By the end of each year, we had nothing. We often needed to borrow money, five or ten dollars, to make it from paycheck to paycheck. This situation was not entirely different from our tight budgeting in China, but now we had a family to raise. There were things I would have liked to have done with and for my family that we could not afford.

There were good people who gave us eggs or other such items. Some even sent us money. One of those good people was Howard C. Yoder, father of John Howard Yoder and Mary Ellen Yoder Meyer (married to Albert Meyer). He had done well in the greenhouse business and greatly extended his generosity to others.

I had decided to pursue a doctorate and was immediately accepted at Princeton Theological Seminary. When the school year started, I took courses under Professor Paul Lehmann, although I did not agree with him theologically on much of anything!

I never had what would be a classical graduate experience, in which one would go to classes and then maybe go to the library or sit in a café to discuss theology with other students. Instead, during our family's first summer in Princeton, in 1953, I worked at a General Motors plant in Trenton, New Jersey, as well as at Princeton University's Firestone Library as a night watchman. In the library, I had to make a round every hour. It took me twenty-five minutes to make each round and punch the time clock. I had a portable radio with me, so I could hear classical music from New

York City, which helped me pass the time. I frequently fell asleep on the job, once or twice when I was walking! I was also a little scared at times when I heard strange noises and wondered whether someone had invaded the library or a student had fallen asleep. That would wake me up!

At seven a.m. I went home and slept. On the way home, I often stopped for my breakfast at a restaurant called The Balt. When I stopped there, nearly always I would see John Finley Williamson and his wife. He was a choral conductor and musician and was cofounder and musical director of Westminster Choir College in Princeton.

I liked the scrapple they served at The Balt. Scrapple is a combination of head cheese and cornmeal. It is something like mush with pork in it, obviously not very good for one's health. It was a Pennsylvania Dutch specialty. I could get a piece of it without eggs for fifteen or twenty cents. I should have known that having it just before going to bed was not a good idea!

When I got home, Harriet left for the Princeton Inn, where she worked in the restaurant as a food checker.[2] There was an island between the kitchen and the dining room where the food checker was stationed to make sure that what was on a plate was what had been ordered. In other words, if someone ordered an egg and got steak as well, that kind of mistake could be prevented.

---

2   When Harriet Burkholder left in the morning for her work as a food checker at the Princeton Inn, she would drive a short distance down Hibben Road (where her family lived in seminary student housing) and turn left onto Mercer Street, where she would often encounter Albert Einstein as he was leaving his home for his mile-long walk to his office at the Institute for Advanced Study. He eventually began to notice her to the extent that one day when both were returning home, and thus going in opposite directions, in her rearview mirror she saw him run to the corner of Hibben and Mercer and look in her direction, perhaps out of curiosity to see where she lived. One Halloween Eve, Howard and Myrna rang the doorbell of his home, hoping he would be there to give them some candy. Instead, the sister with whom he lived answered the door and gave each of them an apple, which they graciously accepted. Albert Einstein died in Princeton on April 18, 1955, several months before the Burkholder family returned to Goshen.

She learned to know a few of the patrons, including members of the Rockefeller family, who stayed there. She took room service orders by phone. Once she encountered Lowell Thomas, who was a radio broadcaster at that time. She happened to know a person in northern India whom Thomas had written about. Over a cup of tea they had a pleasant conversation about that person.

Harriet worked until early afternoon. I slept until she returned, and then I got up and drove to the General Motors plant, where I worked until midnight. As soon as the midnight bell rang, I would walk as fast as I could to exit the building. It was strictly enforced that we were not to run in the factory, so we had to carefully define the difference between running and walking: when a person is walking, one foot is on the ground at all times, and when a person is running, both feet are sometimes in the air at the same time!

As soon as I got to the door, I ran to the car and then drove to Firestone Library as fast as I could—by the back way, as we called it then. I arrived at twenty-five minutes after the hour. Then I would be there for the night.

That summer, in June of 1953, Julius and Ethel Rosenberg were executed as communist spies. Once when I went into a mechanical room in the library on one of my rounds, I heard sparks fly and imaginatively tied together the two things, electrocution and what was happening in that room.

During the winter I did not work for General Motors, but I was still working frequently at Firestone Library. I could not be with the children much in those days. I bought Howard a bicycle, and we turned him loose in Princeton. He was good in athletics and always wanted me to play ball with him, which I did when I could.

What I really wanted was somebody to help me understand theology and philosophy. I wanted the kind of learning that comes in conversation with others. There was just nobody at Princeton of that sort. So I worked independently as a student and managed to do quite well. I was invited to be a teaching fellow at Princeton

University in the Department of Religion, which I thoroughly enjoyed.

The part of graduate study I dreaded most was language study and the French and German examinations. I had trouble with languages. I was never in a situation where I heard French or German being spoken, so I learned by way of artificial memorization. I could never think in terms of a German sentence. I would just think about how to string words together. Thankfully, I did pass the German examination—by the grace of the professor, I suppose. I had to read a citation from Karl Barth, and I am told that his German is difficult to read.

For one year I became a teaching fellow at Princeton seminary. We were reading lots of Emil Brunner, so I studied a German edition of Brunner and picked up some German that way. My father claimed to know Pennsylvania Dutch, but he never spoke to us at home in that German dialect.

The French examination was arranged by Otto A. Piper, a New Testament professor. I had heard that the French examination was quite different from the German examination. I needed to demonstrate reading comprehension.

I had heard that the examining professor would often take an article from a journal, and the student had to read it and then summarize it: read for forty-five minutes and then summarize for fifteen minutes what you had heard. My examination was on Monday morning. Sunday afternoon, I went to the seminary library and picked out a French journal and started to read an article by Emil Brunner on the Reformed doctrine of election. I took it back to my room and read the whole article, with the aid of a dictionary. To my surprise, I got that article the next day for the examination! I wrote a long essay on the article, because I already understood what was in it! When I told Dr. Piper about having already read it, he said, "Well, if you can read it on Sunday, I guess you can read it on Monday."

The students I had as a teaching fellow at the seminary seemed to find me quite interesting, perhaps because I often brought up extraneous questions. I would ask a lot of questions that I could not answer and which nobody else could answer either. I also did that as a teaching fellow at Princeton University in the Department of Religion. I got along well with the university students. They often stayed after class to talk, which someone seemed to notice. Even though I was only a teaching fellow, once I was asked to give two lectures to the entire class of about 150 students. Those lectures were well received.

Soon after that, I was invited into the office of the department head, George F. Thomas. He invited me to stay on and teach. He did not say much about the circumstances and what rank I would have. I probably would have been an instructor, and I suppose I would have had the lowest pay. I knew I would just have to turn it down, and I did.

It is not to my credit that I did not tell him why, though I did have a reason. This was during the early stages of what was later called the Cold War. I realized that the issue of atomic weapons would have to be dealt with by someone teaching Christian social ethics. I could only approach the issue by presenting a Christian solution to what appeared to be the greatest problem in the world at that time and probably still is. And I had no answer.

I was aware of documents floating around, emanating from George Kennan ("the father of containment"), who was at the Institute for Advanced Study at Princeton and who taught the containment theory, the idea that the Soviet Union was fundamentally expansionist and had to be contained. I felt that this theory could work, but only if someone in a position of power were very courageous or would back down. I was at least conversant with the idea of providence, although I had no answer that would have been considered distinctly and uniformly Christian.

I am rather ashamed of the fact that I did not explain to Dr. Thomas my real reason for turning down his offer. I think that Paul Ramsey, who was on the faculty in the Department of Religion, as well as Malcolm Diamond, a professor of Jewish studies, were likely in on the decision to call me.

I felt disqualified and could not with integrity take the teaching post. If I took it, my approach to ethics would be historical—

examining historical positions throughout the ages. That seemed to me to avoid the issue of atomic weapons, and thus to be less than honest and forthcoming. I took refuge in the predominant Mennonite assumption of the time—that we as Mennonites were really not responsible for the world. We were responsible to our own community, to our own fellowship, and to our own congregations. At least in the Christian community, we would try to live out ethics as best we could. We did not have an answer for every plight that the world got into, and especially not for this one, which seemed to be an ultimate issue.

I said no to the offer to teach at Princeton. I also realized that if I stayed to teach at Princeton, I would be subjecting my little children to a non-Mennonite environment, and I was not quite sure I wanted to do that.

An event of significance for me happened in 1954, during my second year in Princeton. In the fall of that year, I was taking my final doctoral examination. It took the form of questions, which I received in five or six envelopes on various subjects. I was supposed to respond in writing to one a day and rest the next day, and so on, until I had finished all of them. On the second day of writing, I got a telephone call from the World Council of Churches in New York City and was told that someone attending a WCC meeting in Evanston, Illinois, was trying to contact me. At that time, the conflicts in Vietnam were becoming a serious issue, and the separation between North Vietnam and South Vietnam had been determined in conversations in Paris. On the basis of my experience in China, I was asked to go to South Vietnam on behalf of WCC to survey the situation. They wanted me to go immediately. When I contacted my professor and told him about the request, he told me to go.

I went to South Vietnam and met with government authorities and with Christian and Missionary Alliance missionaries. There were few other missions in Vietnam at that time. I stayed in South Vietnam for six weeks. A big decision had to be made about where to settle the North Vietnamese who were coming down to South Vietnam. I happened to go to the American embassy, where

I met with Duncan Alexander Duff MacKay, son of John A. Mac-Kay, then president of my school, Princeton Theological Seminary. He was in Vietnam in foreign service at that time. I was being looked on as someone who had come from the World Council of Churches with a lot of money!

I went to see the prime minister (later president) of South Vietnam, Ngo Dinh Diem, who invited me to spend a weekend with him. He spoke French but no English, even though he had lived for a while in exile at Maryknoll seminary, Lakewood, New Jersey, as a guest of Francis Cardinal Spellman. It was a rather awkward situation linguistically, though I must say, the bouillon or fish concentrate that he served was marvelous!

During that weekend we stopped at a little village where he gave a political speech, and I stood beside him feeling somewhat scared. There was so much opposition to him that he could have been shot. Later on, in 1963, he was.

After that visit, I returned to Saigon, the capital of South Vietnam, where I was told that the government had a car ready

Market scene in Saigon, Vietnam, in 1954, taken by J. Lawrence Burkholder when he was representing the World Council of Churches

for me to go to the Mekong Delta, a region at the southwestern end of the country. My purpose in going there was to talk to religious sects about the possibility of settling North Vietnamese people in that area. The delta, known for its rice paddies, had soil that is deep, rich, black, and covered with thick, heavy grass. It seemed like a natural place to settle these people, who could develop it and depend on it for growing rice. That is what I wanted to recommend.

Some other people in the government were recommending that the refugees be settled to the north of Saigon, in the Central Highlands near the city of Ban Me Thuot. I felt that this solution would be a tragedy, because there was no way that these people could make a living in the jungle. It was thought that little industries would develop along the road between Ban Me Thuot and Saigon. My idea presupposed that it would be better if they were given farmland for tilling in the delta. I went to the American embassy and looked at a trade journal that came from Japan and noticed an ad for low-priced, large, heavy hoes that could break the soil. Then I went to Japan and met with my sister Evelyn and her husband, Carl Kreider, who were spending several years in Tokyo at International Christian University (ICU). With the help of a missionary, I finally found the office of the company that made the hoes I had seen in the ad. I went into the office, announced who I was, and held the catalog before them and asked, "Do you make these?"

"Yes, we make them," they said.

"And do you have a sample here?" I asked.

"Yes," they responded, and showed me a sample.

"And how much would you charge?" I inquired.

"How many do you want?" they wondered.

I told them, "Ten thousand."

Their faces fell right away, and they said, "We can't produce that many, because we have no money."

I then telephoned Church World Service and got the money to start making the hoes. I worried about my examinations and was not being paid much for this trip. I felt I had to return home as soon as possible. CWS then sent someone else to Vietnam to continue the project I had started, and he apparently did an excellent job.

While in Saigon at the airport, I sat in an airplane that I had originally flown in China. The Flying Tigers from China, and many others who had joined them, had moved to Vietnam and were stationed in Saigon and in Haiphong, a city in North Vietnam.[3]

I returned to Princeton and took my examinations, but I felt I had forgotten so much in the meantime. But I passed the exams, and we left Princeton in the spring of 1955. We did not have the finances needed to stay any longer. Prior to that, we had been helped with an interest-free loan from Harriet's friend Ruth Weidman Hershey from Pennsylvania. It was only through her generosity that we were able to make it financially for as long as we did in Princeton. We later repaid this loan.

That spring, before we left Princeton, I wrote to President John MacKay of Princeton Theological Seminary and told him I would have to leave and did not know whether I could return. After moving back to Goshen, I worked for the summer at Miles Laboratories in Elkhart, loading and unloading products on railroad cars.

I did not know whether I would ever get a doctoral degree. I had not finished several required courses. At a certain point I returned to Princeton and was advised to do my thesis. I believe that since I was an older student and a former missionary I was thought to be a little different from other students. I was respected for what I had done in China.

The Presbyterians recognized me for things that Mennonites did not. When I came back from China, I was a nobody in Goshen. Oddly enough, when I went to Princeton, they knew something about me through Church World Service. I had a standing there that I did not have in Goshen. There were Mennonites who had

---

3 After returning from this trip, J. Lawrence wrote an article related to it, "There Is Hope for Indochina," published in *Theology Today* 12 (July 1955): 180–88.

been many places during World War II, so what I had done was not anything new for Mennonites. But my work in China was not recognized by Mennonites, since I had worked primarily for Church World Service, although I reported occasionally to Mennonite Central Committee.

I appreciated Princeton Theological Seminary very much, though I realized that there was a significant difference between my views and those of the Presbyterian Reformed tradition. I thought that there was a little too much triumphalism in Calvin-

ism. I just could not participate in the kind of Calvinism that was supported there. It was that side of my Mennonitism that would not allow me to change. They were quite accepting of me. It would have been much easier for Harriet and me if the kind of financial aid that was later available to graduate students had

Harriet Burkholder holding Gerald Paul, born in Princeton, New Jersey, January 18, 1955

been available to us at that time. In the early 1950s in the United States, everyone was still recovering from the war and financial aid was unheard of.

When our family came back to Goshen, I had more or less finished my course work after living in Princeton for two years. On January 18, 1955, several months before we left Princeton, little Gerald Paul was born.

5

Back in Goshen and Dissertation Completed, 1955–60

After we returned to Goshen and I resumed teaching at Goshen College in the fall of 1955,[1] we discovered that our little boy, Gerry, had cystic fibrosis. He was not expected to live long. We were visited by a friend of ours, Richard Yoder, a pediatrician from Elkhart, who saw Gerry and said, "Harriet, that child is sick."

Harriet said, "I know he is, but what shall we do about it?"

Dr. Yoder had just attended a medical conference where they took up the question of cystic fibrosis. Most doctors did not know anything about it at that time, but there was a research program in Boston where they had isolated it as a genetic disease. Dr. Yoder recognized Gerry's problem and formally diagnosed it for us. Gerry had an impressive appearance and grew up to be a delightful young man. He died at the age of twenty-six. We had great satisfaction and great joy in him while he was with us.

At Goshen College I realized that some things had not changed, one of which was the statement on the Bible in the catalog. The word "inerrancy" in it just astounded me, and I just could not take it. I also thought there was a new kind of openness at the college.

In 1958, I became chair of the Department of the Bible and Philosophy, and I made a proposal that we apply to the Eli Lilly

---

1 J. Lawrence was associate professor of Bible and theology. He was faculty sponsor for the Goshen College class of 1959.

Christmas 1956: Howard, Gerald Paul (Gerry), Janet, and Myrna Burkholder

Foundation for a grant that would enable the entire faculty to study theology for two-and-a-half weeks, with pay. The foundation made the grant, so we called it the Goshen College Theological Workshop, and it went well. While I was encouraged by that, I had to deal with problems that emerged beforehand.

John Howard Yoder, who was teaching at the college that year, called into question our use of H. Richard Niebuhr's book *Christ and Culture*.[2] The debate was around the problem of whether there is an intrinsic conflict between Christ, the real Christ, and culture as it is presented in that book. One can argue, as Yoder did, that nobody can live without a culture. No one can honestly be against culture—it is what we live in, in the same way that a fish lives in water and cannot live outside it, though the fish may not be aware of that fact. Nor does the fish understand whether it is

---

2 New York: Harper & Row, 1951.

living in clean or dirty water. The question was, what did Richard Niebuhr mean by culture?

I thought that Niebuhr meant the culture in which we are living, as in American culture or European culture—in other words, culture in a concrete sense. I claimed that if we choose to be deeply involved in culture and be responsible for it, we may have to make troublesome decisions for one reason or another. At the least, I was saying that Mennonites face a problem because of our traditional view of culture. The traditional Mennonite view was

J. Lawrence Burkholder leading the 1958 Goshen College faculty Theological Workshop

that we are not involved in and thus not responsible for culture. Therefore Neibuhr's use of the term does not apply to us. Some, including President Paul Mininger, were very opposed to my view of Neibuhr's work.

By the late 1950s, I was so discouraged with my situation at Goshen College that I did not see any future in staying there. I thought that I was carrying around ideas that were not Mennonite, as Mennonitism was defined then. Why should I appear as a Mennonite when in some respects I was not a good Mennonite? I was a good Mennonite in some senses. I was willing to live with sacrifices, as did my dear wife and my children, to some extent. I was somewhere between mainline theological thinking and where Mennonites were then.

I did not return to Princeton Theological Seminary until I had finished my thesis. I worked on it while I was teaching at Goshen. My thesis topic had not been officially approved, because Paul Lehmann, under whom I had worked, had gone to Harvard Divinity School by that time. When I had finished writing it, I phoned Hugh T. Kerr, head of the Department of Theology, and said that I had a thesis and wanted to be examined. He arranged a date, and I borrowed a small airplane, a little Cessna 150, and flew into the Princeton airport. I went directly to the seminary, where Dr. Kerr, George S. Hendry, and Emile Cailliet met with me. I had no idea whether my work would qualify as a thesis or would just be considered a glorified essay. They discussed my thesis and had me explain what I had written and why I had written it. They asked some good questions—from their perspective, of course. They handled the situation with some sensitivity, because they knew I was subjecting my own tradition to critique.

The title of my thesis was "The Problem of Social Responsibility from the Perspective of the Mennonite Church." I did not know whether it would qualify as a thesis, because the material was well documented but with secondary sources. Many theses deal with a little part of a little problem. Mine was a sweeping critique in which most references were from *Mennonite Quarterly Review* or from *War, Peace, and Nonresistance*, by Guy F. Hershberger.[3] It was a large essay. I had some chapters on what Mennonites have done in the world as a form of social concern, but different from what was being called "social responsibility."

---

3 Scottdale, PA: Herald Press, 1944.

The idea of social responsibility was relatively new. Richard Niebuhr had written on the idea of social responsibility and presented a broad definition for it. I took most of my references from the World Council of Churches assembly in 1948. I digested that material and gave Mennonites much credit for doing good things. I said that they stop when it comes to assuming the kind of responsibility represented by management of and accountability for the world. I believe it still is like that for Mennonites, but with some inconsistency because some Mennonites now function in political roles. I could have gone on to say that there were quite a number of Mennonites who started down that line of responsibility and left the church. All of this was discussed in the last chapter of the thesis.

In my thesis I tried to describe the plight of any denomination that is sectarian. There had been some discussion among sociologists about the problem sects get into in the second or third generation. This meant that my thoughts were not completely new to them, though my examiners were entirely complimentary. I did not have to defend any errors, and Dr. Hendry said, "This is the cleanest thesis I have ever seen." It was clean, though that fact was not to my credit. Rather, it was the work of Marilyn Klassen. She did a beautiful job of typing, and she confesses to this day that she also did a little bit of editing! It worked out beautifully, and they congratulated me and told me I would graduate summa cum laude.[4]

I did not know what to make of that result, except to rejoice for having made it! I got on the little plane and started home. I flew as far as Pottstown, Pennsylvania, where Harriet and I had honeymooned and where there is a little airport. And then I came home.

I sensed right away that my thesis was not going to be accepted in Goshen. I was approached by Robert Friedmann, a Mennonite professor who taught at Western Michigan University in Kalamazoo, Michigan, and who had read it. He conveyed to me the attitude of some people toward the thesis and pleaded with

---

4   J. Lawrence received his ThD in 1958.

me to repudiate it, as if I were a sinner! I said I could not do so. His position at that time was to elevate the Anabaptists for their ethical position, not just their theology. He saw in my work a note of rebellion, as he called it, and said it was "too bad that you've done this."

My thesis went to the Goshen College library and just stayed there. Nobody talked about it until I was invited to speak about it at a conference in Scottdale, Pennsylvania. But Guy F. Hershberger was the first speaker, and his topic was my thesis. He spoke of it in very critical terms. It would have been most logical for me to speak first and interpret it, explain it. That courtesy was not extended to me. He was very critical of it, in terms that made me out to be almost morally suspect, although he said to me later on that the thesis was brilliant. I think I left a copy of it at Mennonite Publishing House in Scottdale, but I never heard from the editors about it. I just let it go, although I felt totally defeated.

Sometime later, Guy Hershberger wanted to speak with me. We met in the Goshen College library, in the Horsch Room. He started out by saying, "This is a brilliant thesis."

Then he went on to be critical of it. He had gone through my thesis and had written comments on it, page after page. It was as if he were correcting a term paper by making commentary such as "Good" and "Excellent" and "Did you think of that?" And he penciled in a lot of question marks.

At the end of his critique, I said, "What should I do? Shall I leave Goshen College?"

Then he just got up and walked out.

That left me in a difficult situation. I did not know what to do. Hershberger had said, in effect, that I had departed from the tradition, and he did so in discourteous terms. I was ready to leave Goshen College, but he would not tell me to do so.

I was also called to the office of President Paul Mininger and was criticized by him as well. I had rubbed him the wrong way because I had said in the thesis that there is tension between Christ and culture, between Christ and his many manifestations in history. Mininger's line was that there is no tension, and it is quite possible to maintain an unambiguous course between Christ and culture, if we only try hard enough.

If I had had the financial resources to do so, I would have left Goshen College there and then. Atlee Beechy, dean of students at the college, had finished his thesis just when I did, and Mininger held it up as a model for me, which was difficult for me to hear. (Ironically, I would preach Paul Mininger's funeral sermon in January of 1997.)

Dean Harold Bender never said a word to me about my thesis. I have been told since then that no one else paid much attention to it in those days, that I should not have felt so bad about all that fuss from Hershberger and Mininger.

Howard Charles, professor of New Testament at Goshen Biblical Seminary, then located on the campus of Goshen College, was also in some trouble because of his thesis, though he did not experience the kind of encounters that I had. He wrote a thesis on the gifts of the Spirit and charismatic life in the New Testament. We were both insecure in so many ways. I had been hoping that my thesis would be read, and I pondered the rejection of it among my Mennonite colleagues, in contrast to the fact that I had graduated with highest honors. I continued to teach at Goshen College with some sadness.

I taught philosophy, Old Testament, and New Testament. It was rigorous material. For the Introduction to Philosophy course, we used a text by Alburey Castell entitled *An Introduction to Modern Philosophy in Six Philosophical Problems*.[5] It was about modern philosophy and metaphysics; the problem of God; the theistic problem of the existence of God; and the philosophy of politics, epistemology, and history. The text was mostly citations from representative writers who covered all that material. I understood the material as best I could and passed it on to the students.[6]

---

5 New York: The Macmillan Company, 1943.

6 On a cold, stormy winter day early in 1959, J. Lawrence was driving with six-year-old Gerry and twelve-year-old Janet through the countryside on his way to Middlebury, Indiana, to pick up a new plain coat and/or vest. When the car skidded off the road, he leaned over to break Gerry's impact

I asked the students to prepare in advance for an exam question in which they were supposed to trace epistemological developments from Locke to Dewey or another modern philosopher. So they had to go through Locke, Hume, Kant, Feuerbach, and finally Dewey. Some of the students did very well.

I also taught the course in ethics that I had taught before returning to Princeton for studies. I was teaching about the problem that I have been working on ever since—the issue of social responsibility—and the students knew this. I was asking what happens when one assumes responsibility for the social order in the form of administration and political reality. At one time I also taught a course on this topic at Associated Mennonite Biblical Seminaries[7] in Elkhart.

Howard Charles was the best friend that I ever had in my academic work anywhere. He and I talked together a lot. He was a little less combative than I, to be sure, and a better scholar than I. He used a fine-point pen all the time and worked out everything to the last detail. I am just not that kind of person. We liked each other very much, and I hated to leave him when I decided to teach at Harvard Divinity School. He did not discourage me from going to Harvard though. He knew that I was not in good standing at Goshen College.

To Dean Bender's credit, he never scolded me. And when I resigned, he called me in and thanked me for having taught and for not having made any trouble with the church. That was important for him. I can see why he would have been afraid of me—of my embarrassing myself or of embarrassing him in the eyes of the church constituency.

There is no doubt that theologically I was not where many people in the church were. Insofar as I was able, I was incorporating the historical-critical approach in the interpretation of the

---

with the dashboard and broke his own back in the process. During his hospitalization and recovery, he recorded his class lectures from a bed, as can be seen in a photo on page 25 of the 1961 edition of the Goshen College Maple Leaf.

7 Now Anabaptist Mennonite Biblical Seminary.

Bible. I was not as good at it as Howard Charles was, but at least I knew that that was the approach that would satisfy my needs.

As far as going to Harvard was concerned, people just shook their heads and wondered why I would go. I guess I should have spoken out then and said, "One of the reasons for my leaving is that I have been rejected, that my thoughts have been rejected."

I did not do that. I just wanted to leave it behind me and not make too much trouble about anything. It was common knowledge that going to Harvard was a step up, so why wouldn't I take the offer of the job there? In truth, I would not have left Goshen College if it had not been for the tension. Without it, I wouldn't have left, even to go to Harvard.

6

Harvard Divinity School, 1961–71

In 1960 I got a telephone call from Harvard Divinity School in Cambridge, Massachusetts. I was asked to submit a statement with respect to a new department they were starting. The divinity school had been reorganized under the aegis of Harvard University's president, Nathan M. Pusey (1953–71), and they called in professors from the University of Chicago and other places to help revitalize the school. They had done well in systematic theology, Old Testament, and New Testament, but they had no one to head up a program in practical theology. My specialty was not exactly theology, but the question they posed for me was about the kind of program I would propose for Harvard Divinity School.

I wrote out a few pages about how Friedrich Schleiermacher had suggested that a genuine systematic theology should proceed from the practical situation. I said that the department would need many courses in the study of ecclesiology, and I made some reference to the distinction in emphasis among Catholics, Episcopalians, and other denominations. The program would include training for preaching. I suggested that the department might be called the Department of the Church. As a result of those few pages, I received a call to speak to the faculty. I met with them when they were on retreat and defended my ideas as best I could.

Theologian Paul Tillich was on the divinity school faculty at that time. He had already seen the proposal and had criticized it. He said, "Because we already have departments in systematic

Burkholder family photo, ca. 1961: J. Lawrence and Harriet with Harriet's stepmother Fannie Lapp and children Gerald Paul, Janet, Howard, and Myrna, at home in Arlington, Massachusetts

theology, New Testament, and Old Testament, we ought to have another two words for the title of the department." It might have been wise to say, if I had thought of it at the time, "Let's call it the Department of Church and Society."

I knew that New England churches were weak. Liberal theology needed the kind of reinforcement that comes through attention to the nature and identity and work of the church. I was uncompromising on that point. They agreed to call it the Department of the Church, as I had suggested, and I was called to chair the department.

Should I go? That was the question. I felt totally unqualified. I was young and had little experience of the kind it called for. I did not know what Harvard Divinity School was like. I had never even been to New England before that first visit.

I got in touch with a friend of mine, Ronald Goetz, who had graduated from Harvard Divinity School and was a frequent contributor to *Christian Century*. He said, "Take it!"

In January of 1961, I bought an old car from Howard Charles and drove to Boston. I took my son Howard with me. Even though it was the middle of the school year, he wanted to make the move, because he was restless. We lived together there, and he finished high school in Cambridge, while I began to teach in the middle of the year, during the second semester. Later on in the spring, Harriet and the other members of the family came to join us.

On arriving, I had my doubts about whether it would work for me at Harvard, but the faculty was gracious and kind. At the beginning I did not know what to teach except ecclesiology. And the only ecclesiology I really knew was the one I had grown up with—some form of sectarianism. I had an idea of what Christian ethics should look like, from my point of view, so I taught a course in discipleship, using Dietrich Bonhoeffer as a reference.

I knew *The Cost of Discipleship* (first published in German as *Nachfolge* in 1937) practically by heart, and I was familiar with Bonhoeffer's work *Ethics* (originally published posthumously in German in 1949 and in English in 1955). I was also aware of what was coming out of the World Council of Churches at that time, in terms of the renewal of the church. I was somewhat conversant about the theological academies in England and Germany and their retreat centers. I knew of churches that were becoming socially conscious, and I even knew what was happening in a general way when churches, including those in New England, added fellowship space to their buildings.

Social action was relatively new then, and of course I was in favor of movement in that direction. I was addressing the whole question of how to get out of the church building and into the world, into social action, which was a new concept at that time. Most churches were not engaged in social action at all. The renewal of the laity and how laypeople could become socially and theologically educated was the big issue then.

My course on discipleship was probably the best course I taught at Harvard Divinity School.[1] It dealt in part with a dialectic between the sectarian theology in Bonhoeffer's *The Cost of Discipleship,* as we read it, and his *Ethics,* which he wrote in a monastery and which presupposed a political situation and background of responsibility. His whole position was given a new dimension when he entered into the conspiracy to murder Adolf Hitler. One of my students, who became president of a college in the South, said that it was the best course he ever took. I believe its success was rooted in the fact that we posed a question—the question I mentioned—in a fresh form. My first semester went well.

The next year I was teaching as I had the first semester. A young Catholic student, Father J. Bryan Hehir, became my teaching assistant. I had given several lectures at St. John's Seminary, a Catholic seminary in Brighton, Massachusetts, where he introduced himself and said he wanted to come to Harvard Divinity School to study the social aspects of Christianity and the role of religion in the world of politics and American society.

I liked him very much. It was a beautiful situation, because he brought the perspective of older Catholicism with him, and yet he was open-minded. He was a wonderful man, of sterling character and commitment. He spent every weekend in a parish somewhere. When it came to political thought, he was quite liberal on war issues. He held to the Catholic just war theory, but we had a wonderful relationship, and we taught together easily. He was better informed than I about ethics; he had come through the discipline of Catholic schooling. It made for a solid dialogue between

---

1 J. Lawrence sometimes told of the time when Maria von Wedemeyer, who had been Bonhoeffer's fiancée, visited class when he was teaching this course.

us: he with his traditional Catholic views and I with views that had come from a sectarian position.

He continued on at Harvard Divinity School until he completed his doctoral work after I left the school. I introduced him to Henry Kissinger, then director of Harvard Defense Studies, and Stanley Hoffmann, chairman of Harvard's Center for European Studies. His later accomplishments include being the Chief Ethics Advisor to the United States Conference of Catholic Bishops, a consultant for the Vatican, professor and dean of Harvard Divinity School, and president and CEO of Catholic Charities USA.

I was brought in as associate professor, but after a few years I was given tenure and was appointed to the Victor S. Thomas Chair of Divinity. I was treated well at Harvard, and Harriet also enjoyed being there. We lived in a nice house in nearby Arlington. It was not a lavish house, by any means, but it was in a pleasant setting that overlooked Mystic Lake. We learned to enjoy our Italian neighbors, some of whom were becoming wealthy. There were many Italian neighbors down the hill from our house who were not as well off, which would suggest something about where we lived. I was not totally happy with our living situation, but we did appreciate learning to know so many of our neighbors. We also loved hearing the Boston Symphony Orchestra.

Some of my Harvard Divinity School colleagues were Samuel Miller, dean; Amos Wilder, New Testament scholar; George Williams, historian of the Radical Reformation; James Luther Adams, scholar of Christian ethics; and G. Ernest Wright, an Old Testament scholar. I knew quite well another colleague, Krister Stendahl, professor of New Testament and later dean of the divinity school. Harvey G. Cox was invited to teach in my department in 1965, the year his book *The Secular City*[2] was published; it brought him fame overnight.

One person I got to know well was Charles E. Merrill, Jr., whose father was cofounder of Merrill Lynch. Charles was the rebellious one of the family. He had departed from some of the policies of his family regarding investments. He used some of his

---

2 New York: Macmillan, 1965.

money to start the Commonwealth School located in Boston's Back Bay, among other philanthropic ventures. He was headmaster of the school.

I worked with Charles Merrill to start the Merrill Fellows program, which enabled four or five ministers to come to Harvard Divinity School for a year—all expenses paid. It went well.

Every year we had a guest minister at the divinity school for two weeks to give lectures on what the ministry is like. Since the students in those days did not know much about parish ministry, we were trying to entice a few of them to consider going into that vocation.

The professor with whom I met most frequently was Gordon Kaufman, professor of theology; he was a Mennonite who came to the divinity school after I did. He and his family lived in a different part of the city from us, but our families were good friends. Another Mennonite friend, Owen Gingerich, was an astronomer who taught a much-appreciated history of science course at Harvard University. He had been one of my students when I taught philosophy courses at Goshen College. He has done well professionally and is still living in Boston, though retired now.

During April of 1969, a student protest against the escalating war in Vietnam was met with violence—including use of billy clubs and mace—when police were called to the Harvard University campus. Some divinity school students declared that they were going to take over the divinity school. At times their behavior became almost irresponsible.

I was identified with student protests partly because I had gone to Florida in 1964 and had participated in an attempt to integrate public accommodations in St. Augustine, Florida, with Mary (Mrs. Malcolm) Peabody, wife of a retired Episcopalian bishop and mother of Endicott Peabody, governor of Massachusetts. This involvement became known to Mennonites because my picture was on the front page of many newspapers, including the *Philadelphia Inquirer*. I appeared there sitting beside Mrs. Peabody in the back of a county-owned limousine on the way to jail.

I had no intention of getting involved with the civil rights movement in that way. It had been a tough year, so during spring break Harriet and I went to Palm Beach, Florida, for a short vacation. At that time Robert Hayling, a young Black dentist in St. Augustine, Florida, put out a call asking college students from the north to come to St. Augustine for spring break—not to go to the beach but to participate in racial integration demonstrations under the leadership of Martin Luther King, Jr.

On Easter Sunday morning, March 29, 1964, I listened to the news and heard that King might be coming to St. Augustine the next day. I realized that this event could be of national significance. I asked Harriet whether I could leave her and go up to St. Augustine. She reluctantly said, "Well, all right. If you must go, you must go."

On Tuesday, March 31, I took a bus to St. Augustine, and on arriving I went to Robert Hayling's dental office. He was known to be leading the upcoming event. As soon as I walked into his office, someone said, "Here's the man who will go with us." Gathered in the office were, among others, Mrs. Peabody and Mrs. Hester Campbell, wife of Donald J. Campbell, dean of Episcopal Theological School in Cambridge. They were planning to go with five local women—Mrs. Nellie Mitchell, Mrs. Lillian Roberson, Mrs. Georgia Reed, Miss Cuter Eubanks, and Mrs. Rosalie Phelps—to the Ponce de Leon Motor Lodge for lunch. They would just go in as an integrated group and ask to be served. For some reason, these women wanted a man to go with them, and I just happened to walk in on their discussion.

Mrs. Peabody knew of me because she had heard me speak about a month earlier in Boston. An article about her appeared in the *Saturday Evening Post*, entitled "Don't Tread on Grandmother Peabody," indicating that she was a strong woman.[3] She was also a gracious, cultured woman, as was Mrs. Esther Burgess (wife of Bishop John Burgess of Boston), who had been arrested with Dr. Hayling the previous day. I said, "Sure, I'll go along."

---

3 Robert K. Massie, "Don't Tread on Grandmother Peabody," *Saturday Evening Post*, May 16, 1964, 74–76.

I was not eager to go, but I would not have turned them down. We were driven to the restaurant. We entered the dining room, with Mrs. Peabody as the obvious leader. It was full of other people, because it was a kind of vacation holiday. The manager of the restaurant asked us to leave, and Mrs. Peabody politely said, "No, we'd like to be served."

He retreated and then returned and asked us again whether we would please leave. Mrs. Peabody just repeated her desire to be served. By that time, a black car had pulled up at the entrance of the restaurant, and behind it was a police car with a county con-

[AP Wirephoto]

Mrs. Malcolm Peabody (left), mother of Massachusetts governor, being asked by county policeman in St. Augustine, Fla., to leave a motel restaurant yesterday. When she declined to halt sit-in demonstration, she and others of party seated at the table were arrested.

Newspaper clipping of J. Lawrence Burkholder with Mary Peabody and others, refusing to leave the Ponce de Leon Motor Lodge restaurant during their civil rights protest on March 31, 1964

stable or an official of that sort. We were very politely marched off to those cars and taken to St. Johns County Jail.

Mrs. Peabody was treated well and was even given the privilege of holding a press conference on the steps of the jail. It was recorded by CBS, so the nation was alerted to our arrest. I was taken outside to the other end of the jail. Since they were not prepared for me, a junior officer of the police force with a police dog guarded me. I must say, I tried to be friendly, and I entered into a nice conversation with the young officer. I tried to pet the dog,

AP Wirephoto

Mrs. Malcolm Peabody, 72, mother of Massachusetts Gov. Endicott Peabody, is driven in police car to jail in St. Augustine, Fla., after her arrest with a biracial group seeking service at motel dining room. Man is not identified.

Newspaper clipping of J. Lawrence Burkholder with Mary Peabody after their arrest while having lunch at the Ponce de Leon Motor Lodge restaurant as a civil rights protest on March 31, 1964

which was a mistake. I did have a little radio I could attach to my ear, a gadget for that time, so I could hear Mrs. Peabody through CBS broadcasting!

Eventually I was taken into the jail and fingerprinted. I was able to talk with the jailer and had a pleasant conversation with him, even though he went through the routine of saying, "Why did you come down here from the north to trouble us? You're a troublemaker." I told him that I did not intend to make any trouble, but I hoped that our protest would remind local people that the situation was not good for African Americans.

The situation was very serious. Some African Americans had already lost their lives. Robert Hayling's hands were so disfigured by the Ku Klux Klan that for a while he could not continue his practice—or so I was told. I tried to remain polite and respectful and yet make my point. I was told that I could make a telephone call, so I called Harriet—it was now her birthday—March 31! I said, "Happy birthday. Sorry no flowers!"[4]

Then I told her about the situation, and she was very sympathetic, of course. Next I called a member of the Mennonite Congregation of Boston, which we had helped to start in 1962. I believe I spoke to Owen Gingerich, who said the congregation would do everything that they could do to be helpful.

---

4 Among J. Lawrence's personal papers, his family found a letter written to Harriet about his incarceration. It was published by the Center for Mennonite Writing (http://www.mennonitewriting.org/journal/7/4/letter-st-augustine-jail/#page1), in the October 2015 issue of the *CMW Journal*, on social justice, edited by Ervin Beck. Here is a brief excerpt: "The cell in which I am writing this is fairly large. There are a number of ministers and ministerial students here from Yale, Colgate, Brown, etc. I hope they will provide bedding. So far I have none. But I have no reason to complain since most of the Negros will sleep on the floor. . . .

"Some of the fellows here have not been eating [by choice] for three days. They suggested I eat and so I did. The supper was pretty good—rice and stew. The other prisoners (regulars) say that the food has improved since we came. The cell is quite dirty, however. The beds are steel [bunks]. I only hope I get a mattress. Unfortunately, my suitcase is at the Greyhound bus station."

I was in jail for three days. It was not long until the place was full of young African American students who had been involved in demonstrations in St. Augustine. A group of them had come into a segregated restaurant to be served, even though they had no money to spend! When they came into this restaurant and sat down on the chairs, they were arrested and put in jail. Some of them were only high school students.

Several theologians began to appear, one of whom was William Sloane Coffin, chaplain at Yale University at that time. We had a nice conversation. He was a wonderful man, and we just decided we would sit it out as patiently as possible. What else could we do? At a certain point, some of us were taken out of a smaller cell and were put into a dormitory-type situation, where many more of us could talk to each other.

By that time, several civil rights lawyers were working to bail us out of jail. Because it was so hot in the jail, I wondered about how Dietrich Bonhoeffer kept his sanity when he was not only in jail but also in a place being targeted for bombing.

After two or three days of this existence, I was visibly affected by being sequestered and not having anybody to talk to much of the time. It was helpful to be in the presence of Coffin. He was preparing a sermon, which he was going to deliver at Yale the following weekend! I was preparing some lectures that I was to give at Elizabethtown College. As it turned out, I did not get out in time to give these lectures and never returned to do so. I believe that Coffin was released later than I, so maybe he was not able to give his sermon the following weekend either.

On April 1, the second day of our incarceration, those of us who had been arrested at the Ponce De Leon Motor Lodge restaurant were taken before Judge Charles Mathis. Mrs. Peabody was the first to be interviewed, and she talked forthrightly to the judge, as one might expect of a governor's mother! I was second or third, but I did not say much.[5] I do remember hearing Judge

5 Hester Campbell, in her book *Four for Freedom* ([New York: Carlton Press, Inc., 1974], 57), noted that a young African American man who was to be interviewed asked Judge Mathis whether he might go and telephone

Mathis say to an African American woman in our group who had been a servant of his, "Now isn't it wonderful to live down here in Florida?"

She said, "Yes, yes."

"Well, what is so wonderful about it?" he asked.

She would only go so far as to say, "There's so much sunshine here."

The press was everywhere. Most likely because of the pressure the media attention brought to our situation, I was released from jail the next day, along with the others with whom I had been arrested.[6] I understand that the arrest is not on my record, though I do not know for sure. After I got out of jail, I returned to Boston.

Of course, my experience was recognized by the faculty at the divinity school as being a little unusual, even though it was a time when students approved of that kind of involvement. It tended to identify me with the radical fringe on campus. This was in the earlier stages of the civil rights movement.

The momentum of the civil rights movement led to other civil rights developments in Boston, and I was called on frequently to march and speak in churches in behalf of civil rights, though I really did not know that much about the subject. I was involved and had at least taken a stand on civil rights.

---

his parents. When the judge's response was a curt refusal, J. Lawrence told him with indignation, "That was a perfectly legitimate request and deserved a courteous answer." Mrs. Campbell wrote that she does not remember the response from Judge Mathis except that he looked angry and retreated to his inner office for a while.

6   William Kunstler in his book *Deep in My Heart* (New York: William Morrow & Company, 1966), 275, writes that he and several other civil rights lawyers were able to arrange for bail bonds to be issued by Allegheny Mutual Casualty Company for all the demonstrators who were in jail at the time of J. Lawrence's arrest. The *Episcopal News Service* (Press Release #XX-10; http://episcopalarchives.org/cgi-bin/ENS/ENSpress_release.pl?pr_number=XX-10) reported that J. Lawrence and several other chaplains and ministers, including William Sloane Coffin, Jr., each had bail bonds set for them for $100.

Harriet and I helped entertain Martin Luther King, Jr., when he came to Harvard occasionally. At that time, Harvard Memorial Church was full and overflowing whenever he spoke. On one occasion I sat beside him at a dinner given by Charles Price, chaplain of Harvard Memorial Church. It was difficult to strike up a conversation with him. He just seemed to be in another world. I attributed some of his aloofness to the fact that I was new to working with civil rights and not a notable person. I have heard others say they had the same experience with him. He was, of course, a great preacher. He combined philosophical knowledge with the cadences of African American preaching, and his preaching was very dramatic and well received.

I had to think about what it means to make a public witness, and I made a distinction in my mind. It is one thing to speak to the faithful: to your own congregation or to your own denomination or to other Christians, with certain expectations. It is another thing to talk publicly about public responsibilities. I refused to carry certain banners that contained Bible verses, because as a person who believes in the separation of church and state, I felt that I could not expect the state to live by biblical principles.

There are many passages in the Bible, in the Old Testament and the New Testament, that could qualify as representing civil reality rather than what Europeans would call "evangelical truth." One could quote Jeremiah or Isaiah or Amos in a call for justice. I would not do that, because I was not going to press my religion on the public.

I was aware that I was living in something of a pluralistic society, where many people were not Christians. Many were students from foreign countries; some were Confucianists, Buddhists, or Muslims. As a matter of principle I was not going to press my ethics and my sources of authority on the state. I would say, however, using whatever language or quoting whatever secular sources, that justice should prevail. I would not call for biblical justice or a justice grounded simply in the Judeo-Christian concept of God. That posture characterized my whole civil rights effort. I did come to be known as a person who was on the side of the racial revolution taking place in those days.

The next year, in March 1965, I went to Selma, Alabama, along with hundreds of others, to participate in the second of several marches that in some ways marked the peak of the civil rights movement.[7] A large group of Unitarian ministers had gone there for that march, scheduled to be held on March 9.

I knew one of these ministers, Rev. James Reeb, from Boston. During the evening after the march, he and two other Unitarian ministers were accosted as they walked down a street past the Silver Moon Café, which was located near where I was staying. He was struck on the head with some kind of a club. The other two men escaped serious injury. Once Reeb was on the ground and appeared to be unconscious, his friends took him to a local doctor, an African American named William Dinkins, who realized that he needed an X-ray. He called for an ambulance to take Reeb to a hospital in Birmingham, sixty-five miles away. The ambulance was old and had a flat tire on the way to the scene of the incident. Then they had to wait for a second ambulance. Reverend Reeb died several days later. If I remember correctly, President Lyndon B. Johnson sent a jet airplane to transport Mrs. Reeb back to Boston from Alabama after her husband's passing.

These demonstrations in Selma were of such a nature that President Johnson became involved, particularly by telephone communication. I overheard a conversation between Martin Luther King, Jr., and President Johnson, as they were testing each other about what kind of an approach to take. In Selma, the question was how far to go. They recognized that if the protesters marched outside the city limits, they would come under the jurisdiction of Montgomery County. In that case, the leadership would

---

7 J. Lawrence was one of about four hundred ministers urged on short notice to attend the March 9 march because of what had happened during the march across the Edmund Pettus Bridge two days earlier. The March 7 event came to be known as Bloody Sunday, since many of the six hundred demonstrators were attacked and injured by Alabama state troopers.

have to deal with Governor George Wallace, and it was likely that some heads would roll.

When it came time for the march on the March 9, I was about five rows behind Martin Luther King, Jr. On each side of the street were hostile people with their feet spread apart and carrying batons. I suppose some had hidden weapons. It was very tense as we walked down certain streets away from the Brown Chapel A.M.E. Church, which was the headquarters for Martin Luther King, Jr., and others from the Southern Christian Leadership Conference (SCLC).

Return visit sometime in the 1980s by J. Lawrence Burkholder to Brown Chapel A.M.E. Church, Selma, Alabama, starting point for "Turnaround Tuesday" civil rights march across the Edmund Pettus Bridge on March 9, 1965

We walked toward the Edmund Pettus Bridge, that famous bridge seen in photos, and then we walked over it. Just at the end of the bridge, heading east, was the line between the city and the county. Martin Luther King, Jr., had been warned that if he stepped over that line, there would be consequences. Just when we came to the edge of the bridge, Reverend King stopped. He turned around and said, "Let us pray."

There were no bullhorns that I know of, but the word was passed back, "Prayer. Prayer. Prayer."

After Rev. Ralph Abernathy of SCLC led in prayer, Reverend King turned around and walked back over the bridge, and the crowd followed him. In this way, he averted what could have been a very bad situation.

J. Lawrence Burkholder seen in the crowd returning from a march across the Edmund Pettus Bridge in Selma, Alabama, in a civil rights protest led by Dr. Martin Luther King, Jr., and others on what was later called "Turnaround Tuesday," March 9, 1965

As mentioned before, Martin Luther King, Jr., and President Lyndon B. Johnson were working very closely together. LBJ, as he was called, had had a tragic presidency in some ways, especially because of the Vietnam War, which caused domestic unrest. He was sensitive about racial integration issues; as a Southerner from Texas, he wanted integration to happen. He wanted this march to be an event of national significance. He also did not want it to get out of hand.

I came back from Selma, having learned a thing or two about how such an event works from behind the scenes and about how important it is to have the support of the government. The event was shared by many people. It would have been possible to have had a theological gathering at this event, because so many theologians, seminary students, and preachers were in attendance. It reminded me that King's genius was, in part at least, the genius of a social strategist. He was provocative and insistent but knew how far to go.[8]

One ethical question for me was how far I, as a white Christian, could enter into a movement which was of and for African Americans. One evening in a part of Boston, I was meeting with some African Americans. A big burly blind man told me, "Get the hell out of here, Whitey." I felt that was the time for me to leave the meeting, and I did.

During the school year of 1968–69, I was made chair of a student-faculty committee at Harvard Divinity School to devise a curriculum in Black theology. This was very difficult: it was considered insulting to speak of theology for Blacks or theology of

---

8 The third march, begun in Selma on March 21, continued for four days until March 24, when the marchers arrived in Montgomery, Alabama, the state capital. They were protected while marching by US Army soldiers, members of the Alabama National Guard, and many FBI agents and Federal Marshals. Some 25,000 people converged on the capital on March 24 in a show of support for federal legislation to enable African Americans to register and vote without harassment. The Voting Rights Act of 1965 was signed into law by President Lyndon B. Johnson on August 6, 1965. Many years later J. Lawrence learned that his successor as president of Goshen College, Victor Stoltzfus, participated in the first day of this march.

Blacks. While I became a part of the movement, I did not go far with it. I related to the African American students, but they criticized me for not being a fighter. They wanted somebody who was less sensitive than I was about insulting people and taking a position. I was too much of a Mennonite, I think. As a white person, I could not use Black rhetoric. Yet if I tried to represent Blacks, it was difficult to do so in my language.

I worked with the Black students for quite a while, and we tried to incorporate some Black theology in our department. We made some progress but were not too successful.[9] I remember identifying with Students for a Democratic Society (SDS). In a newspaper photo I was pictured sitting with a group of SDS students on the steps of Harvard Memorial Church. They were protesting the suspension of sixteen Harvard students for the takeover of University Hall on the Harvard University campus on April 9, 1969. Despite that act of solidarity, President Pusey of Harvard gave me some credit for dealing with the most radical students.

I think the greatest honor that has ever come to me was on the occasion of the death of Martin Luther King, Jr., on April 4, 1968. President Pusey asked me to speak at Harvard's Memorial Church in a special service in honor of Dr. King, held on April 9. The university had "come to order"—that is, everything stopped. Very few times in the history of Harvard had that happened. The only office that was supposed to be open was the telephone exchange. While the university was closed in the morning, the faculty was invited to come to the service. The service included words from President Pusey and Rev. Charles P. Price, the min-

---

9 J. Lawrence was chair of a student-faculty committee at Harvard Divinity School seeking to develop a curriculum in Black theology. An article, "Divinity School Students Question Report on Blacks," in the March 7, 1969, issue of the *Harvard Crimson*, the student newsletter, explained that a report by the committee called for "extensive efforts to recruit black students and to improve the black curriculum" and listed seven recommendations from the report for doing so. The article reported that the Black Caucus rejected the report because of lack of sufficient Black representation on the committee.

ister of The Memorial Church; Scripture reading by a rabbi; and four speeches, the last of which was mine.

The occasion had a negative side to it, in that there were very few African Americans present. Where were they? They were out on a pillared porch at the entrance of the church, where they were meeting in criticism of the whole service.

On April 9, 1968, J. Lawrence Burkholder spoke at a special service at Harvard's Memorial Church honoring Dr. Martin Luther King, Jr., who had been assassinated on April 4, 1968

That evening I went on national television as one who was supposed to understand the movement. I was totally unprepared, but I was interviewed by a rather famous commentator at that time from New York. I tried to extol Martin Luther King, Jr., as a moral hero and a man who in a responsible way had developed a strategy of nonviolence. That is what I had said in the speech that I made for the university service, with only one night for preparation.[10]

10 J. Lawrence began his speech by saying: "Dr. Martin Luther King, Jr., will be remembered as one of the few men who have changed the course of American history. That it is possible for an individual from a deprived minority to lead a great nation to moral confrontation and to a reassessment of its ideals and goals speaks for the power of the man." He ended the speech by saying: "He was a man sent from God, and I trust that the eulogies of this day will not be forgotten in the days ahead. I trust, indeed I believe, that by his tragic death he will have brought us closer to the fulfillment of our cultural and religious heritage."

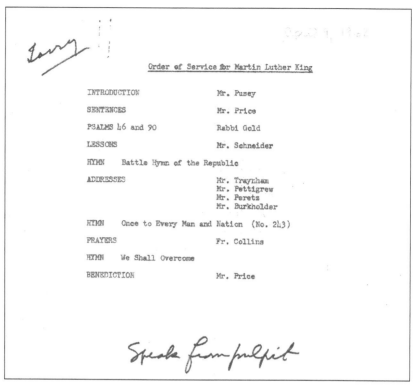

J. Lawrence Burkholder's copy of the program honoring Dr. Martin Luther King, Jr., at Harvard's Memorial Church on April 9, 1968

President Pusey remained my friend and supporter after that event, as he had been beforehand. In 1983, during my presidency at Goshen College, I became a member of the United Board for Christian Higher Education in Asia, which met in New York City six to eight times per year, and he was also on that board. We met many times while I served on the board until 1992.

I enjoyed living in New England for a variety of reasons, one of which was that I had opportunities to fly. One evening I was trying to help some students understand Paul Tillich. The seniors were preparing to take final examinations in several areas, one of which was philosophical theology. Tillich was all the rage then, though he has been relatively forgotten in the meantime. These students could not understand his ontological approach to life. I offered to give a little lecture on Tillich, quite apart from the curriculum and in excess of my normal requirements. The lecture included the ontological concept of being and nonbeing, which is the core of Tillich's theology.

That evening a middle-aged man came in. He was a stranger, and after our meeting he introduced himself to me as Joseph McVicker, the man who with his uncle Noah McVicker manufactured Play-Doh for children. He said he was from Cincinnati, Ohio, and was at the school because of his interest in supporting a particular student. We got into a conversation about being and nonbeing. He was interested in Oriental religions, but he was a Methodist and said he would like to become a Methodist minister. He wanted to know how he could become a student at Harvard Divinity School.

This encounter led to further conversations, in which he told me that he had had a difficult childhood, had been sent to a military school to be reformed, had graduated from Brown University, and then went to join his uncle's company. They made a putty for use as a wallpaper cleaner, which was then marketed as a modeling clay for children, called Play-Doh. It was made by mixing flour and several others ingredients in a machine, and then it was put it into cans. From this invention, McVicker made millions.

I also learned that he had an airplane, a two-engine Piper Aztec that had been altered to make it more powerful and faster. A navy pilot had taught him how to fly that plane. He kept it at a local airport. He took me out to see it.

I helped him get into Harvard Divinity School—as a special student, because his grades were not so great. He sold his company for many millions, and then he—with his wife, Harriet, and their children—moved to Wellesley, Massachusetts. He brought his plane with him. It was kept at Hanscom Field, an airport north of Boston. He said I could fly it, but I did not have a multiengine rating, even though I had flown larger airplanes in China. I was not really qualified to handle it. There is quite a difference between flying a single-engine plane and flying a multiengine plane.

I had someone help me get ready for a multiengine rating, and McVicker would not even take money for the gasoline I used.

The plane was just there, and I could fly it anytime I wanted to, without checking in with him about it. He and his wife came to our home occasionally, and they invited Harriet and me to their home. My wife and his wife—both Harriets—became friends!

It was wonderful to fly at night. Sometimes I flew up along the coast toward Maine, or down over Bridgeport, Connecticut. I would fly northeast around Mount Monadnock in New Hampshire and circle around there at night. I had to be careful, because a lot of airliners were coming in nearby to land.

This airplane flew beautifully. It was fast and powerful. I remember flying up at a sharp angle early one morning, getting above broken clouds, and going up over Mount Washington, which is also in New Hampshire. The sun was shining on the snow on Mount Washington. Harriet and I would occasionally fly to a town in Vermont where we would land and get lobster at a restaurant at the end of the runway! I also enjoyed flying over the ocean.

One time I told Julia Kasdorf about my flying adventures over the ocean, and she wrote a poem, "Flying Lesson," about them. It reflects her poetic imagination more than the facts, but it nevertheless represents something real in my life. I flew frequently to Cape Cod and across the Atlantic north of Boston, where I turned west and landed at Hanscom Field. Thanks to McVicker's generosity, I had a wonderful opportunity to do what I had always wanted to do.

McVicker did graduate from Harvard Divinity School, but we lost contact with him afterward. He decided that philosophically his position was one of ultimate unity. He felt that unity is not represented by Christianity as he defined it, philosophically, mystically, ontologically. So he separated from his wife and went to India to live in an ashram, and I did not hear from him again. His ex-wife married Glenn Johnson, who was connected with Johnson & Johnson, and they lived in New Jersey, where she said she could see the skyline of New York City from her bathtub! She had a great sense of humor and would make jokes like that. Eventually we lost touch with her also.

While at Harvard, I thought it would be good for the students to understand what evangelical faith looked like as it was manifest at that time. I took one of my classes to visit various kinds of churches in Boston, from the Unitarians to the Salvation Army. Many of them liked the Salvation Army better than any of the other groups, because of the social work they did. Students were judging the groups on the basis of what they did during the week by serving others.

I was ready to say at one time that the Salvation Army was just the kind of church to which I would like to belong. Instead of going to church on Sunday to sing only to ourselves, why not be primarily people who live for others and who secondarily go to church services for the sake of that image? Almost everywhere in the world, if the Salvation Army is mentioned, everyone is favorably inclined toward them. I know they are not pacifists, but at least they are living for others, which is an important dimension of Mennonite life as well.

I invited the Reverend Billy Graham to come as a guest of the divinity school. One time when I invited him, I failed to tell Harriet. One day she got a call from a person who said, "This is Billy." Harriet asked, "Billy who?" Oh my! Then he said, "Billy Graham." That settled the confusion, but we never forgot the incident.

Reverend Graham spoke to the students and was received with great enthusiasm by many of them. They appreciated his sense of humor and his humility. He was appreciated for the person that he was, if not for his theology. One of my students, Denton Lotz, had a brother, Daniel Lotz, a dentist who married one of Reverend Graham's daughters. Denton eventually became general secretary of the Baptist World Alliance. I still hear from him now and then.

While there were some who did not accept my theology, those who did were more likely to be Unitarians than Presbyterians or Catholics. In my class on discipleship, the nuns would listen and nod their heads in agreement. They understood what I was talking about. The Unitarians took to my teaching because they were social activists. I showed them how social activism could come from the life and teaching of Jesus.

The church I was presenting as a model at that time was Church of the Savior in Washington, DC. I made numerous trips there with students. Many of them had had an uphill battle if they have been involved with congregational ministry in New England, particularly with Unitarian churches. New England Christianity was at a low ebb, so far as any kind of external marks were concerned.

When speaking at churches, I was sometimes taken by surprise. One evening I spoke at a sophisticated Methodist church in Wellesley. I was called there to give a speech, but I did not know who the audience would be. My theme was "Don't just sit there; do something." There were two or three hundred people at the meeting, including many Jewish rabbis and Episcopalian priests. When I realized that I had a mixed audience, I quickly shifted some of my statements!

One evening I went out to a little Baptist church to speak to their men's group. We were meeting in the basement of the church, where we had chicken for supper, and they told lots of jokes. I thought I was about to be introduced, but they said, "We'll have George play now." George went to the corner of the room and pulled out a trombone. I did not consider the trombone a solo instrument, and I thought, "Do I have to listen to this?" He played, and it was magnificent. As it turned out, he was first trombonist for the Boston Symphony Orchestra. I never knew whom I might meet up with in Boston!

One time after I had been in Florida in the spring of 1964, I went to a Unitarian church to preach a sermon. It was a church in which one of my students was the pastor. I gave the congregation the usual line about social action. After the service a little woman came to me and said, "You know, I've been hearing this for years now, and I'm tired of it. Why don't you preach the gospel?" In a Unitarian church, a question like that!

I preached a number of times at King's Chapel, a historic Unitarian church in Boston that used the Church of England liturgy.

I was invited out often to preach, and I found it an interesting experience. I ran into a variety of strange situations.

When our family moved to Massachusetts in 1961, there were occasional Mennonite student gatherings in the Boston area. In fact, in 1960, when I traveled from Goshen to Boston to be interviewed for my position at Harvard Divinity School, I gave that group a lecture on Paul Tillich. The meeting was held on the campus of Boston University, and the turnout included about twenty people. It was one of many such Mennonite student groups at that time who were meeting in university settings perhaps once or twice a year.

A group of Mennonites attended Harvard's Memorial Church when George A. Buttrick was pastor there, and we began to meet after the service. For a while we met in the basement of Harvard's Memorial Church, and the sexton of the church said he enjoyed our singing more than that of their choir! Yes, we sang well together!

Later it was suggested that we could become a church. That raised an ecclesiological problem: How does one start a church? By what authority?

I went to the phone and called John Mosemann, pastor of College Mennonite Church in Goshen, Indiana. We also called S. C. Yoder, former president of Goshen College, and J. D. Graber, general secretary of Mennonite Board of Missions. The guidance we got from them was to just declare ourselves a congregation! On Good Friday, April 20, 1962, nineteen of us gathered together in a rather solemn way. We prayed and accepted each other as brothers and sisters in Christ. Then we declared ourselves a congregation.

Of course, that raised the issue of conference membership, of what conference we should join. We decided to just let that go for the time being—which turned out to be a long time.

The group had a wonderful evening together and eventually began to meet in our home in Arlington on Sunday evenings. We did not have a big house, nor did we have a large living room. We were crowded into that space. We sang well, and we enjoyed our discussions. Later, when Gordon Kaufman came to teach at Harvard, he made a fine contribution to our discussions, which were rather learned. We discussed many, many topics.

When we first met, we consisted of only three or four families. In the summer in our backyard, we had a Sunday school for the children, which they enjoyed. The subject for discussion was always, how do we bring our Mennonite faith and tradition to bear? How can we sustain it and perpetuate it in an urban setting and a university situation? We went over and over those concerns, Sunday after Sunday.

Some of my students became interested in this issue as I laid out for them a kind of ecclesiology in which the church consists of small groups. Some of them even showed up for several of our meetings. They noticed that we always talked about ourselves as Mennonites, which we were aware of doing. We were also visited by a number of young people in volunteer service work of various kinds, but our level of conversation was a little too intellectual for most of them. While we did not appeal to the Mennonite Harvard undergraduate students, we did attract Mennonite graduate students attending Harvard University, Massachusetts Institute of Technology, Boston University, and Northeastern University.

Quite soon we found that we were there with only one another. We still enjoyed being together and got along well as a group. Since we had no minister, we passed around pastoral responsibilities and had a meager budget. We were also cognizant of social issues being addressed in the city. We identified with the efforts of Martin Luther King, Jr., and other activists for social justice. We often studied philosophical ideas, which included the idea of creation and various kinds of ontology.

We called ourselves the Mennonite Congregation of Boston. Harriet and I got many calls from visitors who were in Boston for vacation or who would notice that there was a Mennonite church in Boston. Sometimes unexpected visitors came knocking on our door in need of lodging, so we put them up in our basement. Harriet made comparisons between what had happened at the Mennonite home mission in Chicago when she was there and what was happening at our house!

We were faced with the problem of women in the congregation not participating much in our discussions. We also did not know what to do with the children during meetings. Most were going with their parents to other churches on Sunday mornings for Sunday school. In fact, most of us were still going to Harvard's Memorial Church to hear Reverend Buttrick and other notable preachers.

Then along came the "death of God" theology, which took many forms. Some of our members became critical of our theology as it pertained to our understanding of God. This caused a little crisis. Shall we pray? Shall we not pray? That led to other questions having to do with radical interpretations of the Bible. We did not really settle our disagreements, which was somewhat disturbing. We also found that there was an unstable character to our worship.

It was difficult to maintain continuity because of the unstructured nature of our worship and life as a congregation. We tried to resolve these issues by moving our worship to a large Congregational church located in Harvard Square. J. Richard Burkholder was working for his doctorate at Harvard at the time. We installed him as an administrator for a while. We thought that since we were Anabaptists and had so much foreign experience, we could maybe appeal to the international students who were coming to Harvard. We failed; they were not interested in us.

After moving into the church building, our services began to take on a more formal format. We would have someone speak or give a talk during the meeting. I tried to construct a liturgy or form of worship for our small group, but it did not work for us. It seemed arbitrary. Even though I was not sufficiently sophisticated musically to put notes and words together, I tried. One member, Mrs. Lois Jungas, who was an organist, just shook her head when she saw my "musical" liturgy!

We had to concede that we were a group of people with certain affinities as Mennonites in a university situation. We were trying to maintain a Mennonite identity, as much as we could, and we were recognized and appreciated as Mennonites. At the divinity school, I was always introduced as a Mennonite. I remember the time Paul Lehmann, then my professor at Princeton Theological Seminary, introduced me to a famous mathematician. She put on her glasses and looked up at me and said, "Oh, I always wanted to see one." I fear she was disappointed.

Although it took a fair amount of energy for Harriet and me to be supportive of the congregation, we were glad to be identified with it and regretted having to leave it. The congregation continuously faced the problem of their identity. Nevertheless, it continued. In September 1979, a booklet about the history of the congregation was published. It had been written at the request of the congregation by David Haury, who had just completed a PhD in history from Harvard.[11]

I returned for their twenty-fifth anniversary celebration on September 20, 1989, and met with the congregation and spoke to them. A few of the old-timers, pillars of a nonpillared church, were still there. Of course, many students were still coming and going, as before. The congregation has been quite successful, I would say. From time to time they have had a regular minister.

In a way, our lives as Mennonites were somewhat lonely during my tenure at Harvard Divinity School. Some of us from the congregation met each other through the divinity school. Others were teaching at Boston University, MIT, or another school outlying Boston. We found no natural community there, in contrast to traditional ways of living in Mennonite communities, where people were united not only by faith but also by fields and trees and lanes and villages!

Harriet lived with the limitation that the wives of divinity school professors hardly ever got together—partly because they were scattered. Something I learned about living in the city is that one mile in a city is about the same as six or eight miles in the country, because it takes so long to get anywhere. It is as if liv-

---

11 An abridged version was published: David Haury, "The Mennonite Congregation of Boston," *Mennonite Life* 34 (September 1979): 24–27.

J. Lawrence Burkholder with Paul Varghese at La Bosse, Switzerland, in August 1967

ing in different parts of the city means living in different worlds. There were also few occasions when faculty wives were properly recognized, though they accompanied their husbands to dinners and various celebrations.

In spite of these limitations, Harriet found her way wonderfully during our years there. She became a librarian at the Arlington Public Library and thoroughly enjoyed her work. And she had a good relationship with our neighbors, some of whom were Italian Catholic immigrants. We had interesting discussions with them. At that time, Catholics and Protestants were just beginning to talk to each other more openly, whereas that kind of discussion is not so unusual now. Back then, there was a division between Catholics and Protestants that had to be penetrated with kindness and consideration.[12]

---

12 J. Lawrence's academic life while teaching at Harvard Divinity School also included several experiences not mentioned by him:

August 1962: J. Lawrence spent three weeks in Europe visiting church renewal centers to prepare for a class on that subject which he was scheduled to teach in the fall at Harvard Divinity School. According to letters written to family members while traveling, he visited the Iona community in Glasgow, Scotland; the Taizé community in Taizé, France; the church of Saint-Séverin in Paris, France; and the World Council of Churches in Geneva, Switzerland. In Tutzing, Germany, he attended a conference for the directors of the Evangelische Akademie. He mentioned his great pleasure in hearing beautiful organ music during his stay at the Taizé community.

1963: J. Lawrence was mentioned in the February 22, 1963, issue of *Time* magazine (p. 69) in an article entitled "Seminaries," with the subheading "The Ministers of Tomorrow." He is quoted as saying that theological students, given the uncertainties of the times (including concerns related to disarmament and radiation), were somewhat apprehensive when it came to their faith.

September 1965–June 1966: J. Lawrence had a nine-month sabbatical from Harvard Divinity School, which he spent at the University of Cambridge (England) as a research scholar. His family went with him. Myrna taught art and music in a local secondary modern school, Howard was in undergraduate studies at Cambridge, Janet was in high school, and Gerry was in grade school. A particularly happy experience for the family was enjoying occasional meals at Indian restaurants in Cambridge. In November of that year, Harriet travelled from England to Dhamtari, India, where she was a guest speaker at the twenty-fifth anniversary of the Mennonite women's organization in India.

1967: J. Lawrence and Harriet attended Mennonite World Conference held in Amsterdam July 23–30. They can be seen on the cover of *Mennonite Life*, October 1967, standing in the balcony during a worship service at the Singel Mennonite church in Amsterdam. After the conference, in August 1967, J. Lawrence met with Paul Varghese (later Paulos Mar Gregorios, first Metropolitan of the Delhi diocese of the Orthodox Syrian Church) at La Bosse, Switzerland.

7

From Harvard to President of Goshen College, 1971–84

I was treated well at Harvard Divinity School, but I felt that my concept of the church and its place and importance was not. Many students majored in my department, the Department of the Church, but we never had a place in the curriculum that satisfied me. The courses in our department were the last to be scheduled, while all the traditional studies— New Testament, Old Testament, systematic theology, ethics, et cetera—were well established and could not be moved. Our courses were scheduled for early in the morning, before the students cared to get up, or late in the afternoon. Of course, we could schedule classes in competition with those major courses, but students had to get ready for the examination at the end of four years, and they were scared.

We were operating at a disadvantage, and we knew that there were many areas of practical theology that we did not have the financial resources to support. I had to design my own courses, mainly in ecclesiology. I tried to give them a biblical and a historical basis by asking questions. What does it mean to be an Episcopalian, and why? What does it mean to be a Methodist, and why? What does it mean to be a Baptist? What does it mean to be an Anabaptist or Presbyterian? The course having to do with the renewal of the church was well received. I was respected by the faculty, but I noticed a sense of condescension when it came to the ministry. The preference was toward doctoral preparation— the "higher degrees," as they were called there. That was where financial resources in the school were going. That was where the professors would get their students to consider their wares; that was where their own professional advancement lay. I felt that the faculty was not as committed to the church as I was.

I began to wonder whether the position I supported had any future. I felt I was in a sense without a profession, a professional niche. I was not trained in sociology or psychology; I had no secular discipline behind me. I had a little philosophy, and I was always sure to move through the theoretical and push the theoretical, the ecclesiological. I tried to suggest how the practical embodiment of church life would precede from theory and from theology.

I also began to sense something that later would be called postmodernity. I knew of a few Catholic churches where they were doing some experimental things, and some Protestant churches where they were using guitars in worship. The unity of the church that I thought was an expression of integrity—in that one does what one really believes in—did not seem to be there anymore. I wondered about the point of telling Episcopalian students how to be good Episcopalians, if it did not matter. I sensed that and wondered whether there was a future for me at Harvard Divinity School.

In addition, on the Harvard campus there were political problems with which I became involved. On April 10, 1969, there was a serious campus revolt, and President Nathan Pusey had to call the police. This incident is described in *The Harvard Strike*, by Lawrence E. Eichel.[1]

Another issue for me was that I was ill with a serious kind of diabetes. I did not know it, although the family knew that something was wrong with me. I found it more difficult all the time to go to work, and I was gaining weight. One summer, Samuel Miller, dean of the divinity school, went off to Europe and asked me to be in charge of the renovation of a section of a campus building. I declined because I did not feel that I was up to doing much of anything. Finally I went to a clinic and was found to be

---

1 Boston: Houghton Mifflin, 1970.

diabetic, and the staff wondered how I had managed to live with such a serious condition untreated!

When a call came in 1970 asking me to consider the Goshen College presidency, I wondered whether I should go. It was a difficult decision. It was difficult for Harriet to think that she would have to leave New England, which she loved so much. And she enjoyed our friendly neighbors and the job at the Arlington public library. Our children loved it there as well. And our son Gerry, who had cystic fibrosis, was one of the subjects in an experimental study being conducted by a clinic in Boston.

We also had some connections with Black churches in the Roxbury area of Boston. I went to their services sometimes, and Harriet and I had marched against Louise Day Hicks, chair of the Boston School Committee who was not responsive to the concerns of African American residents seeking acknowledgment and correction of the de facto segregation of the public school system.

A move meant leaving our Mennonite congregation, a city we loved, and many friendships.

At Harvard Divinity School I had a wonderful relationship with many students. The school had no dean of students, no counselor, and no pastor for the students, so quite a few of them sought me out. Many came from backgrounds similar to mine. Some came from Texas with Baptist backgrounds and were trying to make the adjustment to liberal theology. I was able to help them.

When I went to Harvard's president, Nathan Pusey, and told him that I was considering the move, he said, "How much endowment does Goshen College have?" I said, "$470,000." He just laughed and said, "You cannot maintain a college on that." This was a time when even Harvard was in some financial trouble, despite its many supporters. I chose to go to Goshen College, although no one at Harvard could understand my decision.

What I had foreseen back then has happened: Harvard Divinity School is no longer committed to Christianity in the way that it was when it represented the tradition of Christian liberalism. It is now a place for the study of world religions. The position of Christianity is not being defined by the liberal tradition; rather it is included as one of many religions. I could not argue with that being valid for the divinity school, although it was not my conviction as a Christian. So I left.

I first came to Goshen College in 1970 to look it over. I found the college somewhat stark, maybe a little discouraged, and not

Goshen College president elect J. Lawrence Burkholder speaking with a group of Goshen College student journalists in 1970

in a strong relationship with the Mennonite churches around it—with several exceptions. Goshen Biblical Seminary had left the campus in the 1960s, which meant that professors Howard Charles, Ross Bender, and John Howard Yoder were not there. Much of the intellectual capital of the college was gone. These people had taught undergraduates as well as seminary students. Because the seminary building was on the same campus, they had a presence at Goshen College. Another professor, John C. Wenger, who was so trusted by the constituency, was also gone. I thought, "This place is in a little trouble."

I found out after visiting Goshen that some issues related to the separation of the seminary and the college had not been resolved, including the issue of the location of Mennonite Historical Library. The seminary had moved and only then decided what the terms would be! That is no way to do business, I thought. I was not sure that I wanted to come to a situation like that.

Furthermore, the town of Goshen was upset with the college, because the students had marched on the county courthouse lawn in protest against the Vietnam War. There were also racial tensions and other problems in the town. The students, the baby-boomer generation, were expressing their distrust of their parents and displaying their anti-institutional attitudes. I was told: "The church has the college, but the college is not the church."

I had to agree that the college was not a congregation. Students met several times a week for chapel, and a prayer was sometimes said at the beginning of class. In this way the college was similar to the church. I said to students, "To the extent that I believe that this college belongs somewhere within the body of Christ, I'm a catholic." Well, that did not go down well with anyone!

Soon I felt that Goshen College was really in trouble. I thought that maybe I should accept the presidency because it was my duty to do so and not because it was so desirable! That is what I took to Harriet and our children.

On the positive side, in contrast, was the recent creation of a study-service term, which had started in 1968. Through this program, the college sent students to many countries of the world for a term of study and service. This pioneering program of international education was far ahead of what most other colleges offered. And the program had been conceived imaginatively and was being run responsibly. It was something I could really promote. This innovation confirmed my decision to say yes to becoming president of Goshen College.

Harriet was uneasy about the move, although she agreed to it. It was not that she did not love Goshen and Goshen College; it was because of what she had to leave. That said, we hoped that in Goshen our son Gerry could get the kind of affection, attention, and personal support we thought he needed. To be sure, the best medical understanding of cystic fibrosis was in Boston. In fact, that is where the work on cystic fibrosis started.

Our house in Boston did not sell, because the National Aeronautics and Space Administration was moving out of the Boston area at that time. Housing sales were down. I had borrowed $7,500 from Harvard to put my children through school, and when I resigned I did not have the money to pay to the university back, but a Mennonite businessman generously loaned me the money. Within two weeks, he sent me a letter and cancelled the note. He just gave the money to me! Eventually, we were able to sell the house—not to an advantage, but we sold it.

The question for us was whether to buy a house in Goshen. Our financial situation seemed so risky that I did not want to invest in a house. That was not good judgment, because housing prices went up later and it would have been better to have invested in a house when we first moved there. We spent the first few months in Goshen living in a house near the college on Eighth Street, just sort of camping there. Then a very suitable house along the Elkhart River became available for us to rent. It belonged to Calvin and Freda Redekop. Calvin, a Goshen College professor, was on sabbatical and they were away. We lived in their home for about a year, before moving into another lovely home conveniently located near the college on the dam pond. It had been donated to the college for our use by Lala and Marner

Miller. He was a local businessman. We deeply appreciated their generosity and enjoyed the home.

Adding to our personal financial stress were heavy medical expenses associated with Gerry's medicine and hospitalizations.

Tree planting on the Goshen College campus during presidential inaugural, October 30, 1971: J. Lawrence with Harriet, Myrna, Janet, Howard, and Gerald Paul Burkholder

Some generous people in Ohio sent us money to help with these expenses, for which we were also thankful. We had begun to find the good part of Mennonite community coming through in many ways.

My first task in the fall of 1971, after the inauguration,[2] was to establish an administrative staff. The first two people I asked

---

2 On October 29, 1971, the day before J. Lawrence was formally installed as the eleventh president of Goshen College, GC students performed their own—informal—installation ceremony. Two students escorted J. Lawrence from his office in the Administration Building to Schrock Plaza, where they dipped him in the fountain and sang the college alma mater. The next morn-

Four Goshen College presidents. Seated (left to right): Sanford C. Yoder (1924–40) and Ernest E. Miller (1940–54); standing: J. Lawrence Burkholder (1971–84) and Paul Mininger (1954–70); on the occasion of Yoder's ninety-third birthday, December 1972

turned me down. In retrospect, I am not sorry they did so, because I was able to get John A. Lapp as dean, Henry Weaver as provost, Robert Kreider as business manager, Daniel Kauffman as development officer, and Paul Gingrich as director of church relations. Harold Bauman was campus pastor, and Russel Liechty was dean of students. They were all good—really good!

The administrative council got along beautifully. I cannot remember a single fight or a real argument. While I can remember some disagreements, at no time did I feel that any member was in a difficult relationship with another member. I was glad that I was working with people whom I could trust and with whom I could relate in perfect openness. We got along well.

---

ing more than a thousand people gathered in the Goshen College church-chapel for the service of inauguration. A luncheon followed in the Alumni Memorial Dining Room on campus. During the afternoon, the Burkholder family (J. Lawrence and Harriet, and children Myrna, Howard, Janet, and Gerry) and guests planted 138 trees on campus and attended an informal inaugural reception in the Union Auditorium.

I more or less let these people run the school while I worked on college and church relations, including major fund-raising. I needed to find a way to get Mennonite churches and the college together, and I did not trust Madison Avenue techniques for doing so. I felt that the way to do it was to go to the churches personally and talk. In fact, I resigned from Harvard Divinity School at mid-year, early in 1971, and spent the remainder of the school year, the second semester, going out to churches.[3]

When I came to Goshen College, I knew about a number of pressing financial issues. At that time the general financial condition of colleges and universities was not good. Many were in financial trouble. Among the fine presidents who weathered the difficulties was Father Theodore Hesburgh of Notre Dame. There were many other good university presidents who did not make it, including President Pusey of Harvard. Many small colleges were getting into financial trouble because of the recession in 1971. We made it, but there were many downdrafts at that time.

I have a tendency to think in terms of theology, philosophy, and ontology, and I thought that the ontological status of Goshen College was not properly accepted by the churches. I thought, "This is a church college, and the church and the college ought to be organically and legally related to each other so that the college belongs to the churches. And then the churches would be obligated legally and financially to support it."

That situation obviously did not exist. I thought that the methods being used by most colleges to get support were just not for us. We were being outdone by Hesston College at that time; they had an excellent development officer who understood fund-raising and went after donors and students. They were growing

---

3 J. Lawrence left Harvard Divinity School and toured Mennonite churches and several Goshen College study-service term units in preparation for his presidency, which began officially on July 1. Goshen College at that time had study-service term units in East Germany, Poland, Costa Rica, Nicaragua, Haiti, and Guadeloupe. Each group of twenty to twenty-five students spent sixteen weeks in one of those countries.

when we were not; we used older methods. I still insisted that whatever we did should be done with integrity.

I must give much credit to Dan Kauffman. Dan was a man of great intensity and total dedication. He worked hard, almost too much, all the time, in an attempt to get support for the college—which, in time, worked for us. In a few cases it did not, but he was persistent. Paul Gingrich was also very good. Paul went to churches and heard a lot about the college that was negative. He then brought the information to me, and I tried to patch up the differences. We developed relationships, good relationships, with many people. I used the telephone a lot. Instead of writing a personal letter, I would often just phone someone in the evening. That was when people were likely to be home and when phone calls were relatively inexpensive! They would communicate their concerns verbally, which they would never have done by letter.[4]

I also learned to know a lot of people in Goshen and Elkhart.[5] I was called out to preach funeral sermons, many of them, and weddings, too. I was very busy, but I was not reading or writing. I thought that when I came to Goshen, I would take every Monday off to do something for myself. Then I had to figure out, "How many thousands of dollars are we losing if I take this day off?" I was afraid of having a deficit.

The Goshen College board of directors at that time was loyal, with competent people. They were not asked by the church to do anything but come to the college to see that we were behaving ourselves! I did not feel free to ask a board member to contact someone on behalf of the college. That was not the way the board functioned then; this just was not part of its tradition.

Eventually one of our members, Arlene Mark, went to a symposium sponsored by the Lilly Foundation and read through some

4 According to the *Phoenix Gazette*, March 11, 1972, J. Lawrence and Harriet attended six alumni banquets in five different western states, including Kansas, Colorado, Arizona, California, and Oregon.

5 From 1974 to 1985, J. Lawrence was a member of the board of St. Joseph Valley Bank, later renamed Midwest Commerce Banking Company, Elkhart, Indiana.

J. Lawrence Burkholder meeting in Elkhart, Indiana, in 1973, with John Brademas, who represented Indiana's Third Congressional District in the United States House of Representatives from 1959 to 1981

studies about the work of a board. She came back to the board with the suggestion that it become a working board. We started in that direction, but I still did not feel that it was in any sense my board. Other presidents used to talk about "my board."

We had another little problem at one time. I felt the time had come when Goshen College had to increase its endowment. After paying off the seminary for Newcomer Center, we had less than $200,000 in endowment for the college. Other colleges typically had as much as $50–$100 million. So I proposed that we start an endowment campaign, and we would call it "The Uncommon Cause." That raised a theological problem with our board: Should we not just live from day to day and not worry about the morrow?

I wished that it could be that way, as did some on the board. Some other Mennonite institutions claimed that the only legitimate endowment is a living endowment—that is, an endowment that one makes through having good relationships with others. If a person lives righteously, they believed, support will come. I felt it had to be structured and organized, and we should try to do it in our own way.

We looked at our neighbor, the University of Notre Dame, which had a marvelous campaign going on at that time, in which they raised many millions. They flew in their supporters for weekends. They brought them in on a Friday, and the first thing that they did as soon as they got off the plane was go to mass. Then Father Hesburgh talked to them about the university. On Saturday, they were taken various places, and on Sunday they were asked to help the university.

I thought that would be a wonderful way for us to do it, especially if we could use private airplanes to bring people to Goshen! I did ask one person for his airplane to be used for this purpose, but he said no. I did not ask anyone else with a private airplane about this possibility.

We started to bring groups of people to the college for this purpose, and it began to work well for us. They would come on Fridays, some from a distance, as far away as California, and some more locally. We first showed them a movie about the college and then explained some things. On Saturday they visited the campus, and on Sunday they went to church and came to our home for dinner in the evening. We served them the best food we could think of, though it was almost always the same menu for every group!

By Sunday evening, people were tired, but they were very much in favor of the college, we thought. Of course, they were in favor of the college to begin with, or we would not have invited them! The visit convinced many of them to feel even more strongly about the college.[6]

---

6 The *Goshen College Bulletin*, September 1984, reported that thirty-four groups of guests visited the campus for a weekend each as part of the Uncommon Cause endowment drive effort from 1982 to 1984. The guests were hosted by J. Lawrence and Harriet.

J. Lawrence Burkholder cooking with a wok, as reported in the Goshen News, *April 5, 1978 (page 13), in a feature article entitled "College President Enjoys Chinese Cooking Hobby"*

J. Lawrence Burkholder in conversation with weekend guests visiting the Goshen College campus

By the time I left the presidency in 1984, we had $38–$40 million in the endowment fund. And after a few more bequests, it went up to $100 million. That was after I was no longer president, but the commitments had been made during my time as president. One commitment was for a donation of stocks amounting to $37.5 million. By the time we got it, the stocks' value had gone down, and the bequest was worth $27.5 million. Even so, we were thankful. Most of that bequest came from one person, Harold Good. Both he and his deceased wife, Wilma, had graduated from the college. Wilma was the daughter of the founder of the J. M. Smucker Company in Orrville, Ohio, and Harold had worked for General Motors for thirty years.

The bequest would have been missed, had it not been for Harriet. Harriet spoke with Harold after he had gotten a negative impression of the college, having heard in a roundabout way that there were communists at Goshen College. Actually, the "communist" was Father Philip Berrigan, who had been invited to speak at the college. Our administration was a little divided about whether he should come to the college, because he was so controversial. He

Harriet Burkholder in conversation with Harold Good at his retirement home in Florida in 1983

did come, and Harriet was responsible for persuading Harold to shift his attitude in favor of Goshen College.

The Uncommon Cause endowment campaign was a success. We acquired contributions toward the endowment with dignity and with honesty and not with big displays of any kind. We just openly explained to the supporters what we were trying to do and what we hoped to do. In that sense, I have felt good about what we were doing!

One problem we had at the college during the earlier part of my administration was the issue of drinking alcoholic beverages. We had faculty meetings to discuss this. There was a strong feeling against drinking, so I wrote a little book about it called *To Drink or Not to Drink? Toward a Mennonite Consensus on Alcoholic Beverages.*[7] I did not particularly like the title, but that is how it was published. In this book I said that we would take the position that Mennonite Central Committee takes. After some theo-

---

7 Scottdale, PA: Herald Press, 1981.

logical and social arguments, I said that ordinarily we would not drink, but that there were certain social occasions when we may feel it is in the best interest of everybody to participate in drinking with moderation. And I said that that was my personal policy. I think we handled the issue quite well.

Today a lot of people in the constituency have beer in their refrigerators. Mennonite young people come from homes where drinking is not an issue. Goshen College students are still not supposed to drink on campus. I mention this matter simply because I would not be honest if I were to say that the problems were not real. They were very real for us and cut right into what we were trying to do.

Another problem at the college was the question of co-ed residency, because students wanted to live more communally. We did permit them to live together, in the sense that women were allowed to live on one floor of a dormitory and men on another. Some students wanted to live off campus in co-ed residences. It was worked out that they could do so after having had a co-ed dorm experience first. We wanted to make sure that they knew one another and trusted one another well enough to make communal living workable for themselves. Then several of the houses the college owned were made available to these student groups. That arrangement created a considerable amount of criticism from the constituency.

There was also a little smoking now and then by students. On this issue, I felt that the reaction from the constituency was out of proportion to the problem.

We had another serious problem in those years, which was that College Mennonite Church (located on the college campus) spawned a new congregation. Most of the founding members of the new congregation, Assembly Mennonite Church, had withdrawn from College Mennonite Church. The wider church did not know how to interpret what was going on. Was it a split from College Mennonite Church? And if so, in what sense were they leaving? What was the word to describe their leaving? Assembly members felt that they simply wanted a more intimate community in which to do their own mission work. College Mennonite Church did well in not making too much of it. All this was happening on the campus when I was president. In the end, it turned out all right.

There were also groups that wanted to come on campus and evangelize our students and start something from their own perspective. There were Pentecostals among them, and others who were ultraconservative. I had to face the issue in a theoretical as well as a practical way: Who was going to control this ambience? Somebody had to be responsible for it. Somebody had to draw some lines. The question was not settled as long as I was president, and I did not feel like settling it. I just let it go. It was a matter of real concern for me, but I did not want to be heavy-handed about it.

My administration was characterized by informality, openness, and honesty, as far as one could be honest. Administratively, we could let people assemble around problems, if they wanted to do so, and we left our doors open. We still needed to accept responsibility for what went on at the top. We tried to do that.

Shortly after I became president, I became aware of the fact that the move of the seminary from Goshen to Elkhart had potentially weakened the ability of the college to serve the church, and I realized we needed to address that issue.[8] Of course, we would continue to try to prepare many young people to go to the seminary for ministerial training, which indeed we did. What we would have liked was to have had students come to Goshen College for religious purposes as well as for academic study.

We decided to start what we called the Center for Discipleship to make available special theological study and related programs of various kinds. C. Norman Kraus became director of the program. It was difficult for us to know how to proceed. Sometimes it seemed that we were manufacturing programs for their own sake. Even so, the program did some good and remained for

---

8 Among J. Lawrence's church-wide involvements was a period of membership (1973–80) on the Mennonite Church Council on Faith, Life and Strategy.

a few years, but it never turned into what we had hoped it would become. We recognized that it was difficult for students to come to Goshen College for religious purposes without more structure and continuity. The loss of the seminary to Elkhart was with us as a permanent feature. We had to somehow or other create a reality of religious life and piety on campus. And we had to try to incorporate it into the college program and hope that something would come from it.

Related to that concern, one fine campus event occurred in May of 1972 with what we called the Festival of the Holy Spirit. This event came about at the suggestion of Nelson Litwiller, a retired missionary to Argentina with Mennonite Board of Missions who visited my office and told me that the Spirit was moving in many, many ways in other denominations as well as ours. He believed that we should recognize that and make provision for it. Then I got the idea for the festival and hoped that people would respond to it. Actually, they did respond in a big way. Associated Mennonite Biblical Seminaries and a number of (Old) Mennonite Church congregations cosponsored it with Goshen College, and more than 2,000 people attended the event.

The theological question that surfaced for me when planning this event was what we really mean by the Spirit. It was evident to me that the Bible speaks of the Spirit in different ways. In the Old Testament in particular, there are many references to the Spirit of God, even in the creation story. That observation led me to think of the Spirit as a certain kind of immanence in God's creation, which would be analogous to natural law. This was rather farfetched, as Mennonites had never taught the concept of natural law and in fact were suspicious of it.

In the New Testament there were also many references to the Holy Spirit, and it seemed that the charismatic movement at that time focused primarily on the book of Acts and several other passages in the New Testament. I was enough of a philosopher to suggest that at least we ought to think in two ways about the Spirit, as seen first in the Old and then in the New Testament. That is, we should think of the Spirit of God that has been infused in this world, but which is nevertheless a part of God's creative force, along with the Holy Spirit. We simply called the event "Festival of the Holy Spirit."

Led by Mary Oyer, we sang hymns "in the Spirit," and we even had the college orchestra play for a few events, which was a way of celebrating the broader idea of the Spirit. I gave a speech on the idea of the Spirit, particularly as it expressed itself in idealistic philosophy—that is, in metaphysical idealism. I said that we could make a distinction between the Holy Spirit and the Spirit, but living under God we should celebrate both. So we did, and it was a big occasion. We had several other speakers, all of whom spoke to a full auditorium of listeners. The students loved the event, and it did something to make us realize that from day to day we should be aware that God is moving, that God is present, and that we should not only celebrate God's presence and movement, but we should incorporate the Spirit of God in our lives.

We were looking for other such events to sponsor in those days, to make sure that the college would not turn into a secular institution. These events included discussions about the relationship of religion to science. We called not just on the department of theology, Bible, and religion but also on the science department, to hear what they had to say.

I was pleased with the help that some of the faculty members gave to our son Gerry. He was a bright boy and handsome—just a beautiful young man in every respect. Because of his cystic fibrosis, he had to have so many surgeries. And he had some accidents. A bicycle ran into him shortly after he had had a surgery, and he developed an adhesion. Gerry had to have surgery after surgery after surgery. When he lived on the campus of Goshen College, almost every morning I would go to his room to pound his back so that he could spit up the phlegm in his lungs. These were good times for us, because we had time to talk to each other, though I may have been more preoccupied than I should have been. There were others who were very good to him, especially Atlee Beechy.[9]

---

9 Gerry's health situation did not allow him to participate in an overseas study-service term. Instead he went to Seattle, Washington, where he lived

Gerry majored in psychology. His hope was to counsel veterans of wars. He identified with victims of war. He died on Easter Sunday morning, on April 19, 1981, at the age of twenty-six. He had lived in Goshen for ten years and had graduated from Goshen College in 1979. We appreciated how kind the community had been to him.

Gerald Burkholder died on Easter Sunday morning, April 19, 1981, of complications of cystic fibrosis

A significant event that happened during my presidency at Goshen College was the development of the China study-service term program in 1980. It was big when it happened, although it would not be considered so big now. Its development was preceded by several related events.

---

with his sister and brother-in-law, Janet and Lauren Friesen, who helped him with his daily breathing treatments. There he did a trimester of volunteer work at the Northwest Native American Center. The work of the center included making referrals for those seeking assistance of various kinds, assisting with organizing local festivals, and publishing a monthly newsletter. Gerry was particularly involved with editing the newsletter.

In July of 1975, toward the end of the Cultural Revolution, I was able to go to China. Mennonite Central Committee had a relationship with an organization in New York City that made an arrangement with the Communist government of China for a delegation of twenty-one educators and others to go to China for a three-week tour of the country. MCC made it possible for me to join the group. MCC also sponsored Benjamin Sprunger, then president of Bluffton (Ohio) College, to go on this tour.

It was quite a revelation to go to China at that time. We traveled extensively throughout the country. We even went to Mukden, Manchuria, a place I had helped evacuate when in China in the 1940s.

We saw oilfields, factories, schools, art institutes, communes, and hospitals. Our guides showed us, presumably, everything. Of course, when we went to a hospital, we knew it had been cleaned up beforehand! On our visit to a May Seventh Cadre School, a correctional school for professionals who needed "remolding," we saw fresh vegetables on a table but no students. We were told that they were all out somewhere, so we could not talk to anyone at that place. We went to a factory where nothing much seemed to be happening, because—we were told—"It is a holiday today."

At a People's Liberation Army camp, they showed us a mock battle between two armies. We saw this from a reviewing stand, where we were joined by television personality Steve Allen and his son, who were also touring China at that time. He later wrote about this trip and several other trips he made to China in *Explaining China*.[10]

In Shanghai, I was able to see the office where I had worked some thirty years earlier. It was located in what had been Moore Memorial Church, [11] which was then being used as a high school.

---

10   New York: Crown Publishers, 1980.

11   The Mu'en Church, formerly known as Moore Memorial Church, is a large nondenominational church in Shanghai where J. Lawrence had an office when he worked for the American Advisory Committee, the operating agent for Church World Service in China. Reverend Xie Songsan was a pastor at Moore Memorial Church from 1937 to 1989 and was pastor-in-

I also went to Young Allen Court, the apartment building where my family and I had lived. I looked for a former neighbor, but I could not find him. He was in jail at that time, I later found out.

Overall, I found the trip to China a most interesting experience. Several years later, in 1977, I had a half-year sabbatical (January-June) in Concord, California, to study at the University of California, Berkeley.[12] While there, I focused on "the analogy between Maoism and Christianity" as a study project. Upon returning, I spoke at the University of Notre Dame about my trip in 1975 and about my study project in California.[13]

---

charge from 1941 to 1958. The Burkholder family became well acquainted with Rev. Xie Songsan (1900–89), and his wife Yuqing (1906–85) and their two sons, Luke and Paul, since both families lived at Young Allen Court. Years later, Luke Xie and his wife, Mary, and their son, Donald (Xie Daming), also lived at Young Allen Court. At the urging of J. Lawrence and Harriet, Donald attended Goshen College and graduated in 1990. Donald now lives and works in Shanghai with his wife, Meilin, and daughter, Alysa. Widow Mary Xie is still living at Young Allen Court in Shanghai.

Another large nondenominational church in Shanghai is Shanghai Community Church. J. Lawrence, Harriet, Myrna, and Howard attended this church, now called Hengshan Community Church. In the 1940s the services were nondenominational and held in English. The church now has services in Chinese and English. It is considered the largest, most active Protestant church in Shanghai. According to Harriet's diary, she and J. Lawrence attended a sunrise service there on April 6, 1947, where they heard John Leighton Stuart, US ambassador to China from 1946 to 1949, preach.

12 As J. Lawrence and Harriet traveled west, they met with ten Goshen College alumni groups. While in Concord, Harriet broke her wrist, so J. Lawrence took that opportunity to learn how to cook Chinese food. After their return to Goshen, Harriet Burkholder became a member of the planning committee for the college's Afternoon Sabbatical Program—from its beginning in 1977 and for many years thereafter. It was started by community women and college personnel as a way to draw on the expertise of Goshen College faculty and community members. A yearly series includes on-campus programs as well as off-campus bus tours.

13 In June 1977 at a conference entitled "China: The Religious Dimension," held at the University of Notre Dame, J. Lawrence gave a presentation entitled "Rethinking Christian Life and Mission in Light of the Chi-

In early 1979, I spoke to the Elkhart Rotary Club about my vision for an educational exchange with China. A man named Edward Hou, who happened to be at this meeting, was favorably impressed with what he heard. A native of China, he was the corporate representative to China for Miles Laboratories in Elkhart, and he had connections with education officials in Sichuan Province. He thought that it ought to be possible for me, with the help of an interpreter, to go there to give lectures on education.

After he had communicated this idea to them, two older, powerful Sichuan Province officials—Mr. Ding Genglin, director of the Bureau of Higher Education of Sichuan Province, and Mr. Han, the minister of Science and Technology—invited me to go there.

Harriet and I left for China on December 13, 1979. En route we enjoyed a brief visit with friends in Warsaw, Poland, where I signed an agreement to continue a Goshen College student/faculty exchange with Warsaw Agricultural University. We then flew to Peking and on to Chengdu, where I gave several lectures.

It was a fascinating to be in China some four years after I had toured there in 1975. The Chinese were just coming out of the Cultural Revolution, which had started in 1966. And because there were hardly any foreigners in West China at that time, whenever we walked out of a building a crowd came toward us.

Zhao Ziyang was the much-appreciated governor of Sichuan Province. He later became a high-ranking Chinese politician, although during the Tiananmen Square incident in 1989 he sided with the students and was silenced and imprisoned for fifteen years. He died in 2005.

I gave several lectures for professors at Sichuan University. I was supposed to speak about American higher education, with an emphasis on the responsibilities of administrators and the moral responsibilities of professors to tell the truth! I said, "My experience is with Goshen College, a small religious college, and

nese Experience," which was published in *China and Christianity: Historical and Future Encounters*, edited by James D. Whitehead, Yu-Ming Shaw, and N. J. Girardot (Notre Dame, IN: University of Notre Dame Press, 1979).

Harvard University, a large secular university. The two schools do things differently. Which do you want to hear about?"

They said that they wanted to hear about both, so I spoke about both. I noticed that as I spoke, many of them fell asleep and others were looking around. Because they were just coming out of the Cultural Revolution, they were lost or disinterested. A lot of these "teachers" were on the government payroll but were not teaching. Many of them had been rounded up for this experience, I was later told.

Since they were in transition, they knew that eventually administrators would be selected to lead their institutions. It was being put on me to try to address their Communist leadership issues. I did the best I could.

I was scheduled to give one more lecture, at the Sichuan Teachers College. And then I got sick. I was at our hotel, the Gungyuan Hotel, when I became ill. A little roly-poly Chinese doctor was sent to help me. He was afraid I might die! I was only having a stomach problem. I had been given some pills to take as needed on the trip, so I took them and soon got better.

In the meantime, since the people at the teachers college were expecting a lecture, Harriet went to speak for me. She had been told that in order to qualify for this trip, she needed to be an expert in some area of education. She had taught English at Soochow University School of Law in Shanghai when we were there in the 1940s. She had not kept up with the field of teaching English as a second language, but she had read several books on the topic before going on this trip.

Our hosts took Harriet by surprise. First, she spoke for a short while to a small group of English teachers about educational theory. Then they said, "Now we'll go to the lecture hall."

"Well, what will we do there?" she asked.

"You'll give us a speech," they said.

She was ushered into a room of about five hundred students and faculty, who greeted her with applause. She again gave her lecture on teaching English. She spoke rather slowly, and they got it. They could understand her. And she happened to have taken with her a large red scarf with Chinese writing on it. It had been given to her by her students in June 1947 at the Soochow law school. About half way through her presentation, she held it up and showed it to them, and they clapped and clapped!

When she was finished, they again clapped and clapped and then asked questions. They asked, "Is it true that Christians pray five times a day?"

She said, "Probably not. Maybe you are thinking of Islam."

They had also read in *Time* magazine about troubles in our schools, such as University of California, Berkeley, and they wanted to know about that. Then they wanted to know something about the sexual standards of young people in the United States. She told them that they were not very good but probably not as bad as they thought.

Overall, this session was wonderful for them, because they had not heard from or seen a foreigner for a long time. They seemed to trust Harriet.

Harriet Burkholder, Chengdu, China, in January 1980, giving a speech at the Sichuan Teachers College on teaching English as a second language

I went on that trip with a plan that had evolved in my mind after I became president at Goshen College, and which I had processed with John A. Lapp and Arlin Hunsberger, director of International Education. It was probably about 1972 when I began to think about extending the study-service term program to China, which was unthinkable at that time because of the cold relationship between the United States and China.

I had sent a letter to the Chinese embassy in Ottawa, Canada, thinking that maybe they would respond. I suggested that as Mennonites we believe in working hard and serving the neighbor and we also believe in community life. I explained that we live in communities—not communes, but at least communities—and that our students were going to various parts of the world to try to learn about the cultures and languages of other people. I also said that we all hope for peace, and our hope was that a student exchange might help to bring about a better relationship between China and the United States. I did not hear back from anyone. When I heard that there was a Chinese embassy in Warsaw, Poland, I sent a letter to them, but they did not respond either.

I had in mind to establish an exchange between China and Goshen College that would be very favorable for them: if they took two of our students for one semester, we would pay for the education of one of their students, or for one of their teachers to come to Goshen College for a year. That was a good deal for them. I knew I had to make it good or they would not be interested.

Before leaving Chengdu, we sat down with our elderly official hosts, Mr. Ding Genglin and Mr. Han. One of them explained that many years before, he had been on the Long March, that difficult march in 1934–35, led by the Red Army of the Communist Party of China, which started in South China, went westward and then up through China, and which marked the beginning of the Communist era in China. I was able to talk to them about what happened to me when I was in China in the 1940s and about all the cities I had traveled through. They had not been to many of these cities themselves. I spoke about my affection for the Chinese people and said that I felt that China was making good progress. Harriet also talked about her experience of being in China.

I suggested that there be a student exchange, and they said, "Wouldn't that be good?" They took the plan to Governor Zhao

J. Lawrence and Harriet Burkholder receiving a gift after their visit to Sichuan University and Teachers College in January 1980

Ziyang, and he approved of it and worked it out in detail right there. Next it was given final approval from the central government. This happened in just a few days. Word about the plans for the exchange quickly went out all over China.

From Chengdu we went back to Peking, where Harriet and I were escorted from location to location. Never did they let us out of their sight. Our hotel room was always at the end of a hall, so that we had to go by officials to leave.

People from other educational institutions came to the hotel to talk with us. One was an old man—illiterate, a Communist Party member—from north of Shenyang,[14] who was head of an agricultural school. He wanted us to come to his school.

People from various schools in Peking also came to see us. We do not know how the word got out so quickly. Of course, these educators were all glad that the Cultural Revolution was over, so they could go about schooling more normally and possibly even come to the United States.

---

14 Formerly Mukden, Manchuria.

When we went to the US embassy in Peking, we learned that the staff could hardly believe what had happened. They had sent out a prospectus for the possibility of an exchange program with China. They had been told it was possible only on the graduate level, not on the undergraduate level. Well, we had done it!

Back in the United States, these negotiations were seen as a breakthrough for Goshen College and its study-service term program, which gave me tremendous satisfaction. We immediately began to develop plans for groups of students to go to China and for some to come from China to Goshen. Since we needed funding to do so, I met with two people, prominent businessmen from Elkhart representing the Martin Foundation. I had already been asking them for help to complete the financing of the John S. Umble Center for the Performing Arts, which had been built at Goshen College and dedicated for use in 1978.[15] They said, "We're

---

15 The center was designed by architect Weldon Pries, who devoted many months to research, including a stint in Greece, before beginning the project. Roy Umble, then director of theater, had been a Fulbright Scholar in Athens during a sabbatical year and served as a resource for the design. As a result, the building has features found in ancient Greek theatres, including the steep rise and semicircular rows for audience seating. As in Greek theatres, a whisper on stage is heard—even the back row. Modern theatre elements include trapdoors, a fly-loft, and stage rigging system. The initial funding for the facility came from Lyle and Erma Yost, Goshen College graduates from the class of 1939. Mr. Yost was at that time chairman of the board of Hesston Corporation, Hesston, Kansas. Charles Ainlay, chair of the President's Advisory Board, remembered the time when J. Lawrence in 1976 convened the board on short notice to ask for help with meeting funding deadlines to complete the facility. Board members were able to acquire pledges from community members for a total of more than $300,000 within seventy-two hours.

The President's Advisory Board had been formed in 1963 by President Paul Mininger to help build bridges between Goshen College and the local Goshen community. J. Lawrence increased the number of board members and included members from Elkhart and Middlebury. Goshen attorney Charles Ainlay had been chair of the board since its inception and continued as chair during J. Lawrence's presidency.

very much interested in that project, but we're more interested in China." I said, "That's fine."

After our meeting, they had a private consultation of their own and returned with an offer. They said, "We're ready to give $100,000 toward the building project, and we're ready to give $125,000 a year to this exchange program, as long as we feel that it is helpful." With their help, the exchange program was launched, and the Martin Foundation was able to continue to support the program year after year until 1988, for a total of more than a million dollars. The exchange program got underway quickly and made a positive contribution in the area of human relationships.

Geraldine Martin, J. Lawrence Burkholder, and Atlee Beechy with two professors from the Sichuan Teachers College in Chengdu, China, during the fall of 1980, when J. Lawrence and Harriet Burkholder took Lee and Geraldine Martin, co-founders of the Martin Foundation, to meet with the first group of China study-service trimester students from Goshen College. Atlee and Winifred Beechy were the faculty leaders for this group.

In the fall of 1980, Harriet and I took Lee and Geraldine Martin, cofounders of the Martin Foundation, to China to meet with the first group of Goshen College study-service term students there, being led by Atlee and Winifred Beechy.[16] The Sichuan Teachers College in Chengdu had constructed a new building for our students and called it the Panda Palace. (The panda is native to Sichuan Province.) The students had been having a good experience, though their freedom was limited. They were not allowed to leave the campus alone under any circumstances. The reason given was that with so many bicycles on the streets, they could be hurt! There was real comradeship and fellowship between the students and those with whom they worked. That was the start of the study-service term program in China, and it went on for many years.[17]

In 1981 the Sichuan provincial education bureau suggested that the time had come for the Mennonite Church to send teach-

---

16 Lee Martin was chairman from 1976 to 1995 of NIBCO, a leading manufacturer of pipe fittings, valves, and plumbing fixtures, located in Elkhart, Indiana. The Martin Foundation's strong financial support for the study-service term program made its implementation possible. The China study-service term program was the first undergraduate exchange between a college in the United States and a Chinese educational institution since the reopening of China in 1977. This trip for Lawrence and Harriet included going to Shanghai, where they attended a service at Mu'en Church. Harriet reported in a March 1981 letter to friends that there were three services on Sunday mornings at this church, with 1,200 people attending each. When the church reopened in 1979, it was the first church with a public worship service in Shanghai in thirteen years.

17 Other China involvements during the early 1980s included the following: J. Lawrence went to Taiwan as a delegate to the Sino-American Conference on Higher Education held from March 30 to April 4, 1982. On this trip he also went to Peking, where he met with US Ambassador Arthur W. Hummel Jr. and Betty Lou (Firstenberger) Hummel. On January 11, 1984, as one of four hundred guests, J. Lawrence attended a reception for visiting Chinese Premier Zhao Ziyang in Washington, DC. According to the *Goshen College Record*, January 20, 1984, "The invitation to Burkholder by the sponsoring Chinese Embassy displayed their recognition of the importance of GC's exchange program with China."

ers to China to teach English. I knew that this kind of a program would have to be managed outside the administration of Goshen College, because we could not afford to sponsor it, nor did we have the personnel to manage it.

As it happened, four Mennonite church agencies formed what was called China Educational Exchange (later renamed Mennonite Partners in China), now managed from Harrisonburg, Virginia. In 1987 CEE had thirty-six teachers in China. We had two Chinese teachers come to Goshen College from China recently through this program, though fewer are coming now than before.

What has happened in China between then and now is amazing. Through our study-service term program, we were in on the early stages of something important in China, though it has not been clear exactly what that was. I have done a little reflecting about what happens when one starts something: history takes over, and the instigator does not know whether it is for good or ill.

First-graders from Parkside Elementary School, Goshen, Indiana, visiting J. Lawrence Burkholder in February 1981

Given my philosophical inclinations, I have to say it will likely be both good and bad—which is another way of speaking of ambiguity.

What the future will hold for the Goshen College relationship with China, I do not know, though I do know that the contact has been positive thus far. Diana Tsu, who had served as my secretary in Shanghai and who later lived in Peking, informed me that an article in a daily newspaper had reported that there are three major universities in America: Harvard, Yale, and Goshen College!

Overall, we had some good years at Goshen College, though we always faced pressure to get enough students. Oh, how we worked and worked to do the right thing and say the right thing. I felt the downdraft all the time. I felt that the relationship between the college and the churches was fundamentally wrong. If Goshen College was going to be a Mennonite school, there ought to be

J. Lawrence Burkholder at a sibling reunion with (left to right) Harold Burkholder (Peoria, Illinois), Evelyn Burkholder Kreider (Goshen, Indiana), Mildred Burkholder McDannel Hackman (Palmyra, Pennsylvania), and Verna Burkholder Troyer (Goshen, Indiana)

some firm commitment on the part of the churches to support it—and not just Goshen College but all Mennonite schools. It is an obligation on the part of the churches.

Now if I understand correctly, the Reformed church has such a system. The Reformed colleges are never without money; the Reformed church taxes its congregations. They even use the word "tax." Calvin College is financed like that, and their president is chosen by church ballots. Two candidates run against each other. After all, these colleges stem from John Calvin's Geneva, and that is not too different from the way Calvin operated in Geneva, where on one corner was the church and on the other was the academy! When we as Anabaptists started our churches, we were not interested in formal education, and it was not just that we were persecuted; it was that as a sect we did not know how to relate to the broader church and society.[18]

---

18   Other significant developments during J. Lawrence Burkholder's time as president of Goshen College include the following:

Merry Lea Environmental Learning Center. In 1980 after several years of negotiation with J. Lawrence and other members of his administrative team, Lee and Mary Jane Rieth gave the college responsibility for operating and managing what is now called the Merry Lea Environmental Learning Center of Goshen College. Larry Yoder was appointed as its first fulltime director in 1981, and in 1997 Luke Gascho became executive director. Located near Wolf Lake, Indiana, the land and property consisted of about 525 acres. An additional 425 acres was transferred and leased to the college in 1997. In 1967, Lee and Mary Jane Rieth had established Merry Lea as a natural habitat. In keeping with their original vision, Merry Lea now offers a variety of collegiate programs, including a master's degree in environmental education. The total acreage of the Merry Lea Environmental Learning Center has risen to 1,189 with the transfer of all Merry Lea land parcels.

Lee Rieth was a former co-owner, with his brothers Bill and Blair, of Rieth-Riley, a large construction company headquartered in Goshen, Indiana. In 1996 Mary Jane, widowed in 1984, established a foundation which now allows Merry Lea Environmental Learning Center to operate financially independently of Goshen College.

Chair in Moral Philosophy and Carl Kreider Chair in Economics. In the late 1970s Howard and Myra Brembeck gave Goshen College a contribution for a Chair in Moral Philosophy and also endowed the Carl Kreider Chair in Economics.

J. Lawrence and Harriet Burkholder Merit Scholarship Fund. Also in the late 1970s, it was recognized that the college needed to raise significant funds to help establish scholarships for worthy students. In 1983, as part of the Uncommon Cause capital campaign effort, the board of overseers established this scholarship fund to help attract academically strong students, and they honored J. Lawrence and Harriet by naming it after them. The goal was to get the fund to $500,000; as of January 2016, the value stood at about $300,000.

Fourth Freedom Forum. Howard Brembeck was founder of Chore-Time Brock Inc., located in Milford, Indiana, which invented and produced innovative poultry and swine feeding and storage equipment. In 1982 Brembeck founded Fourth Freedom Forum, with headquarters in Goshen, Indiana. It is a nonpartisan, nonprofit foundation seeking to provide discussion, development, and dissemination of ideas focused on solutions to global security threats. When Brembeck decided in the early 1980s to use his wealth to create this foundation for world peace, he said publically and at board meetings that it was J. Lawrence's encouragement that led to his decision to invest in the foundation. In June 2008, J. Lawrence was honored by the Fourth Freedom Forum for his twenty-six years of service on its board.

Sagamore of the Wabash Award. Sometime during the 1970s Indiana governor Otis R. Bowen (1972–1980) presented J. Lawrence Burkholder with the Sagamore of the Wabash Award, an annual award begun in the late 1940s given to those rendering a distinguished service to the state or the governor. The honorary title "Sagamore" was used by Native American tribes in northeastern United States to describe a great man among the tribes, to whom a chief would look to for wisdom and advice.

8

Retirement, 1984–2010

When I retired from Goshen College in September of 1984, Harriet and I went to Florida to visit Harold Good who, with Wilma (now deceased), had contributed so generously through the years in support of Goshen College.[1] Later in the month we drove to Boston to see our son Howard. When we got there, I was approached by Gordon Kaufman about the need for the appointment of a new dean at Harvard Divinity School. Acting Dean George MacRae had died at the beginning of the school year, in early September. Some of the faculty had been meeting to decide whom to recommend to Harvard University president Derek Bok as a replacement.

They had two choices. One was to choose someone from the divinity school faculty, and the other was to go outside the divinity school. They could not agree on anyone inside the faculty, and then I came along. Richard Niebuhr and Gordon Kaufman asked me whether I would be interested in being the dean on an interim basis. I was not looking for employment at that time! I was looking forward to having less responsibility, and I was still struggling with my diabetes.

"Would you talk to President Bok?" they asked.

---

1 The Burkholders returned from this trip with an embroidered Chinese wall-hanging which Harold had donated to Goshen College. Measuring 6½ feet by 7½ feet, it is now mounted and hanging on campus in the Good Library. Harold and Wilma Good had purchased it at an estate sale of opera singer Enrico Caruso. It is thought to be at least a thousand years old.

I said that I would. He had been dean of Harvard Law School and came from a prominent Philadelphia family: his father had been a justice on the Pennsylvania Supreme Court. He was married to the daughter of the Swedish economist Gunnar Myrdal. When we met, we got along easily. He asked me what I thought the divinity school should do and be, and I felt free in his presence to say what I thought. I think I gave him good answers.

"Would you take the position if asked?" he wondered.

"Well, I would at least like to discuss this with my wife, but I am a little concerned about whom I'd be working with," I said.

"I think we can make arrangements for that," he responded.

He arranged for a faculty committee to meet with me. When we met, I felt right away that some of these people did not want me. When they asked questions, I gave evidence of the fact that I had not been around there for a long time and had not kept up with their line of thought. I probably sounded old-fashioned, and soon the discussion became personal, which amplified my inadequacy for a position of that sort.

Some committee members brought up certain women's issues and asked me how I would handle them. They had brought into the meeting some women from the administrative council to represent women's interests. I cannot claim to have performed well at this meeting, and it was evident that except for Gordon Kaufman, Richard Niebuhr, and one other faculty member who was there, they did not want me. When the meeting came to an end, as we were walking out of it, Gordon Kaufman said to me, "Such people!"

And I said, "It just wouldn't work."

Then Gordon said, "I think the school could stand you, but I'm not sure if you could stand the school!"

I did not take the position, and President Bok was disturbed about it and discussed his concern with Gordon.

I was a little tired after fourteen years at Goshen College, and it may have been good that I did not get the position. It was the older faculty who wanted me, because they remembered me from my years as a professor there. The younger faculty of course did not know me. Harvard Divinity School had advanced in many ways during the years since I had been there, and it was in so many respects a different school.

In the fall of 1989, I went on an extended trip to China, Vietnam, and East Germany. It had many surprising twists and turns. When I arrived at the airport in Peking, Diana Tsu, my secretary in the 1940s, met me, and I stayed at a hotel near Tiananmen Square. She was interested in talking with me, but she could not be seen entering a hotel where there were so many foreigners. We met in a certain restaurant and stayed there for a while. She said she was in favor of the position of the Chinese government at that time. She had been a victim during the Cultural Revolution. She was sent to Manchuria and was treated badly there; her teeth had been knocked out. By this time she had become convinced that the Communist government was a legitimate government, and she was in support of it. Her husband, who was chief engineer at a factory for electrical circuits, took the same position. We had an interesting time. Her brother, Daniel Tsu, had also worked in my administration in Shanghai.

The Tiananmen Square student-led protest demonstration, known as the June Fourth Incident, had happened several months before I came to Peking. I was there rather inconspicuously and on my own initiative at my own expense. I did not have a chance to go to Shanghai, which I would have liked to do. It was new and interesting to be in China without a Chinese official escort.

Following my meeting with Diana Tsu, I flew to Chengdu, where I met with a number of former Goshen College students— that is, Chinese teachers who had been to Goshen College for one year. They were there to celebrate the tenth anniversary of the Sichuan University/Goshen College study-service term exchange program, held October 14–15. The celebration was put on by the government with great fanfare. It included fireworks, television coverage, toasts, and banquets. It was a memorable experience. The former students had come from all over Sichuan Province for our meeting; we had Chinese alumni who were greatly interested in Goshen College and were very loyal to it.

These Goshen College alumni were having a remarkable influence linguistically in Sichuan Province. Since they had been at Goshen College to improve their English, by this time they knew something about teaching English to speakers of other languages (TESOL), both scientifically and sociologically. They had become leaders in their schools—including medical schools and other kinds of schools—where they were teaching English. One former student, I was told, had written a book and had been invited to teach at the university in Guangdong Province, and he was understandably proud of his achievements. It seemed that those who had been to Goshen College were being recognized for their special abilities. This brought joy to me.

From China I went to Vietnam, where I was hosted for several days in Ho Chi Minh City (formerly Saigon) by Mennonite Central Committee workers Stan and Janet Reedy. I went there out of curiosity, having been there briefly in 1954 as a representative of the World Council of Churches. One lasting impression was seeing so many motorcycles!

Then I went to Germany, where I was joined by Gerhard Reimer, professor of German at Goshen College, then directing the Brethren Colleges Abroad program at the University of Marburg. We drove from Marburg to East Germany and visited former Goshen College study-service term unit locations, including the one in Naumburg. We heard over the radio at about 9:00 on the evening of November 9 that the Berlin Wall had come down. We got up early the next morning and started driving west. We finally came to where the wall should have been, and people were lined up there by the hundreds in their cars, ready to go through the wall. Many of them were stopping to celebrate. And many children were riding their bicycles from East Germany to West Germany, which had been separated by the wall. Some people were passing out flowers and chocolates. It was a time of great celebration. That was one of the most meaningful experiences of my life. We stayed there for a short time and then went on, but we felt that a new era had begun.

Two years later, on August 9, 1991, I went to Lithuania as a member of the board of Lithuania Christian College,[2] started through the support and influence of Art Defehr, a Mennonite Brethren businessman from Winnipeg, Manitoba. We had a productive meeting there. I had been a member of the board for several years and had been in discussion with Defehr about its initial location, because of difficulties in that Baltic nation. The school was finally moved to its present location in the city of Klaipeda, and it has become a strong institution.

J. Lawrence Burkholder in an ultralight airplane

I also happened to be in Moscow when a coup attempt failed. I had gone with Art Defehr and several other members of the board to Moscow for several days and had arrived on the morning of Tuesday, August 20, 1991. The coup had begun the night before, on Monday, the nineteenth. We had the interesting experience of being among the crowds in Red Square where the demonstrations

---

2 Now LCC International University.

were happening. Remarkably, not a shot was fired; it was a peaceful coup.

When I returned, I was met by the press in Goshen, as one who had been in several hot spots in the world in recent years. They remembered that in addition to having just been in Moscow during the failed coup, I had been in China several months after the Tiananmen Square protests in 1989 and had passed through the Berlin Wall in Germany the very morning after it fell in November of that same year. I was asked whether I planned to visit hot spots elsewhere in the world the next time special events were unfolding!

9

Musings on Pressing Issues of My Time

On Luther and Grace, Mennonites and Evil

I'm a follower of Christ, but I do not imitate him in all respects. There is a Lutheran character to my theology. Of course, I know what Luther actually did. He started regional churches, and he was against the serfs. He did some awful things, and he said "Sin bravely" and all that. He also said that he would like to be a follower of Jesus Christ and live like Jesus did. But he couldn't do it, and I understand why he couldn't do it. He was in a tough political situation. He had hordes of people who were becoming Protestants of a sort, so he had to define what that meant. In one place he said that he would like to have a small group of serious people who would record their names in a book and live together. He had high ideals that went with that vision, which Dietrich Bonhoeffer described in *The Cost of Discipleship*. In principle Luther thought of doing this, but then he couldn't do it, because people are sinful. And there were just too many of them. How do you organize all those people? He changed his mind out of practical necessity. He then said that the primary thing is not following Jesus. We ought to try to follow Jesus, but we can't make it. So for him the doctrine of grace came to be the key to Christianity, as a result of his experience as a human being, in a political situation within Christendom, which included the public order.

We have to make a distinction between Luther at his best and Luther at his worst. When Luther was at his worst, he went right off; he became a sour old man, and his theology corresponded to that outlook. He was a human being, and he had his dark moments and attacks—*Anfechtungen*. So he said: What we have to do is rely on the grace of God through Jesus Christ and the atonement, and then his ethics becomes one of love. God's love must come through us. The idea that we are priests for each other, preachers to all believers—that's his idea, not a Mennonite idea.

Eventually he backed away for practical purposes, because he had to answer the question (which Anabaptists have never answered clearly): Who is my neighbor? He had an awful lot of neighbors of all kinds. They weren't all priests, and they weren't all good people. They were all just ordinary people. I've always been willing to grant that he became a sour old man, and his theology was misleading in the sense that it ended up in cheap grace. But I don't think he started out that way.

For Luther there was an ontology of evil; this is behind his theology. You get into situations when you can't do what's right; you're caught. The Anabaptists would never be caught, because they always thought there was a moral way out. If they would try hard enough, by the grace of God, they could get out. The kind of thing I was told by Harold S. Bender and others, as I interpreted it was: It's tough, but if you try hard enough, pray hard enough, there is a way out.

John Howard Yoder wrote a book[1] and found about a couple dozen ways by which you can worm your way, intellectually, out of a situation in which somebody wants to beat up your grandmother. I've been in situations where it wasn't my grandmother that was facing harm, but I couldn't help the person who was, and I felt guilty for it. That's one of the differences between me and John Howard Yoder. With him there is no such thing as a dilemma. One time when I was at Princeton and he was visiting

---

1 See John Howard Yoder, *What Would You Do? A Serious Answer to a Standard Question*, expanded ed. (Scottdale, PA: Herald Press, 1992).

there, he pulled me aside. He said, "Lawrence, keep your norms up. There's no such thing as a dilemma."

I came back from China full of thoughts of ambiguity and conflict. What Yoder wanted to save us from is an ontology of evil. He would say, you might figure there was evil, but there's no ontology that is comparable in terms of being to the being of God and Christ. In other words, there is no devil. I don't think there is a personal devil, but I think there are evil forces which are collected and systematized and organized, and just like a tar baby you get caught up in them. You can't get out by your best efforts, particularly if you're in certain political positions. Yoder's position would not acknowledge that as being the case, and Mennonites love it. But one of these times they're going to learn.

On Goshen Biblical Seminary and Goshen College

I have moments when I say that sometime I'll learn about John Howard Yoder—not only what kind of a person he was but what kind of a theologian he was. When I became president of Goshen College, he was president of Goshen Biblical Seminary, and I had to deal with him for two years. A lot of things were not settled. When I came into the presidency of Goshen, they had decided to separate the seminary from the college, but they hadn't agreed on the terms.[2] It took ten years of discussion to settle where the Mennonite Historical Library should be. The toughest letter I ever got as president came from John Oyer.[3] He thought that I had put

---

2 In 1969 Goshen Biblical Seminary moved from the Goshen College campus to nearby Elkhart, Indiana, to share a campus with Mennonite Biblical Seminary (which had moved there from Chicago in 1958). Eventually the two fully integrated to become what is now Anabaptist Mennonite Biblical Seminary. See Harold S. Bender, "Goshen Biblical Seminary (Goshen, Indiana, USA)," Global Anabaptist Mennonite Encyclopedia Online, http://gameo.org/index.php?title=Goshen_Biblical_Seminary_(Goshen,_Indiana,_USA)&oldid=101331.

3 John S. Oyer taught in the history department at Goshen College for thirty-eight years beginning in 1955, served as director of the Mennonite Historical Library (1975–87), and edited *Mennonite Quarterly Review* (1966–74 and 1977–92).

on the table the possibility that the historical library would go to Yoder and the seminary. Eventually it was decided that it would remain at Goshen, but there would be financial advantages to the seminary.

Those first few years were fierce. The college was going down, the seminary was leaving, the faculty was dispirited, and even some of the faculty members said we ought to become a state school. I went to Goshen to save it for the Mennonite church; that's the reason I left Harvard. If Goshen College had been doing well, I wouldn't have gone. But I thought it was being lost. And John Howard Yoder's father later said to me, "You saved Goshen College."

But so far as John Howard Yoder is concerned, I found an awful lot of dishonesty. He dealt dishonestly with the board about his marital problems, and with the church too. But he had a quick mind, and a great ability to talk and to write. He would always frame the argument or the discussion in a way that would favor him. I heard him, for example, give a talk over at Notre Dame one time on something having to do with the economic order. The question was, what do you think of capitalism? He got up and he talked around and around and around it, and then he said, "I have appreciated the assignment," and sat down.

When I went back to Goshen after having received a doctorate—I think it was 1958—I thought it would be good for the faculty to do some theological reflection, not on Mennonite themes necessarily, but just to become better theologians. I had given a little speech at Harvard when I got there, on the function of the teacher in the congregation, on the office of resident theologian. I thought it would be good for faculty members at Goshen to get in some theology. So I went to the Lilly Endowment and asked for enough money to pay the salaries of our faculty for two weeks, and the endowment gave us the grant. The one book I suggested that we all read was a book that was highly touted then, H. Richard Niebuhr's *Christ and Culture*. Well, John Howard didn't like that, and he did everything he could to disrupt the meetings. Mary

Oyer really told him off.[4] He set out to make my project a failure, but he didn't succeed entirely. There was a kind of mean aspect to him, but at the same time he got some good ideas out.

Yoder talked about middle axioms. That idea came out of Union Theological Seminary, and before that it was in England. Yoder used the term but really didn't go into it deeply enough, so one doesn't know whether for him the middle axioms are describing what the state will do or what we as Mennonites will do as well. The middle axioms are somewhere between the absolute ideal and the real. Another word for it would be compromise. In German the word *Kompromiss* means making a deal, or just working it out, doing the best you can, making something good out of something; it isn't shady. I figure I can't live without compromise. I'm very sympathetic with car dealers who have to make a living, and college recruitment officers who have to get their students, and presidents who have to meet a budget. You have to choose between this person and that person for a position on your faculty. They're both good, but they bring different things, so you have to say no to one of them. That may not be a moral problem, but it comes through to me as a moral problem—something I would rather not address if I could avoid it.

Ethical Dilemmas

I was told by many people that there is no such thing as a dilemma; there are just *seeming* dilemmas. This would suggest that if we pray hard enough and think well enough and are smart enough, we'll find that there is a way of escape. So what seems to be a dilemma is not a dilemma after all. I think you recognize the problem, and you hope and pray that you make the better choice in an evil situation, that you choose the lesser evil, and then you act, because there are certain situations in which you *must* act. Now the prophet does not necessarily have to act. He can go and cultivate his trees, like Amos, or he can go somewhere else, but the king must act. The president of the United States must act.

---

4 Mary K. Oyer was on the music faculty at Goshen College.

The governor must act. Mennonites who are running caregiving homes must act.

At the Mennonite Church national assembly this year [2005?], Mennonites are going to get into issues of medical ethics. Dr. Willard Krabill[5] says there are certain dilemmas we have to meet and we are setting up committees to anticipate that and to work through them. But in many cases this approach doesn't solve our dilemmas; it just suggests how we're going to muddle through. I look at complex reality as situations in which with the best of intentions we can have some influence but they are not situations we can always solve.

When Jesus sometimes got into such a situation, he just didn't answer the question. Shall we pay taxes? Jesus said, "Give to Caesar what is Caesar's, and give to God what is God's." He didn't say what to give, though. It's the same as saying "Just do it." That response was just a way of repeating the question. And if you pay taxes, well, go and catch a fish and there'll be a coin in there. You have to ask: If a good Samaritan came along when five or six people were being half killed, whom should he save? He has only one ass and he can't take all of them to an inn, so whom would he save? It's that kind of question that the New Testament does not face and which is faced only by those who go into Christian ethics.

Christian ethics must include the question of what you do in these kinds of situations. Now fortunately, not all of life is of that sort. You know when you get up in the morning and your child has a bowel movement in his pants, you clean it up. You see? You *know* what to do. And when it's breakfast time, you go and cook your kids some food. And you protect your children, up to a point. But in some extreme situations, what should you do? Should you

---

5 Willard S. Krabill (1926–2009) was a family physician with a master's degree in public health and advanced training in obstetrics who also served as Goshen College physician and associate professor emeritus of health education. He did pioneering work among Mennonites in medical ethics, public health, family-centered childbirth, and sex education. See https://mla.bethelks.edu/mediawiki/index.php/Krabill,_Willard_S._(1926-2009).

deter the assailant? I would say yes. Kill him? That's the question. When Jesus said in his prayer "Lead us not into temptation," what did he mean? I think he meant, don't let us get into the situation of an ultimate sort, where we have to decide on life and death. Protect us from that kind of situation. That's what I put into it, but maybe that's not what he had in mind. I don't know. My position is: Work like the dickens, do the best you can, seek the council of the church, and then act. And probably your action will be partly good—mostly good—but there will be some evil in it. So as a good Lutheran, or I hope someday a good Mennonite, you ask for forgiveness.

Grace

I think it's only been in recent years that we Mennonites have discovered grace. In my discovery of grace maybe I have taken too much of Luther's counsel, sinning bravely. That seems to be a terrible contradiction. But what did I do on that airplane?[6] I pushed a woman out, and I pushed other people out. Now that's not a big event. I'm sure the pilot, the marine officer, has long ago forgotten about it, and to bring it up to him would be crazy. Oh, what's the difference? But I was sensitized by my Mennonite background, and if I was instrumental in somebody's being left behind, in separating an old man and his wife by what I did, I felt bad about it. Maybe you do have to just get tough, get calloused. But I don't like that. I hope not to get calloused.

Jimmy Carter Speaks to Mennonites

When Mennonites met in Atlanta, the main speaker was President Jimmy Carter. The reason they invited him, they would say, was because he does so many good things of a charitable nature, because he has a foundation that helps many people in Africa. And he has worked with Habitat for Humanity, even hammering nails so people who need homes have them. But he also presided over deadly weapons in a defensive manner, and if he had been called to respond to a first strike, it would've meant the end of civilization.

---

6 See account on pages 88–89 of this volume.

And we Mennonites made him the chief speaker at our convention and told our young people, "Here is a great national hero." Now what does that mean? To me it means that Mennonites don't know the implications of our own position.

Jimmy Carter has never renounced what he did as president. I talked with him. He came to Goshen to our Fourth Freedom Forum,[7] and I got on this whole question of atomic weapons. I didn't press it, because it's so difficult to handle, and I knew that he was a sensitive kind who taught the Sermon on the Mount in Sunday school class in Americus, Georgia, where he lives; I knew some Mennonites who had been under his teaching. But what do you do if you're president of the United States, presiding over many millions of people—people of different kinds of faith and no faith? What do you do? He did what he thought he had to do, and I have to admire his courage and the faith. As a Christian, he believed that maybe if he were president, he wouldn't have to use those bombs.

I like President Carter very well and I admire him, but I felt that the Mennonites were calling on him without proper justification and acknowledgment of the dilemma involved.

Dr. Don Minter, a thoughtful member of our congregation, is now a member of our city council in Goshen. Under a city initiative of some kind, he went to school with police officers and participated in mock exercises of various kinds. In one situation the instructor said, "Now, there's somebody coming here with a gun. What you can do is just put up your hand and kind of push them or at least indicate to them 'Don't do that.' Or you can reach for a gun." Don reached for a gun. It's been an education for him. He says he's been part of that group and they get along fine and it's almost like being in church.

There are similarities. There is civility in public situations. But I like to feel that there's more than that in the church. Most people are nonviolent all their lives, but in church you become nonresistant. I've been so imbued with nonresistance that I would have a hard time suing somebody. I don't say I never would

---

7 For more information, see http://www.fourthfreedomforum.org/.

have, because as president of Goshen College I might have had to defend Goshen College in court. There is a fundamental difference between what's involved in personal ethics and what's involved in social ethics.

Reinhold Niebuhr

I had a wonderful experience in China, but I hardly read a book while I was there. I was busy morning, noon, and night. But one of the shipments we received from Church World Service was a shipment of theological books. I opened one box and from one book I read Karl Barth on the resurrection. Even though I believe in the resurrection, it didn't make much sense to me. I read Reinhold Niebuhr, *An Interpretation of Christian Ethics*, and it described to me the situation that I was in. I was influenced by that book, I must say, and maybe that was a bit unfortunate. But it was an amazing book. In one little volume it set forth the presuppositions of Niebuhrianism, which is a kind of Lutheranism, an Americanized Lutheranism. It's different from the views of Reinhold's brother, H. Richard Niebuhr, who taught at Yale and belonged to the American school of relativism. Reinhold Niebuhr was not a relativist, although he acknowledged that some things needed to be relativized. But he was a person of principle and dialectics. He was against the Vietnam War, but he could not be against resisting Italy. He wrote this book between the world wars; it was published in 1935.

The question is, did Jesus think that what he said would have immediate application for the state? I shouldn't doubt that he meant it, because there's a theocratic, political presumption in the Old Testament and the New Testament. But I can't go along with all the New Testament theocratic eschatology. I don't care to reign with Christ. I don't care to reign with anybody. To me the book of Revelation is a statement to the Roman Empire: "You've had power long enough. You've been persecuting us, and Jesus is going to come and he's going to get you. Then we will reign with him." My interpretation may be wrong, but the idea of Jesus reigning is there. And what is the meaning of judgment? Well, the whole political complex of the empire will be changed. Now, it didn't happen. Maybe it will happen, I don't know. But I'm old and tired, and I have no desire to rule anybody.

But if it were a matter of responsibility and bringing about civil order and so on, I would think as a matter of principle, and I would maybe take the position which you're defining as Pilgram Marpeck's:[8] you go as far as you think love will let you go. But there is a point where you would withdraw, and certainly I would too. But almost everybody could state positions and conditions that would lead to withdrawal. If I were in the German government in 1938, and knew what was coming, had some idea of that, I don't know what I would've done, what form my resistance would have taken. But at least I wouldn't go along with the government if I could help it.

The Limits of Nonresistance

I did think a lot about death when I was flying in China. I knew that I would never defend myself in a military situation. I was that kind of a pacifist. But I did have to wonder about how far I should carry risks. The fact was that I was the father of two children, and then we had our third child in Shanghai, and I knew that I was putting myself at risk. Somebody asked Dr. Robert T. Henry, "Why does Lawrence Burkholder live such a riskful life?" And Dr. Henry, who was my predecessor as director of Church World Service, said, "I don't know, but I can't stop him."

I felt risk-taking was a part of being a Christian, the risking of everything. The only kind of pacifism I was acquainted with and thought of was a kind of nonresistance. If anyone would strike me, I would never strike back. But I had to face the question, what if your wife was present, and your children? I talked with Harriet about it, and we decided that I would never protect her by use of lethal means, because she was a Christian. But I didn't know

---

8 Here J. Lawrence is addressing his interviewer, C. Arnold Snyder, a specialist in the history of the Radical Reformation, of which Pilgram Marpeck was a part. Marpeck took a more moderate position among Anabaptists, critical of those of a more legalistic and a more spiritualistic bent.

what to do about my children, my little children. Are you going to subject your little children to that kind of decision, which should be made only by those with maturity and responsibility? What do you do with kids? There's a natural bond there, and when you have them you feel responsible for them. Now of course I would protect them in any way short of killing someone else. I'd shoot an attacker in the foot if I could. I'm not nonresistant in that absolute sense, but when it comes to killing somebody, I would not kill anybody for my own safety. Neither would I kill anybody, at least this is the way we talked about it theoretically, for the sake of my wife. But it's pretty hard to know what I would do in case my little children were attacked. And I haven't solved that yet completely. That is, I don't know what I would do. I don't know what I should do. What should I do? I'd be inclined not to shoot. That would be my first inclination, I think. But I just couldn't see my children dragged off and destroyed. So it is a dilemma. Sometimes I wish Jesus had been married and had six kids. Then we would know, maybe. Or maybe not.

We discussed this subject an awful lot in China, because we were living riskfully. Harriet had Janet in Shanghai, and what she got was not very good care, but she survived. Still, that experience in China was the best experience of my life. I learned more than when I was at Princeton or at Harvard or any other time. And I take greater satisfaction in it because I didn't kill anybody, and I didn't lead anybody astray. I just gave and gave and gave and gave. Sometimes it didn't amount to anything, but sometimes it did. And the contingencies of history—how unpredictable history is, the instability of everything—came through to me, particularly living in a war situation. Everything was coming loose at times, it seemed. Life was coping with this and coping with that.

Life here is pretty easy by comparison. I find a lot of loose talk going on now about what's right and what's wrong. Out there you just didn't have to deal with the hypothetical, because it was the real. And a lot of our discussion now is hypothetical. What would you do if . . .? What is right if . . .? If—it's all if. That discussion of hypothetical questions is typical of a classroom situation, if you're teaching ethics. What is the ground for your decision? Is your argument deontological or teleological? Are you a foundationalist or not? The classroom situation is hypothetical, but in China the situations were real.

From Dualistic Nonresistance to Sectarian Realism

Miner Searle Bates, the missiologist and missionary in Nanking, also frequented Shanghai. We talked a good bit about pacifism. He was an old-time liberal pacifist until he had a direct encounter with the Japanese and almost lost his life. He took me through his experience, and I had to digest it as a young person who had never really thought through the pacifist position with the advantage of background in ethics and a good theological education. Pacifism was a matter of discussion among the missionaries there because many of them had been pacifists until they ran into the Japanese in World War II. That was something they had to come to terms with, and a lot of them just had not had time. Not enough literature in the field of ethics had been produced since World War II for them to rely on. When I happened to read Reinhold Niebuhr's *An Interpretation of Christian Ethics*, the outlook was very new to me, and it was new to everybody. The field of ethics was churning, and people were looking for definitions.

I found a clarity in the various positions emerging at that time, which to my mind has been obscured now as language is clouded with time and made so ambiguous. I don't think we know now what our position is, in many respects. We know how we would respond to certain historical events, but the word *pacifism* is not clear now; it was then.

The position with which Bates came to China as a Presbyterian missionary was that war is outmoded, that there is no justification for war biblically or philosophically. So he made no theoretical provision for war under any circumstances in any form. That was the essence of the old pacifist position. When I was reflecting the Mennonite position as I knew it and as I experienced it, I told him that I didn't consider myself a pacifist. I was nonresistant, and that meant that I would not go to war. I remembered something of Schleitheim and the dualism reflected there,[9] and knew that my position would not necessarily be reflected by the state, by the life and performance of the state. The state had a mission to do, which was to defend life and to establish order by use of the sword. In Bates's understanding of pacifism there was no place for the sword, though when I pressed him, he said of course we have to have a police force. But he was making a distinction between what a policeman does on a personal or a communal basis by targeting evil persons and apprehending them, if possible without killing them. That is different from what the state does in war. He had believed that it was possible under God for the state to be pacifist and to never resist. And up to that time, American policy had reflected that approach, because the Japanese had invaded North China with impunity, and war had gone on there since the 1930s, and the missionaries worked around it. This is not to suggest that all the missionaries in China were pacifists, by any means, but by and large those who were products of Union seminary[10] and most of the liberal seminaries—the Chicago School,[11] for example—were pacifists. That position was reflected by the professors I had at the Lutheran seminary in Gettysburg. This was the time between the world wars.

I had more or less subscribed to the liberal position. I was living in the hope, in the confidence of the power of goodness, the power of love. But then World War II came along and I didn't know how to apply that idea to Adolf Hitler and Joseph Stalin and Hideki Tojo, particularly after the invasion of Central Europe by the Germans. Miner Searle Bates found to his surprise that when he was standing between the Japanese soldiers and the young girls in his orphanage, instead of loving the enemy he took a swipe at the Japanese officer. He surprised himself. So he said, "I guess I'm not a pacifist after all." It was the end of pacifism for him.

---

9 The statement known as the Schleitheim confession is an articulation of Anabaptist principles endorsed by a group of Anabaptist leaders meeting in 1527 in Schleitheim, Switzerland.

10 Union Theological Seminary in New York.

11 The Divinity School at the University of Chicago.

We discussed this, and he came out with what he knew as a historian about the just war theory. He said that there must be some justification for what he did, though he also said that he didn't know what now, from a Christian point of view. There was a lot of discussion of these issues among people at that time. The idealism represented by liberal theology was not just a theological idea; it was a product of the Enlightenment, and many of the leaders of China were enlightened. Among them were bankers, some of whom had studied in the United States. One example was the president of the Chungking bank, who was on our advisory committee. He had studied at Johns Hopkins and he was a pacifist until the Japanese came and made him, as president of the bank, get down on his knees and clean the floors. Reality was coming through, and reality then came to take the form of the extreme goodness of some people. I could mention some of the Chinese who suffered greatly out of a Christian idealism. Against this was the absolute cruelty of many of the Japanese.

Now we might bring this into the present: the Japanese are now among the most orderly people in the world. We can go to Tokyo and walk with greater certainty of personal safety than in New York, even though Japanese society is not a Christian society. But there is no reason to doubt the cruelty of the Japanese soldiers. One of the most remarkable things that I noticed, when I came to Hankou before taking that train trip to the north to Jiangsu Province, was that there were many Japanese soldiers still in Hankou. They had black armbands, but they still had their military suits on and they walked like Japanese soldiers did. You could tell right away by the way they walked that they were Japanese. But there was no visible evidence of retaliation against their persecutors among the Chinese. I shouldn't doubt that it went on, but it was not evident. The Chinese did not retaliate; they sent the Japanese back home. You may attribute that to the Chinese long-term view of things; it was a certain kind of fatalism, maybe something of a Confucian ethic. Nevertheless, to this day the Chinese resent the Japanese interpretation of the invasion of China.

Before World War II, I was at Gettysburg seminary, in spite of the fact that I was a Mennonite. At the time I was extending the Mennonite ethic from the church position to a position that would apply to the state as well. Probably there were two sources behind my thinking, as far as my thinking was worth anything and developed at all. One was that I thought that this was the Christian way history was moving. I was missionary minded, in the sense that I thought that there would eventually be enough missions and missionaries and evangelism, in the best sense that it was going to conquer the world. That was not a foreign idea there at that time, by any means. It was an assumption of the missionary movement at the beginning of the nineteenth century: the idea of progress. I believed in that, but I also believed in the Enlightenment. I had gotten enough of the Enlightenment to feel that the world was going to get better through the advancement of knowledge and of science—not to speak of technology, which hadn't yet fully arrived at that time.

I went into that little church there in the middle of New York state with very positive thoughts of the future. But then Hitler came along and the war started. I began to wonder whether the world could survive the onslaught of fascism and totalitarianism. I was not afraid that there would be an invasion of the United States, but I was thinking of humane institutions, and wondering whether they would survive. What would Hitler have done if he had been able to take Britain and had united with Stalin? Of course, Hitler was at war with Russia at the time, but nevertheless there was the possibility that totalitarian governments could take over all of Europe and all of Asia, and then where would the United States be? In fact, that was the thinking of the local gunsmith. It wasn't the thinking of scholars necessarily, or even of a realist like Jack Wolschlager, who was a fundamentalist, a German Baptist of a sort, and head of the local draft board. But I couldn't deny the reality of the threat, and I had no answer from a Christian point of view, because the Christian point of view that I had inherited was that the world was getting better.

What devastated my historical present was what was happening in Europe and what I was reading in the *New York Times*! If I hadn't read the *Times* every morning, I would not have been aware of what was going on and I wouldn't have thought in these rather extreme terms. I had nobody to talk to there in Upstate New York. I preached peace from the pulpit. It was getting hard to know what to say about World War II. But I was so much of a Mennonite that I helped the young men there to get the support of the draft board so that they could go to Sideling Hill Civilian Public Service camp and other places like that. In that connection, I got to know the draft board really well. There was no talk between the draft board and the leaders of the conservative Mennonites there. But the board wanted to talk with me. I actually developed a pretty good personal relationship with Jack Wolschlager. He always wanted to have lunch with me because we'd talk. But he pressed me, pressed me, pressed me, and I simply resorted to what I thought was the best I could do: go someplace where I would be of use to somebody and expose myself to dangers analogous to those experienced by the fighting men. I had friends who had been killed in the war. And of course in the little town of Croghan, a Catholic town, the bell would toll every time there was a casualty from there. So I couldn't avoid the reality.

I wanted to do something. In the *New York Times*, Theodore White, a noted writer, a China expert, described the situation in China, and he had a pathetic piece about a young Chinese couple who went out into a field together and died in each other's arms from starvation. That grabbed me. So without any knowledge of China, without knowing a word of the language or the geography or anything, I thought that was the place I would like to go—particularly when I heard that the Mennonites wanted to start a mission there and that Mennonite Central Committee wanted to do something in the country. So that's the reason I went.

I don't know when I first heard about the Holocaust. I knew the Jews were in trouble. But I hadn't heard about the Holocaust when I went to China. I thought about certain implications of fascism and totalitarianism. I did not believe it would be right to fight in order to save the church, and I did not believe it would be right to fight to save myself. I was thinking of culture, humane institutions, universities, hospitals, and what I guess most people these days mean when they talk about freedom. I don't know how I was moving intellectually. I was handling these ideas which were becoming rather discrete in my head, but I couldn't decide. I felt I would like to remain a Mennonite in the truest sense, whatever that was, because I *was* a Mennonite.

There's nothing like life in a war situation to impress you with the extremities of goodness and evil. But I had to ask myself: what would I do if I had been in a situation like the one the Presbyterian missionary Miner Searle Bates confronted? I don't think I would have struck back, but I would've become a dead man. I don't think my reflex would be to strike with my fist, because I was at heart a Mennonite—a super-Mennonite. I had preached over and over about the cross and its many implications, including the possibility of one's own death. That was my message to the congregation, though I would always pause to say that I'm not sure what I would do in an emergency situation, but that's what our faith holds out for. And I reminded the congregation of the martyrdom in their own history, though Mennonites had been in the United States for two hundred years. They had pretty much forgotten that early history, although there were evidences that there was something left of it, to be sure.

On Political Order

I spent four days between the lines on one occasion. I returned one time to Xinzhou, and then went to Yangqu, where there was a little kingdom ruled by a fat warlord with many women around him all the time there in a big hall with lots of kids, army, soldiers all around everywhere. He was sometimes allied with Chiang Kai-shek. It wasn't too far from Xinzhou; it was about fifty miles, I imagine. I guess it was early 1946. On the way back from that place there was fighting between Nationalists and Communists, and I was caught between them in an anarchist situation, and I was alone. I stayed in an inn of a sort, and I heard cries going

210 • Recollections of a Sectarian Realist

up in the night. There would be absolute silence and then there would be yelling. I was told that there was no police force, no army, Nationalist or Communist, and we didn't know who was going to win the struggle. So I stayed there. The whole trip took four days. I guess I stayed about two days under that situation.

I was impressed then with what could happen in the absence of enforced law, and the way people were paralyzed by the absence of the military. This town had been occupied by both the Nationalists and the Communists, and they had suffered under them, but they were more apprehensive under the absence of law than under a tyrannical law. That gave me something to think about too, I must say.

But I got out of that situation by leaving at night under the custody of somebody driving a government truck. I don't know much about the situation, but I was taken back near Xinzhou, in Nationalist territory. But that was another lesson that I learned. I must admit that sometimes I have difficulty understanding what I thought then and what I know now. I mean, there's that problem! But at least I was made aware of the fact that anarchy is an awful thing. I did not know then that historically people generally would prefer tyranny to anarchy. Sometimes those are the bad choices.

Honorable Nonresistance

There was a US Navy hospital boat, and they had no chaplain. They asked me to preach to a load of soldiers, wounded in a bad way. What do you preach about? These soldiers had been in the South Seas and had been in the Philippines a long time, and they were being transported to the United States from the Philippines. I preached that I hoped for the day when there would be no more war: the gospel of hope for peace. Should I have implied that they were all sinners for having fought? I know that war is absolutely terrible. It's grievous. It entails terrible suffering too, particularly for the children of the world—as with that awful advance of the Germans into Rotterdam, and saturation bombing. The Germans started it, but the Americans continued it and just devastated Germany, even with fire bombing. I could not do that. I couldn't even help train pilots to do it.

Yet here we are. They saved western civilization. They released people from the death camps. They eventually saved Eastern Europe from the Communists, and Russia now has some kind of democracy, some measure of freedom. I find it really a dilemma; I feel it personally. I tried to do an honorable thing, but I have to confess that I don't know whether I was trying to save my honor or trying to save human lives, when it came down to it. But at least I was not going to do something dishonorable, by the standards of conventional morality at least, and that's the reason I went to China and left my wife and family.

I would not criticize those young men who went into Civilian Public Service. We used to think of civilian service as somehow the moral equivalent to fighting in a war. Some of it was, but some of it didn't amount to anything, although that wasn't the fault of the young men. I have to give credit to a lot of people, including Orie O. Miller and Harold S. Bender and others who helped set up the position with the government. But I visited the camps, particularly the Sideling Hill camp. I can't say I was terribly impressed with what they were doing, as they were not! It was honest and it was honorable, but it was not significant, as I see it.

I think that the most profound statement that has been made on behalf of the Mennonite church with respect to war and peace was made by Ronald J. Sider at Mennonite World Conference in Strasbourg, France, in 1984.[12] He said that the proper response would be for thousands of people to stand as peacemakers between armies, at the risk of their lives. I'm very glad for that; I think that's reasonable. And out of that have come Christian Peacemaker Teams, where people are spending periods of time in perilous places, for which I give them credit. But in general the pacifist position is easy these days. It carries no implications except verbal implications dealing with hypothetical situations. Pacifism now is talk, saying the right words to each other and maybe to the state,

12 For the full text of this address, "God's People Reconciling," see http://www.cpt.org/resources/writings/sider.

but for most Mennonites it's not a matter of suffering. So that's my criticism, but in it I'd have to include myself as an old man. I'm here enjoying life.

Compromise and Accommodation

In my dissertation I used the word *compromise*. I meant compromise in the Troeltschian sense of the German word *Kompromiss*. I meant compromise in the sense that the church has always had to shift its position on things as its social position has changed. This includes the idea of accommodation: acknowledging some relativity. It was the only way the church could ever keep alive, and it was first expressed by the apostle Paul when he allowed marriage. Marriage is a big problem. If you marry and have children, then you're within the stream of history in a way that you would not be if you were not married. Then you have to think of the future: property, education, piano lessons. You're tied into culture. Jesus never made any accommodation for that; the apostle Paul did. So the apostle Paul said you could even remain married if one spouse was Christian and the other was not, because the Christian partner might make the un-Christian one holy in some sense. The apostle Paul was the one that started the process of accommodation.

Actually, accommodation was not considered a good word then, either. Everyone must acknowledge that we're accommodating all the time now, but in those days (in the 1950s), we Mennonites could deny that we were doing it, because we were sufficiently separated. Socialization is how we often say it now. It was Ernst Troeltsch, I believe, who coined the term for social studies and used it frequently. Its first appearance in social teaching comes in connection with marriage. With marriage we have another generation and another generation, and there's a social, cultural accommodation going on there and a depth of penetration and roots in the culture, so you get a church-culture problem. It may not be a problem of persecution. In fact, the problem is advanced if there is no persecution; the church is more likely to make accommodation with culture.

In the 1950s, when we talked about the past we used only two references. One was the early church. The second was Anabaptism. We were skipping over the Middle Ages as being inconsequential and of no significance—at least that's what I got from H. S. Bender—and not giving the monastic system the credit that it deserves. Monasticism attempts to be a direct outcome of the teachings of Jesus, both in word and in deed, but it got into trouble because it became institutionalized. You have to run institutions very much as you would in the world, and monastic institutions became large and powerful. There were reforms. Every system becomes corrupt with time and has to be brought back somewhat here and there, but not totally so. You really can't fully restore it.

And of course the Reformation in the widest sense was intent on bringing some kind of correction—*reform* is the word—to Christendom. But as the Anabaptists said, it's still Christendom under different leadership and different military protection, and so the Anabaptists tried once more. Now the same thing is happening with the Mennonites: it starts out as a small group, and then it gets bigger, bigger, bigger, bigger, and deeper, deeper, deeper, deeper in society, and it makes accommodations—but they are called accommodations only when Mennonites become reflective. It's always a question of how far to go with it. Never would Mennonites use the term *compromise*. But Mennonites do it nevertheless. To a certain extent you've got to compromise in order to keep alive; otherwise you end up in a desert.

Christianity could have gone East, or it could've gone West. It went West, spearheaded by the apostle Paul. The apostle Paul is the one who described the terms under which growth would be made possible. Not Peter. Peter was an early reformer of Judaism. And of course certain Jewish forms of Christianity went East into the desert and died. So my thesis is: you either accommodate or die. And that's true of the Mennonite church. The Reformed Mennonites, represented by my grandmother, are dead.

But I can't say this without some qualification. I'm not willing to go along this broad road. I will go along at points here and there, but I do it as a dialectical person. I don't compromise unless

I feel that by compromising I will be helping other people somewhere. When I compromised in China, it was so I could help more people. But the sacrificial ideal goes on. The perfectionistic ideal is in my head. A friend recently referred to me critically as a perfectionist who doesn't live it perfectly.

Mennonites now are living like other people in the world, not only externally but internally as well. I think there ought to be a visible difference, but not a clothing difference. I think there ought to be a difference between Mennonites and the people who live like the world does—that is, those who accept capitalism without critique or accept political involvement without critique of what it may mean, or who become mayors without realizing that they're also responsible for the police force. I can't stand the theology of people who do this and do that as they go out into the world but who don't acknowledge what they're doing.

Calvin had Servetus killed, but he never acknowledged it as a sin. Bonhoeffer participated in an attempt to kill Hitler, but he said, "It's sinful, but I must do it for the sake of humanity." *That* was honest and there's a fundamental difference there. What I'm afraid of is that Mennonites are becoming Calvinists under the guise of the Baptist church as represented by fundamentalism. We're becoming Baptists. We're leaving Anabaptism. Mennonites are joining this new Corpus Christianum, which is represented now most visibly by the president of the United States, and by their hobnobbing with evangelicals. Now they say, "Well, we're still pacifists," but it's not a tested pacifism. If the Mennonite church now were tested by something analogous to Hitler and Stalin and the gulag, Mennonites would fight. I wouldn't. I think I wouldn't.

I'm sorry to say so, but I think all this Anabaptist stuff is not taken seriously. It's good to know where we came from. It's good to line up along the river so we can say, "Oh, we're making peace." But there is no war, and we're being sucked in here and there. We no longer make a distinction between love and justice. Now we're talking about justice, justice, justice, justice, but it's not a sacrificial justice. It's just a call to somebody else to make things more equal, or something like that.

Mennonite Peacemaking

I don't think the Mennonites are going to be pacifists for very long unless there's a general, peaceful situation. Of course we're for peace, aren't we? Who isn't! You're crazy if you're not for peace. A lot of these peace conferences would be like icing on a cake, but down beneath, in the heart of the cake, there's a lot of gravel, dirt, blood, hardship, historical conflict, while on the top there is icing, peaceful icing. We say, "Let's be peace lovers." Well, who wouldn't be peace lovers if they could be! Unless loving peace involves a lot of sacrifice. That makes a difference. That's the reason I liked what Ron Sider said. The logistics of getting a hundred thousand people together and sitting between the antagonists—that is a romantic idea, but symbolically it's a very good idea. I can't see pacifism without sacrifice. In these courses on peace, you're talking about hypothetical situations all the time. Now if connected with it there would be something like going to Hebron, or getting right in there where the conflict is, with a few Mennonite casualties—as awful as that may be and as much as I wouldn't care for my son or my grandson to be the one—I'd have to say, that would have integrity. There's an awful lot of easy talk going on in peace circles right now. And the world is not calling our bluff, calling us on it, because they're half convinced themselves, a lot of them. We're not offensive to anybody, really, not offensive to anybody very much, are we? I don't think so.

I'm just not quite as impressed as some people are with recent peace studies developments. We've got hypothetical situations in which we stand between warring parties, conflicted parties. We become mediators, but we stand over here, not where conflict is. We're not participants in the conflict. We've learned psychological techniques now to try to transform the parties, making them not just reconciled enough to get along without killing each other but trying to transform them! Transformation in Christianity comes to the cross, not by standing in a superior position, telling these dumb and bad people how they are wrong. I don't want to go down as the critic, as an old, sour man, because I might be wrong too!

You might think I'm not a believer, but I'm a strong believer. I just don't mouth it. There is just so much loose talk. It is true that if you take my line, there might be some young high-schoolers who would give up the faith, I'm afraid. They might not be able to handle ambiguity and certain realities of life. The kind of thought I have is not new. It has many roots in Jesus and the apostle Paul (less so Peter), a bit of Augustine, some of the philosophy of Dirk Willems. I like that man, and what he did. But somebody recently told that story in public and people laughed. It was a joke: look what a dumb guy he was: when he could've saved himself, instead he went back to save his enemy![13]

Justice, Power, and the Cross

In my doctoral thesis[14] I was saying that the Mennonites are not being responsible. I defined responsibility as taking public

---

13 Dutch Anabaptist Dirk Willems succeeded in escaping arrest for heresy by crossing an ice-covered river, but then he turned back to rescue his pursuer, who had fallen through the ice. As a result, Dirk was imprisoned and burned at the stake. See Nanne van der Zijpp, "Dirk Willemsz (d. 1569)" (1956), Global Anabaptist Mennonite Encyclopedia Online, http://gameo.org/index.php?title=Dirk_Willemsz_(d._1569)&oldid=129761. Kimberly Schmidt in a November 4, 2013, comment on the May 16, 2013, *Everyday Revolutionary* blogpost writes: "I organized a conference on Mennonite and Jewish ethno-religious history, held at the University of Maryland at College Park in 1997. We invited scholars of Jews and Mennos to speak in comparative sessions on various topics. When Mennonite historian, James Juhnke, told the Dirk Willems story the room erupted in laughter—much to the surprise of the Mennos in the audience, myself included. Holocaust survivors told us they thought of Dirk as stupid. Why would one turn back to save the life of a jailer? The prime directive in their case is to 'survive' so that one lives to teach the faith and heritage to the next generation" (http://everyday-revolutionary.blogspot.com/2013/05/dirk-willems-d-may-16-1569.html).

14 J. Lawrence Burkholder's thesis, *The Problem of Social Responsibility from the Perspective of the Mennonite Church* (published by Institute

administrative positions where persons would be held accountable. When we Mennonites did that, I said, "That's good!" But I
couldn't separate justice from the power involved in the exercise
of justice. Guy F. Hershberger was not against justice; he said there
are times when we have to practice justice, though we should be
practicing love most of the time, almost all of the time.[15] But he
made no place for the fact that when you go into the public, or
when you operate a business or participate in a labor union, there's
a power dimension which can lead not only to corruption but to
dilemmas where love has to become preferential: you love some
people more than other people. That's what the budget means.
That's what a political slate means. Actually, we haven't faced the
fact of power. It is hard to understand that wherever you're in a
commanding position and you act, you're actually using power
so that some people will be preferred over other people. This has
now has become routinized. Mennonites are doing it all the time
but don't think much about it, unless it's really, really, really bad.

Pacifists now have been talking about justice, justice, justice,
and peace, peace, peace, but they haven't faced the power problem yet, which comes to you when you start exercising power
especially in the public sphere. Of course we exercise power in
running a school like Goshen College, though obviously it's not
a violent application of power. But it is preferential. When two
people come up for a position, you choose one. You can't choose

---

of Mennonite Studies in 1989), was submitted to the faculty of Princeton
Theological Seminary in 1958 in partial fulfillment of requirements for his
ThD degree.

15 Guy F. Hershberger taught history, sociology, and ethics at Goshen
College from 1925 to 1966, wrote prolifically on peace and social concerns, and served on the Mennonite Church's Peace Problems Committee and the Committee on Economic and Social Relations. For more
information, see John R. Burkholder, "Hershberger, Guy F. (1896–1989),"
(1989), *Global Anabaptist Mennonite Encyclopedia Online*, http://gameo.
org/index.php?title=Hershberger,_Guy_F._(1896-1989)&oldid=121127;
and Theron F. Schlabach, *War, Peace, and Social Conscience: Guy F. Hershberger and Mennonite Ethics*, Studies in Anabaptist and Mennonite History
45 (Scottdale, PA: Herald Press, 2009).

them both. That is inevitable, but it's a problem. I had to fire one person from our faculty. I did it gently and with conversation, so that the person voluntarily resigned without being fired. If they hadn't, I would've had to fire them. I've never been able to manage to my satisfaction the problem I've articulated here.

The problem with ethics is not only the defective will but the third person. The social character of social ethics makes it complex. Or I might say, complexity is a result of the nature of social existence. If you look at the process of evolution, evolution has no regard at all for the individual. Millions and millions and millions of little animals have been slaughtered as part of the process. Gordon Kaufman says there's a serendipitous aspect to it all— and there may be. But we're caught in that. Social institutions are evolutionary too. The church is evolutionary. In a sense it does a sifting process.

You and I have no idea how many people were dropped out by the Mennonite church in the North American Mennonite situation—people who just fell by the wayside or were expelled. It was an evolutionary process. And that's the way it is in business; that's the way of capitalism. But oddly enough, capitalism is a wonderful thing too! You see, it's ambiguous. Ambiguity is my favorite word, I'm afraid. I've been captured by it too much.

What would I recommend that Mennonites do? That's a tough thing. I think that externally we pretty much live like other people. People have got to live. I can also think of a person living and having a fairly good life, but going to Baghdad now and trying to contact Al-Qaeda terrorists, and dying in the process. I don't have the nerve to suggest who exactly should do it. Maybe I'm the person who ought to do it, since I'm an old man and won't live long anyhow. I don't know. I think the real test of our integrity and sincerity is that point at which we're willing to make sacrifices. This sacrifice will take many forms, depending on the situation and what our capabilities or our gifts are.

What is missing today is the fact that we've lost the cross, and that's what the Anabaptists were for! They said, if you're going to live, you're going to live dangerously and you may have to take up the cross. And a good many of them did. I'm not suggesting that we go out and look for martyrdom so that we're righteous. But I believe in sacrificing something that you have for the sake of other people. That's the essence of Christianity, as far as I'm concerned. It's nice if we can have mystical experiences and spiritual experiences. I've become suspicious of the word *spiritual*. There are people who find motorcycling a spiritual experience.

The Holy Spirit

Of course I believe in the Holy Spirit. The study of the Holy Spirit is the study of how God lives in history, how God inspires and protects and leads. But it's hard to measure the Spirit. What is spiritual, and what is purely historical, and what is psychological, and what is individualistic? And so on and so forth. But I'm sure that we must, as a church, discern the spirits in the sense that we ask, Is this really Christian, or is it not? And should we do this, or should we do that? We should ask in an attitude of testing. Here John Howard Yoder and I agree. But don't say that what we have decided is God's politics. Say it's *our* politics.

There is danger in saying, "This is it, and we know it's it, and it is beyond criticism because the Spirit has told us." That's probably what the sixteenth-century Anabaptists ran into all the time, because these groups of people were reading the Bible for the first time themselves, and some of them would say it says this and says that, and they got around the table, and they had somebody light out about this Bible passage, and somebody else would say "Yea and amen" or "No."

I believe in regeneration, but only up to a point, because I believe Augustine's view of humanity. I have encountered so much evil—not so much personally, but at least I read about it and I was living in a time of evil. I believe that there is a mystery of goodness and a mystery of evil, a mystery of God and also a mystery of the devil, although I don't believe in the devil as a personal being. But there is something to original sin. And *original* doesn't necessarily mean what Augustine said, that it's transmitted sexually and all that stuff, but sin does persist. The only real argument

I have against original sin is that I don't think my mother had it—even though that's heresy.

Anabaptism

I didn't like the Anabaptist vision because there was no appeal there for grace. In fact, Harold Bender was critical of the traditions of grace—I can show you passages. Of course, Steve Dintaman has pointed that out.[16] I feel I live by grace; it's the only way I can live. And our institutions live by grace. But unfortunately, I have had to draw on Luther, because nobody else I knew understood grace. That may have been not too smart, or even correct. There's such a thing as pluralism: Mennonite pluralism, Anabaptist pluralism. That has enabled us to justify almost anything by Anabaptism, because we can always find some Anabaptist who will agree with us.

I had never understood Mennonites as being anything but ultra-Pelagian. The only Anabaptists spoken of [by Bender et al.] were the Conrad Grebel types (the Swiss Brethren) and Hans Denck, who was spiritually irresponsible and who would interpret Scripture individualistically and go on to do his thing. So therefore I have read Calvin. With Luther he would say, "I've tried and tried and tried to be like Jesus, but I can't do it, and part of the reason I can't do it is I've got too many people to serve and I must practice love selectively, and I get into dilemmas and I've got to be forgiven for it or I really have no hope." And so grace comes in, not just enabling grace (or ultimately as enabling grace), but as forgiveness.

---

16   See Stephen F. Dintaman, "The Spiritual Poverty of the Anabaptist Vision," *Conrad Grebel Review* 10, no. 2 (Spring 1992): 205–8. Dintaman's essay is a critique of Harold S. Bender's influential articulation of "The Anabaptist Vision," which had been published in *Church History* 13 (March 1994): 3–24, and reprinted in *Mennonite Quarterly Review* 18 (April 1944): 67–88; and in Guy F. Hershberger, ed., *The Recovery of the Anabaptist Vision* (Scottdale, PA: Herald Press, 1957), 29–54.

The Mennonite Church of the Future

As far as what Mennonites of the future should be like, I would suggest that they do what they're now doing and go into professions of various kinds. I wrote an article on that after I was at Harvard. Get out into the professions and live sacrificially within them, not on top of them but within them. Be good farmers, but take care of the land and sell your supplies so that people might eat. Or be a schoolteacher and be a gracious, loving, and understanding as well as interesting teacher. Or go into science, doing something good. But at the same time, I think that we ought to have a way by which college graduates in particular, but not only college graduates, should be able to do something in peace that we thought was logical in war. So I'm somewhat attracted to what the Christian Peacemaker Teams are doing, though they do many different things. Some of these things seem trivial to me, but others seem to be right on. But a lot more people should be doing it. I don't mean just going to where it's nice. I could name some places where Mennonites have gone to make peace which are lovely places for a vacation. But I mean going to the place where it's not nice, where it's risky. I think that's an idea that is not new by any means, but it ought to be extended far beyond what it has been.

I think that Mennonite Central Committee pushes this kind of thing, but we ought to do more. I do think people in the Mennonite church are going to go more and more out into the professions, and we're going to become increasingly sophisticated and elite. What would be considered elitism, snobbish elitism, in society should be a humble elitism. There was a Canadian, Joseph Martin, who was dean of the Harvard Medical School and chair of the Department of Neurology at Massachusetts General Hospital. He started some real reform work among the hospitals there, instead of duplicating personnel and sophisticated machinery, and he fostered a more cooperative attitude. It was he who brought that about within the last fifteen years and I think it was in the *Boston Globe* that it was attributed to the fact that his father was a Mennonite minister in Canada. That's the kind of thing I think would be very good. Now of course, not everybody is going to go that high in a profession, and there are certain people working here in the retirement community where I live who have that fine attitude of help and service and kindness. Some of them are people who are not highly educated. That's what I really believe in.

Under certain circumstances, maybe a Mennonite of this kind could seek public office and get it. If you were to become well-known as an artist or as a teacher or a football player or whatever, you could use that prestige within the political realm to do what you felt was right, with the understanding that you may have to give and take a little bit here and there. But you would have your limits as to how far you will go, and you'll be ready to get voted out if the people didn't go with your idealism. So you see that my ethic is not exactly simple, but I like to think it's honest.

Love and Justice; Luther and Mennonites

I think justice can take the form of love, but justice very frequently limits what you're willing to do for the other person: I'll give you what is due to you and stop it at that. That's how we do commerce with each other. But at the same time, I think justice can be moved by love. But love and justice are not the same. By love I mean *agape* love, sacrificial love, the kind that takes its purest form in the cross, in death. After all, Dietrich Bonhoeffer said that Jesus was claiming, "Come, follow me, and die," and that's how I think of love. It goes beyond mutuality. You love me and I love you and we'll both get along very well and we'll support each other. That's good! That's one expression of love. But the kind of love Jesus talks about is one that goes beyond scribal love and pharisaic love, beyond mutuality.

And then there's also the question of power. In all my reading for the thesis, nowhere did I read any attempt by Mennonites to come to terms with power. So I insisted that we are using power all the time, and power does not always take the form of coercion. It can take the form of demeanor and a look and a wave of the hand, but it's there. I've had to come to terms with it, particularly when it comes to running institutions—not to speak of the home, where it's obvious too. And power is a problem. In my rather careless moments, I say that I wonder what Jesus would've done if he'd been married and had six kids and had to make a living for them, and what he would've done if he'd run institutions. What do you do when you get into a social situation in which you are responsible?

Here I would speak of the role of the king. The king or those who in democracy are elected to positions are responsible, accountable; they're in charge, just as we are in charge of our homes and our little businesses. That's what people in the ecumenical movement were talking about at the various meetings of the World Council of Churches. They assume that we are responsible and are therefore accountable. But the prophet can come from another country and go and say his piece and then go home. Of course, many times prophets were slain, and prophecy isn't easy. But the person who is in charge is accountable in a way that the prophet is not. Now Moses was both prophet and priest and sort of a king, but in my thesis I tried to make that very important distinction between king and prophet.

What my thesis was supposed to have said is that we would do just what the World Council of Churches and mainline theologians were suggesting. I would have to admit that my analysis of the ethical situation is very Lutheran. But Luther read Jesus, and the early Luther would like to have brought about something like the Anabaptist movement. But he couldn't do it. He had too many ordinary people, too many ordinary peasants, too many princes to deal with—and also his own sin and the sin of other people. But when he read the Sermon on the Mount and Jesus, he said, "This is what we ought to do. This is what is required of me." But then on the basis of his experiences he said, "How can we? And how can I?"

So his doctrine of salvation by grace through faith came after the experience of having tried and failed. Therefore there came this characteristically Christian emphasis on justification by faith; you can't make it by your own power, your own good, and if you try to do it, you'll fail. And if you try persistently, you'll get proud and think maybe you have done it. In that sense I'm a defender of a Lutheran position, but I also know about cheap grace and I also know the history. And then of course the question is, am I trying to lead the Mennonite church down a Lutheran path? And I have to say that it could go that way, but I would hope not. But I would say that the Mennonite church is going down that way anyhow, as I see what the acculturation process is of Mennonites all over the world, particularly in Holland but in the United States and Canada as well. We're making a little compromise here, a little compromise there, but we don't recognize it as compromise. We've watered down Jesus, and we've had a better impression of ourselves than we should.

The Peace Position

Now it comes to my peace position. If I may try to say it, it's not a nice position to be in. I am a nuclear pacifist without knowing exactly what that means. I'm so repulsed by this massive destruction that I don't see how it could be used for constructive purposes under any circumstances. As a general principle, I'm opposed to war for two reasons. One is the deontological position. Jesus does not will it. God does not want it. The other reason is practical: wars don't pay. The just-war position has had a very negative influence on history. But there are difficult cases. In Yugoslavia, for example, Slobodan Milošević and the Serbs in their attempt to take Yugoslavia killed more than 200,000 people. What should the nations who have power do in a situation like that? I think they would be justified in stopping the killing with a minimal use of force, but force nevertheless. There can be times in history when the use of the military is salvific not in a religious sense but in a sense of protecting people who have to be protected. I think the old-fashioned pacifist position is immoral, because it makes no provision for that situation in which the only hope that a mass of people have, however big or small they are, is the interference of some kind of international police force. It is force, but it'll be reasonable force; it'll be thought through and it'll be last resort. I felt that, particularly when Sarajevo was being blasted from the hillsides and shells were falling down into the marketplace, the United Nations or the European Union would be justified in intervening—and they did. The United States did too. That is my position.

Now, I was openly against the Vietnam War. I preached a sermon at Harvard in which I came out very early against the Vietnam War. I marched against it and identified with students who were draft dodgers. Some other wars I wasn't smart enough to oppose, or I didn't take an interest in them. For example, the Korean war, which was a United Nations effort, I just didn't say anything about, and nobody asked me.

I say I'm not a pacifist. I am very much interested in peace-making, if you can do it with integrity and with an element of humility and sacrifice to go with it. That's the reason why I was very much taken with Ron Sider's statement at the 1984 Menno-nite World Conference in Strasbourg: I thought it was an authen-tic statement. But I cannot just come off automatically against the use of force as if there's no other possible response. Sometimes there may be no other possible response, and in that case, it's a matter of judgment. Had I known all that I know now, maybe I would not have been for intervention in Somalia. I've been reminded within the last twenty-four hours that Somalia has become a hotbed for terrorism. But I would remind pacifists who say "Don't ever" that their position means that a lot of human beings may be consigned to destruction, and I'm not ready to take that step. I'll take it as it comes.

Of course, that doesn't answer everything, because you have the question of what sort of standing armies you need and how they should use power in various ways. Who decides, and what are the circumstances? But there are very few pacifists today, if you press people. There were some who call themselves pacifists who have said to me, "When it comes to World War II, I don't know."

I have known pacifists to run away from threats, and I don't blame them. My wife and I came home from China when the Communists were about to take Shanghai. We got out, although I was invited to take a job out there. If I had been in better health,

I think I might have stayed. If you go into a classroom and teach peace studies, it's hypothetical; we have no draft and it doesn't matter what you say. Nobody is going to hold you accountable. Bert Lobe was in charge of the Teachers Abroad Program when he was working for Mennonite Central Committee. I guess it was in 1989, in connection with the China incident.[17] He told me that there were thirty-four Mennonite teachers there, and thirty-two of them came home. I cannot blame them for coming home. The only two who stayed were older people who were outside Beijing somewhere and who didn't know what was going on. In our invasion of Somalia, where were the Mennonites? They'd left, because they didn't want to stick with it because of the danger. I'm not here to blame them, but there's such a thing as consistency and integrity, and I figure if you're going to be a pacifist you have to run some risks, though I'm not looking for risk personally. But as old as I am now, I don't care about my personal safety. Now if somebody should come in here with a gun, I wouldn't respond to it at all.

Some Mennonites say we should not be concerned with how history turns out, but to me that means you don't give a damn about what happens to humanity. And I care. For that reason, I used the deontological argument for myself: I'm going to do what Jesus would have me do. I am enough of a Kantian to suggest that if you make an ethical claim, you ought to at least take into consideration the test of universalizability. You should ask, as Kant did, what would happen if your position were made a position to which all people—or an awful lot of people—subscribed.

Relativism

Reinhold Niebuhr has never been given half a shake by Mennonites. They don't understand his spirit. They don't understand his character. They don't understand the agony he went through during World War II when he shifted the position of the major

---

17 Probably Burkholder is referring to the student protests in Beijing in 1989, which were violently suppressed by the government, most vividly in what became known as the Tiananmen Square Massacre.

denominations. He had Hitler in mind. Niebuhr started off as a pacifist, but most of the major denominations were pacifist until Hitler came along. Then they had to decide. The Nazi threat brought up an awful lot of other questions too. Is it ever right to tell a lie? If you have a Jew in your closet and somebody asks, "Is there a Jew there?" would you lie? I used to put that to my students, and they would ponder and ponder. Put it to students now, and they would say, "Of course you tell a lie if you have to." But this is postmodernity. Now, I shouldn't doubt that I would tell a lie, but if I told a lie I would say, "I am telling a lie and I need to be forgiven for it, even though I'm saving life by it." World War II was a time for ethical dilemmas.

I understand that during the German occupation the harbor master of Rotterdam had to decide whether he was going to continue as harbor master and keep order within the harbor as a place for U-boats to anchor and be reconditioned and so on—assisting the whole Nazi effort—or whether he would quit. If he had quit, he probably would've been shot or sent to a camp or something. Now that was an extreme case, but it was the kind of situation that many people had to face under occupation. Many had to cheat to get food coupons, but at the same time a lot of them were sharing. If they had more, they'd share with other people. That is an ambiguous situation. But this generation has no idea what ambiguity is, because they've got everything. They can say whatever they want to and nobody is going to criticize them, except maybe newspaper writers who say they don't agree with them.

Relativism takes as many shapes as history takes. To be relative in one situation is terrible. To be relative in another situation is just being nice, courteous, sharing. If you were in a situation of occupation and you shared with your neighbor and then some officer came along and said, "What happened to all the stuff?" and you'd say, "Well, something happened," you'd lie. I did not often get into that kind of situation in China, but I was protected to a certain extent. I could leave anytime I wanted to. I could go home, if I wanted to. But most of the refugees and people who lived under occupation were there to stay, and they had to live with the consequences. Those of us who went out under Mennonite Central Committee were in a very privileged position. We were backed by a church, and we were backed by the strongest nation in the world, and anywhere we'd go, people knew we were Americans. So we had it easy, even though we lived on ten dollars a month.

Or take life insurance. We once said, "Don't take out life insurance. Trust God." We set up Mennonite Mutual Aid on that basis, theoretically. But Mennonite Mutual Aid became an insurance company. When you get benefits according to your agreement, legally defined, actuarially calculated, it's not mutual aid. We may still use the term "Mennonite Mutual Aid," but it's become an insurance company. Now we're in this business together, functioning on the same basis that secular insurance companies run on. We want it both ways. *I* want it both ways. I will have it both ways but acknowledge the incongruity of it by reference to the dialectic. What that means is that I'm always pulled toward that perfectionist ideal. But along the way I have made adjustments—call it compromise—in order to help other people. But not in order to help myself, I hope. I'm not a relativist in the sense in which relativism is used now, because I've got this one pole up here and it's drawn toward Jesus. As Bonhoeffer said in *The Cost of Discipleship*, I accept that as drawing me and defining much of my life.

Let's take wealth. In the New Testament there probably are more criticisms of the wealthy and of becoming wealthy than of anything else, in the Gospels at least. There was a time when Mennonites did not approve of going into certain professions because they'd get wealthy and be associated with bankers and people outside. But now we're in it, and in it professionally. Mennonite doctors are making four or five hundred thousand dollars a year here. We travel. One good Mennonite not too far from here engaged a jet plane to take his daughter to New York as a gift for her commencement. That's extreme, but most of us are middle class, and what do you do about that? I see it as a problem, but it isn't a problem to most Mennonites now—certainly not much of a problem. Many could see that employing a jet to take your daughter to New York might be a problem, but what is the answer to that? The only answer I know is to give like the dickens.

I'm trying to be honest by saying, "I'll take Jesus straight as it comes out of the New Testament, in the Sermon on the Mount, and I'll try to do it." The more factors enter into the situation, the more likely you are to run into dilemmas. What we as Mennonites have always done is try to simplify things. Simplify, simplify. It's good if you can do it and if you can come to the state with a simple solution, because it's up to them to take it or leave it, and you're not going to be held accountable for having said it. But when you're running an institution, when you're responsible to administer it and you're responsible to the client, you're responsible to the state, you're responsible to the medical doctors and all that, then you feel that there are a lot of good things that are just piled up against each other. Over here they have a committee that meets fairly regularly, with representation by doctors and staff and so on to go over ethical problems.[18] But, if it's a real dilemma, there is no perfect answer. In a moral dilemma you have to make a decision. We as Mennonites are taking a position where we're now going to witness—that's the term—to the state. But we can say our witness and then leave, and we won't be any problem. Who is a disciple now? Is a millionaire a disciple? A multimillionaire? A Mennonite millionaire?

When I was teaching discipleship at Harvard, I had a Swedish student. I was teaching with the implication that Jesus's life mattered and we ought to try to live like Jesus. But then he said, "This is awful! This is heretical. This is presumptuous. Who are you, making little Jesuses out of us?" He said, "It can't be done, and it ought not to be tried." I said, "Well, what do we do in this life anyhow? We do the best we can and trust God to forgive us." You've got to try, but he had given up. Now, I think you could go on to say, "Yes, if you follow Lawrence Burkholder, you've got to come out eventually right where that student did." I have to face

---

18 Burkholder seems to be referring to an ethics committee dealing with end-of-life issues in the retirement community.

230 • Recollections of a Sectarian Realist

that. But Mennonites now have a roller that goes out in front of them that sanitizes the next move.

Politics

On the subject of politics and John Howard Yoder's book *The Politics of Jesus,* I have to say I agree with a lot of it, but I don't agree with Yoder's understanding of politics. Politics as it is normally used in conversation has to do with the workings of some government authority, whether democracy or another system. But politics was redefined by John Howard Yoder to mean any association of a continuous nature. When people organize, and possibly become legally organized and continue in association or community for any length of time, that's what he defined as politics!

No, Jesus was a prophet. He wasn't a politician in any sense, because he never made laws, and he never demanded that people respond to him as an authority. It's an abuse of language to talk of the politics of Jesus. Mennonites have been abusing this language for the last fifteen years in particular, at their convenience, and it started with John Howard Yoder. In what sense is it politics? Jesus wasn't an earthly king. Now Mennonites think if we get together and talk and are a church, and we're all related to each other in a continuous way, we're involved in politics. But that is not politics, and to suggest that the "politics of Jesus" is a political possibility as it pertains to the state—that is what the liberals said before World War II, and then Hitler came along and they had to disabuse themselves of that notion. How can you run a state, or run any institution even, on the basis of "take no thought for the morrow"?

John Bennett used the term "middle axioms" to refer to what the state does; John Yoder borrowed this term. What is not clear in my mind is, did John Howard Yoder set forth the middle axioms as what only the state does, or as what the state does and we also do? The question is, is he saying we should really follow Jesus in that literal way—which Reinhold Niebuhr said we should but can't do? Yoder says we can, yes. But when it comes to giving examples, his life was very much like anybody else's life. Now you could ask the question, was Jesus involved in politics when he went into the temple and disturbed the temple? No! Because he wasn't in charge of the temple. He was just there as a prophet would be there. Prophets don't run things.

I can understand the prophetic position when it's taken by the Amish, but what Mennonites now want is the privilege of both sides: we want to hold on to all the benefits and nevertheless be Mennonites. We do what everybody else does, and yet we call ourselves Mennonites. But we don't acknowledge that we're dealing with a contradiction. I do acknowledge it even with respect to myself, and that's the reason I hold a dialectical position. That's an uncomfortable position to take.

Mennonite Compromise

At one time Mennonites wouldn't do many things. But then they'd do such things, and when they'd do them they would redefine them or understand them in some kind of innocuous way. We look at certain activities as being wrong because we feel they are not loving or not sacrificial and Jesus wouldn't do them. That's a Mennonite position. But then history comes along and raises necessities for us. We didn't believe in being lawyers, but now we find that we need lawyers, so we can be lawyers. We can even be patent lawyers. First we raise a question about this, but then we do it, and then it even becomes stewardship. Stewardship isn't the ethic of Christ. The ethic of Christ is what the Hutterites claim: it's the communal life. That's the ethic of Jesus. That's what appears first in the book of Acts. As soon as Christians were gathered together in Jerusalem, they said, how are we going to live here? Then it was thought that they would be there no more than a week or two. They tried to form a community of goods and set up a few authorities over it. But what does the apostle Paul say? He dropped that communal idea of all things and invited people to follow Jesus Christ, or to believe in Christ—not follow but believe in Christ—but meet together as an eschatological community. But where would they meet? They would meet in the houses of people who had big living rooms where the church could meet. These were rich people, and they even had slaves. And the apostle Paul said, "Well, be a good slave owner. And if you are a slave, don't fight it. Just be a slave, because the Lord's going to come soon anyhow." And what if you get married? If you get married, you better get married to a Christian, if you can. But if you don't marry a Christian, remain married, because you might sanctify the non-Christian spouse. And so forth. That's the beginning of compromise.

The first experience of compromise is acceptance of the family and the implications of being a family. If you read the Sermon on the Mount in particular, Matthew finds that there's a great tension there between those who are itinerants, people who move around, and those who stay. Matthew is written from the standpoint of those who go, but those who stay have a problem on their hands. Peter, James, and John were supposed to go out and be itinerants without providing for the family! The family was a problem. It's the first sociological problem of the Mennonite church and of the Christian church.

But the apostle Paul and his missionary work outside the Jewish context, in places like Antioch and Corinth and so on, had to make adjustments, which missionaries do, and so his approach included the rich and the poor, but the rich would love the poor and would help them. But this was charity. There's nothing in the New Testament or in Jesus's teaching that would look like systematic charity. The apostle Paul didn't get to systematic charity, but he began at it, when they started taking up collections. But charity means you all go out and get the money, and then when somebody has a need, you share it. But you're all going to go out and get it. And you could keep the money, unless somebody really needs it more than you do; then ideally you give it to them. But it didn't always happen that way. I would suggest that once you have accepted the family unit, then an awful lot of demands are laid on you. You've got to sustain your children with food, you've got to get them an education, you've got to be concerned about their safety, and you've got to give them piano lessons. You know how complex that is. You can't get up and just leave your family.

If Jesus would come along and say, "Follow me," you can't do it! You run into that problem.

Now, John Howard Yoder kind of makes fun of the Catholic solution to that problem. The Catholic solution is monasticism, and he says that's not the New Testament. Why is that not the New Testament? Because the New Testament doesn't call for that kind of thing? Well, I agree that it doesn't call for that kind of thing on a systematic basis, but something like it was bound to happen. I think I belong to the monastic tradition as a Mennonite, but it is not systematic. If I were a bachelor, I could be a better disciple, because all I'd need is enough to eat and a place to sleep and a few books. Oh, and maybe that stereo over there. Culture comes into it. I have to think of this beautiful organ we've got over here.[19] Seven hundred and fifty thousand dollars I think is what it cost. It's just beautiful and it's a big concert hall; it's beautiful and I love it. And I enjoy it especially when I hear Bach. I think Mennonites are caught in a dilemma here that they're more or less conscious of.

---

19 J. Lawrence is presumably referring to the Opus 41 pipe organ, designed by George Taylor and John Boody, installed in 2004 at Rieth Recital Hall in the Goshen College Music Center.

Epilogue

J. Lawrence Burkholder's narration about his life ended with 1991, several years into his retirement, and the final portion of his narrative has many gaps which this epilogue seeks to fill. He lived nearly twenty years more and died on June 24, 2010.

Following his retirement in 1984, J. Lawrence taught classes at Goshen College and Associated (now Anabaptist) Mennonite Biblical Seminary, Elkhart, Indiana, as well as preaching and lecturing on many occasions in many places.

In October-November 1985, J. Lawrence and Harriet co-led a three-week Goshen College Alumni China Tour with Arlin Hunsberger, director of international education at Goshen College, and Arlin's wife, Naomi. In Chengdu, the tour group of thirty-nine GC alumni and friends visited the study-service term unit led by Wilbur and Fanni Birky.

At the end of the tour, Harriet returned to the United States with the tour group, but J. Lawrence joined a six-person delegation representing the United Board for Christian Higher Education in Asia. They visited several universities and seminaries in China.

J. Lawrence then went to Shanghai and was able to see the Mu'en Church. About three thousand people were attending services at this church each Sunday. He also learned that twenty-three churches were open in Shanghai, including Community Church, the church that he and Harriet and their children attended in the 1940s. J. Lawrence mentioned in a 1985 Christmas letter that churches in China were being organized at the rate of one per day, though numerically the Christian population was still small in comparison with the population of China.

Sum and Substance: Essays by J. Lawrence Burkholder, edited by Edward Zuercher, was published in 1986 by Pinchpenny Press of Goshen College. The book includes essays written by J. Lawrence for the Goshen College *Bulletin* when he was president.

In 1989 J. Lawrence's doctoral thesis, *The Problem of Social Responsibility from the Perspective of the Mennonite Church*, was published by Institute of Mennonite Studies, Elkhart, Indiana.

During the summer of 1989, J. Lawrence and Harriet celebrated their fiftieth wedding anniversary (they were married August 20, 1939). In mid-June, they spent a long weekend at Martha's Vineyard, Massachusetts, with Lauren and Janet (Burkholder) Friesen and their children, Erica and Eliot; Howard Burkholder; and Myrna Burkholder. From mid-July to early August, J. Lawrence and Harriet toured England and Norway. On August 19, their children hosted a private reception for them in the home of Lauren and Janet Friesen in Goshen.

On September 20, 1989, J. Lawrence was the featured speaker at the twenty-fifth anniversary celebration of the Mennonite Congregation of Boston, held at Clarendon Hill Presbyterian Church in Somerville, Massachusetts. The service included the sharing of communion and was preceded by a carry-in supper.

J. Lawrence was the featured speaker for the 20th Annual Thomas F. Staley Distinguished Christian Scholar Lecture Program at Eastern Mennonite College and Seminary, February 12–14, 1990, in Harrisonburg, Virginia. He lectured on the theme "The Redemption of Power."

J. Lawrence and Harriet were given a Culture for Service Award by Goshen College on October 6, 1990. The award is given annually during Alumni Weekend activities to several distinguished Goshen College graduates.

In October 1990, an article by Harriet, "Picking up the Pieces of a Broken Dream," about son Gerald Paul, who had died in 1981 from complications caused by cystic fibrosis, was published in *Christian Living*.

In the spring of 1992 (March 30–April 2), Laurelville Mennonite Church Center hosted a theological conference, "Conversations with J. Lawrence Burkholder on the Church in Society," in which he presented an overview of his theology in an autobiographical, narrative fashion. He was unable to complete the last session because he was hospitalized for an inflammation of the pancreas. He recovered and was able to return home to Goshen shortly thereafter.

In 1993, Institute of Anabaptist and Mennonite Studies, Waterloo, Ontario, published *The Limits of Perfection: A Conversation with J. Lawrence Burkholder*, edited by Rodney J. Sawatsky and Scott Holland. The book includes J. Lawrence's presentations from the 1992 Laurelville seminar and essays by several others, some of which were delivered at the conference. The book also includes a poem written by Julia Kasdorf, "Flying Lesson," inspired by J. Lawrence's adventures in flying over the ocean.

In 1994, Howard and Myra Brembeck gave a substantial gift to Goshen College to establish a scholarship fund for students named as President's Leadership Award recipients. They gave this gift in honor of J. Lawrence and Harriet Burkholder in recognition of their friendship. They also did it in recognition of the academic achievements of J. Lawrence and Harriet and of many Goshen College students. PLA recipients receive awards of one-half the cost of their tuition. As of June 2015, the fund was valued at about $2,000,000.

On June 21, 1994, J. Lawrence gave the opening prayer for the US House of Representatives, at the invitation of Indiana's Third District Congressman Tim Roemer:

Gracious God,

We would begin this day of deliberation in gratitude, for skies above, land below, and oceans around, for "America the Beautiful"—purple mountains, fertile fields, rushing streams, and flowered deserts.

Help us to save this inheritance, lest we become rich while the land becomes poor, imagining ourselves fulfilled but future generations deprived, indulging our well-being without being well.

Not only for this natural inheritance would we be grateful. We would rejoice in the soundness of democratic institutions, which, though vulnerable to human error, persist for the advancement of justice and peace, blessed by the wisdom of founding fathers, caring mothers, and dedicated statesmen.

By your kind providence, lead your servants, our legislators, to make good judgments, to the benefit of all your children everywhere.

Amen.

In October 1996, J. Lawrence made his last trip to China, where he was hosted in Shanghai by Luke and Mary Xie and their son's fiancée, Meilin. (Their son Donald was in the United States at that time.) J. Lawrence stayed at Shanghai Mansion, from which he had a view of the Bund, a waterfront area in central Shanghai. He visited places familiar to him, including the Shanghai American School, which daughter Myrna had once attended. Luke and Mary Xie and Meilin took J. Lawrence to the beautiful nearby city of Hangzhou (formerly called Hangchow) for several days.

J. Lawrence Burkholder in Hangzhou in October 1996, during his last trip to China

Harriet Burkholder as hostess in retirement years

On October 31, 1997, J. Lawrence celebrated his eightieth birthday by planting a tree in the center circle south of the Union Building at Goshen College. This event was organized as a surprise by Harriet, who made arrangements with Clayton Shetler, director of facilities at Goshen College.

On August 20, 1999, in a reception at College Mennonite Church, Goshen, hosted by their children, J. Lawrence and Harriet celebrated their sixtieth wedding anniversary with friends and family.

In the summer of 2002, J. Lawrence had triple bypass and valve replacement surgery at Mayo Clinic in Rochester, Minnesota.

In 2003, Karl N. Stutzman, a history major at Goshen College, completed a J. Lawrence Burkholder bibliography for academic credit. It was published in *Mennonite Quarterly Review* 80, no. 3 (July 2006): 435–53.

On September 14, 2004, J. Lawrence spoke about his life in a presentation entitled "Some Reflections on the 20th Century" at an Afternoon Sabbatical Series program held on the campus of Goshen College.

J. Lawrence Burkholder holding his first great-grandchild, August Franklin, born on September 4, 2008, to granddaughter Erica Friesen and her husband, Blair Franklin

Harriet Lapp Burkholder (born March 31, 1915), died at Greencroft Healthcare, Goshen, Indiana, on September 6, 2007.

J. Lawrence's first great-grandson, August Franklin, was born on September 4, 2008, to granddaughter Erica Friesen and her husband, Blair Franklin. A brother, Max Franklin, was born to Erica and Blair on November 22, 2010. J. Lawrence's other grandchild, Eliot Friesen, and his wife, Carrie Meyer-Friesen, have two daughters: Greta, born July 18, 2011, and Alexandra, born August 27, 2013.

In late July and early August 2009, J. Lawrence visited his boyhood hometown, Newville, Pennsylvania, for the last time. J. Lawrence and daughter Myrna were joined by daughter Janet and son-in-law Lauren Friesen and son Howard. During that trip, on August 1, the family was hosted in Fairfield, Pennsylvania, by Phil Roth and other relatives of the Howard Musselman family for a meal, after which Phil, a pilot, helped J. Lawrence fly an airplane over Cumberland County and Newville. On August 2, John A. and Alice Lapp from Akron, Pennsylvania, joined the Burkholder family in worship at J. Lawrence's boyhood church, Diller Mennonite, after which they all toured Newville and two family cemeteries. This trip had been preceded by two other trips to Newville made by J. Lawrence and daughter Myrna, including one in September 2007 and another in June 2008 (during which son Howard Burkholder and grandson Eliot Friesen joined J. Lawrence and Myrna).

At a Goshen College convocation on January 15, 2010, GC president James E. Brenneman preached on "Getting to Yes and Amen! The New GC School of Thought," honoring J. Lawrence for the contribution his dissertation made to Mennonite thought.

On April 2, 2010, as part of the Arbor Day celebration in Goshen, the Goshen Tree Board recognized J. Lawrence for the planting of more than 130 trees on the Goshen College campus in 1971 as part of his inaugural activities. Since 1971, more than 1,000 trees have been planted on campus.

On June 24, 2010, J. Lawrence died. He was ninety-three years old. The previous evening, a small tornado had struck Goshen, felling trees on South 8th Street (near Goshen College), which brought down service lines and caused a power outage at the

J. Lawrence Burkholder being greeted by Goshen College president James E. Brenneman, January 15, 2010, after a Goshen College convocation honoring J. Lawrence

Greencroft Healthcare facility where he had been receiving care after suffering a stroke several weeks earlier. He died a few hours later, early in the morning of June 24. At J. Lawrence's memorial service at College Mennonite Church on June 30, 2010, James E. Brenneman, president of Goshen College, began his remembrance with these words: "President J. Lawrence Burkholder laid down his life as nobly as it was taken up. Perhaps it is fitting that on a night when tornadoes touched down in the city of Goshen, felling giant oaks across 8th Street, the Spirit came and plucked up and laid down our dearly beloved Lawrence, mighty oak that he was, one last time."

A Chronology of the Life of J. Lawrence Burkholder

October 31, 1917	Born in West Hill, Pennsylvania
1921	Moves to 89 North High Street, Newville, Pennsylvania
1929	Baptized, Diller Mennonite Church, near Newville
Summer 1935	Attends Moody Bible Institute, Chicago, for seven weeks
1936–39	Attends Goshen (Indiana) College, graduating with a bachelor of arts in history; studies summers at Shippensburg (Pennsylvania) State Teachers College
1937	Harriet Lapp graduates from Goshen College, majoring in Bible and biology
1938	Harriet completes bachelor of theology degree
August 20, 1939	Marries Harriet in Manheim, Pennsylvania
Fall 1939–spring 1940	Studies at Princeton (New Jersey) Theological Seminary

1940–42	Attends Lutheran Theological Seminary at Gettysburg (Pennsylvania), graduating with a bachelor of divinity degree
July 25, 1941	Daughter Myrna Rachel born in Gettysburg
1942	Ordained to ministry by Bishop D. A. Yoder of Elkhart, Indiana, at First Mennonite Church of New Bremen, New York; lives in nearby Croghan, New York
July 18, 1943	Son John Howard born in Lowville, New York
October 1944	Leaves for China under auspices of Mennonite Central Committee; stays in Calcutta, India, prevented from entering China; works for Bengal Christian Council Relief Fund; Harriet and children Myrna and Howard live in Goshen, Indiana
December 1945	Enters China; lives in Shanghai and works for Mennonite Central Committee and American Advisory Committee under the auspices of Church World Service, for which he is associate director
October 1946	Harriet and children Myrna and Howard join J. Lawrence in Shanghai
1948	Serves as director of the National Clearing Committee, a commission for United Nations Relief and Rehabilitation Administration

August 18, 1948	Daughter Janet Louise born in Shanghai
November 1948	Burkholder family leaves China
1949	Studies at Princeton Theological Seminary; earns master of theology degree; thesis (dated 1951) is "An Examination of the Mennonite Doctrine of Nonconformity to the World"; Harriet and the children remain in Goshen
1950–53	Teaches at Goshen College as professor of Bible and philosophy
1953–55	Returns to Princeton Theological Seminary for work toward doctor of theology degree
1954	Travels to Vietnam on behalf of World Council of Churches
January 18, 1955	Son Gerald Paul Burkholder born in Princeton
1955–60	Teaches at Goshen College as associate professor of Bible and theology; serves as faculty sponsor for the graduating class of 1959
1958	Receives doctor of theology summa cum laude from Princeton Theological Seminary; thesis is "The Problem of Social Responsibility from the Perspective of the Mennonite Church"
1959	Suffers a back injury in a car accident near Middlebury, Indiana

1961–71	Teaches at Harvard Divinity School, Cambridge, Massachusetts; lives in nearby Arlington, Massachusetts
April 20, 1962	Nineteen people covenant together at the Burkholder home to form the Mennonite Congregation of Boston
August 1962	Spends three weeks in Europe visiting church renewal centers
1963	Named chair of the newly created Department of the Church at Harvard Divinity School
February 22, 1963	Quoted in *Time* magazine in an article, "Seminaries"
1964	Named Victor S. Thomas Professor of Divinity at Harvard Divinity School
March 31–April 2, 1964	Arrested in St. Augustine, Florida, as part of a civil rights protest
March 9, 1965	Marches across Edmund Pettus Bridge and back in a civil rights protest led by Martin Luther King, Jr., and others
September 1965–June 1966	On sabbatical from Harvard Divinity School at Cambridge University, England, as a research scholar
November 1965	Harriet travels to Dhamtari, India, to serve as guest speaker at the twenty-fifth anniversary of the Mennonite women's organization in India
1967	Attends (with Harriet) Mennonite World Conference in Amsterdam

April 9, 1968	Speaks (with several others) at Harvard University's Memorial Church in a special service honouring Martin Luther King, Jr., assassinated April 4, 1968
March 7, 1969	Article "Divinity School Students Question Report on Blacks" appears in the *Harvard Crimson;* it deals with a report coming from a student-faculty committee at Harvard Divinity School chaired by J. Lawrence Burkholder
January 1971	Leaves Harvard Divinity School and tours Mennonite churches and several Goshen College study-service term units
July 1971	Begins work as president of Goshen College
October 29–30, 1971	Installed as the eleventh president of Goshen College
March 8–22, 1972	Attends (with Harriet) six alumni banquets, in Kansas, Colorado, Arizona, California, and Oregon
1973–80	Serves as member of Mennonite Church Council on Faith, Life and Strategy
1974–85	Serves as board member for St. Joseph Valley Bank (later renamed Midwest Commerce Banking Company), Elkhart, Indiana
1975	Travels with delegation of twenty-one educators and others to China for a three-week tour of the country

January–June 1977   Spends (with Harriet) a half-year
sabbatical in Concord, California,
to study at University of California, Berkeley; the topic of his study
project is "The Analogy between
Maoism and Christianity"

June 30–July 2, 1977   Presents "Rethinking Christian Life
and Mission in Light of the Chi-
nese Experience" at a conference,
"China: The Religious Dimension,"
held at the Center for Pastoral and
Social Ministry, University of Notre
Dame; presentation was published
in *China and Christianity: Historical
and Future Encounters*

1977   Harriet begins service as a member of the planning committee for
the Afternoon Sabbatical Program
sponsored by Goshen College

April 5, 1978   *Goshen News* article reports that
J. Lawrence is learning to cook Chi-
nese food, in a development occa-
sioned by Harriet's fracture of her
wrist

December 13, 1979   Travels (with Harriet) to Poland;
–January 9, 1980   signs agreement to continue an
exchange program between Goshen
College and Warsaw Agricultural
University; proceeds to Peking
(China) and then to Chengdu; gives
several lectures on American higher
education at Sichuan University,
and Harriet lectures on teaching
English as a second language; nego-
tiates agreement to begin study-

	service term exchange program between Goshen College and China
1970s (date unknown)	Presented by Indiana Gov. Otis R. Bowen (1972–80) with the Sagamore of the Wabash Award
Fall 1980	Travels with Harriet and Lee and Geraldine Martin to China to meet with Goshen College study-service term students at Sichuan Teachers College, Chengdu
April 19, 1981	Son Gerald Paul Burkholder dies of complications of cystic fibrosis
1982–2008	Serves on the board of Fourth Freedom Forum
Spring 1982	Travels to Taiwan as a delegate to the Sino-American Conference on Higher Education, March 30–April 4, 1982; travels to Peking
1982–84	Hosts (with Harriet) thirty-four groups of guests at Goshen College, as part of the Uncommon Cause endowment drive
1983–92	Serves on the United Board for Christian Higher Education in Asia
January 11, 1984	Attends reception in Washington, DC, for Chinese Premier Zhao Ziyang
June 1984	Retires from presidency of Goshen College
September 6-13, 1984	Travels with Harriet to visit Harold Good in Florida

October–November 1985	Leads (with Harriet and Arlin and Naomi Hunsberger) a Goshen College Alumni China Tour; joins delegation representing the United Board for Christian Higher Education in Asia in visits to several universities and seminaries in China
1986	*Sum and Substance: Essays by J. Lawrence,* edited by Edward Zuercher, published by Pinchpenny Press of Goshen College, Goshen, Indiana
1989	Doctoral thesis, *The Problem of Social Responsibility from the Perspective of the Mennonite Church,* published by Institute of Mennonite Studies, Elkhart, Indiana
June–August 1989	Celebrates fiftieth wedding anniversary
September 20, 1989	Is featured speaker at the twenty-fifth anniversary celebration of the Mennonite Congregation of Boston
October–November 1989	Travels to Chengdu, China; Bangkok, Thailand; Ho Chi Minh City, Vietnam; Germany
February 12–14, 1990	Is featured speaker for the 20th Annual Thomas F. Staley Distinguished Christian Scholar Lecture Program at Eastern Mennonite College and Seminary, Harrisonburg, Virginia; lectures are on the theme "The Redemption of Power"
October 6, 1990	Receives with Harriet a Goshen College Culture for Service Award

October 1990	Harriet's article "Picking up the Pieces of a Broken Dream" is published in *Christian Living*
August 9–23, 1991	Travels to Lithuania as a board member for Lithuania Christian College; then to Moscow
March 30–April 2, 1992	Laurelville Mennonite Church Center, Mt. Pleasant, Pennsylvania, hosts "Conversations with J. Lawrence Burkholder on the Church in Society"
1993	Pandora Press and Institute of Anabaptist and Mennonite Studies publish *The Limits of Perfection: A Conversation with J. Lawrence Burkholder*, edited by Rodney J. Sawatsky and Scott Holland
June 21, 1994	Gives opening prayer for the United States House of Representatives at the invitation of Indiana's Third District Congressman, Tim Roemer
October 1996	Travels to China
October 31, 1997	Celebrates his eightieth birthday by planting a tree at Goshen College
August 20, 1999	Celebrates sixtieth wedding anniversary
Summer 2002	Has triple-bypass and valve replacement surgery at Mayo Clinic, Rochester, Minnesota
September 14, 2004	Speaks at a Goshen College Afternoon Sabbatical on "Some Reflections on the 20th Century"

July 2006	Bibliography of J. Lawrence Burkholder's writings compiled by Karl N. Stutzman is published in *Mennonite Quarterly Review* 80, no. 3 (July 2006): 435–53
September 6, 2007	Harriet dies
June 2008	Honored for twenty-six years of service on the board of Fourth Freedom Forum
2009	Visits hometown of Newville, Pennsylvania
January 15, 2010	Honored at a Goshen College convocation by President James E. Brenneman, who spoke on "Getting to Yes and Amen! The New GC School of Thought"
April 2, 2010	Recognized by Goshen Tree Board for planting of more than 130 trees on the Goshen College campus in 1971
June 24, 2010	Dies in Goshen, Indiana

Index

The letter *f* following a page number denotes a figure.